DEAD MEN TALK

DEAD MEN TALK

Sandra Mara

POOLBEG

Published 2009
by Poolbeg Books Ltd
123 Grange Hill, Baldoyle,
Dublin 13, Ireland
Email: poolbeg@poolbeg.com

13 5 7 9 10 8 6 4 2

A catalogue record for this book is available from the British Library.

ISBN 978-1-84223-365-8

Typeset by Patricia Hope in Sabon 11/15
Cover design by Glen McArdle
Printed by CPI Cox & Wyman, UK

www.poolbeg.com

About the Author

Sandra Mara has been a member of the Forensic Science Society since 1986. The FSS is a professional body representing forensic scientists, academics, researchers and those working in related fields both in the UK and internationally. One of the oldest and largest forensic science organisations in the world, the FSS has long been associated with the Forensic Science Laboratory in Ireland.

Sandra was Ireland's first female private investigator, following in the footsteps of her father, Bill Kavanagh who started Ireland's first detective agency in 1947. As an international investigator for over twenty-five years, she acted for government agencies, multinationals, professional bodies and media outlets around the world. She was on the board of the International Security Investigation Service (ISIS) and was a founder member and former President of the Institute of Investigators. Her book *No Job for a Woman: The Inside Story of Ireland's First Female Private Investigator* was published by Poolbeg Press in 2008.

A regular contributor to radio and television programmes both in Ireland and abroad, Sandra holds a masters degree in journalism from DCU and is currently doing an LLM. She was an investigative journalist with

Magill magazine for four years, exposing political and other scandals such as the Donegal garda story. Sandra was a journalist with the *Sunday Tribune* and a contributor to *The Examiner* and *The Dubliner*.

Acknowledgements

The idea for this book came not from me, despite my long-term involvement with investigation and forensics. It was the brainchild of those wonderful people at Poolbeg, and it came about during a meeting about my last book, *No Job for a Woman*, about the world of private investigation as I experienced it for over twenty-five years.

Kieran Devlin, Paula Campbell and Brian Langan had the great idea of doing an Irish forensics book, telling the true inside story of what happens behind the closed doors of the forensic scientist. All I had to do was write it and let Brian, an editorial genius, deal with the fall-out!

I would also like to acknowledge all those friends and colleagues I've worked with over the years, both in the Forensic Science Society, and in the field of investigation worldwide. Thanks also to the very many good friends I have made over the years within the gardaí and other forces. For them, the job doesn't get any easier and these true stories may just give the reader a taste of how the other half lives, protecting their safety and security.

I'm grateful to those friends and colleagues from all aspects of crime-fighting who shared their war stories with me; you know who you are. I hope I have done you justice.

"If the law has made you a witness, remain a man of science. You have no victim to avenge, no guilty or innocent person to convict or save — you must bear testimony within the limits of science."

— Dr PCH Brouardel
Nineteenth-Century French Medico-legalist

Contents

Introduction

The Killing Fields
of Ireland

The world of forensics holds a fascination for many people reared on a diet of TV programmes such as *CSI*, or writers such as Kathy Reichs and Patricia Cornwell. In these fictional accounts, glamorous detectives, scientists and pathologists investigating murders and other crimes piece together the intricate details of the forensic jigsaw, finding solutions in the most unlikely of places and always catching the bad guys.

But is it really like that? This book delves into the murky world of the forensic scientist to find out . . .

It is almost incomprehensible to believe that over 500 people were murdered in a small country like Ireland during the past ten years – almost one a week. If you add to that the attempted murders, serious assaults, sexual assaults, armed robberies and related crime, it might appear that Ireland could teach the Mafia a thing or two. In 2007 there were eighty-four murders or manslaughters, and 166 attempted murders or serious threats to kill, and that number is increasing, as week after week we hear news reports of not just one, but several murders around the country. Between gangland killings, crimes of so-called passion, and random vicious attacks, Ireland seems more like Miami or LA in the 1980s.

Thanks to the efforts of determined detectives in the gardaí, aided and abetted by forensic scientists, many of these criminals have been brought to justice. Gangland crime is a big contributor to our crime levels, but that alone is not responsible for the surge in the murder rate, as "respectable" members of our society are often indicted for murder, manslaughter and other heinous crimes. Even the leafy suburbs are not immune to marital murder. Often described as a crime of passion, these occur most frequently when a woman wants to split from her partner. What triggers the murder – jealousy, possessiveness, a fear of financial ruin – is almost irrelevant when families are left devastated and children become virtual orphans, with one parent dead and the other jailed.

The vast majority of murders are committed by men, although there are gruesome exceptions, like the Mulhall sisters who butchered Farah Swaleh Noor and dismembered his body before throwing it, minus his head, into the Royal Canal in Dublin; or "Black Widow" Catherine Nevin, convicted of soliciting assassins to kill her husband. Then there was the self-styled "devil in the red dress" Sharon Collins, who tried to hire an Egyptian hit man to kill her lover and his sons, in an effort to get her hands on his money. No wonder they say hell hath no fury . . .

That said, men are far more likely to be the killers and are also five times more likely to be murdered in Ireland, with the majority being shot, stabbed or beaten to death, often in gangland murders, according to the Department of Justice. Other serious crimes are also on the increase – everything from Tiger kidnappings, armed robbery, stabbings, arson and drug-related crimes have combined to make the mean streets of Ireland unsafe.

State Pathologist, Marie Cassidy, believes that murders throughout Ireland have become far more vicious. "You don't get single stab-wound deaths, because if they [a victim of a single stab wound] can get to a hospital they will survive." We have a "more violent culture" now. Dr Cassidy says deaths generally result from multiple injuries, which make it more difficult for the person to be resuscitated: "They stab them, shoot them, then set them on fire . . . things have become much more complex."

This book shows just how the gardaí are fighting this growing crime wave on all fronts, through expert investigative work backed up by some of the best forensic scientists in the world. However, they are not always backed up by the criminal justice system, which often appears to be too lenient on crime and recidivist criminals, not because of a lack of effort on the gardaí's part. We need stronger legislation to ensure the safety of our citizens, courts that are willing to enforce the law and realistic penalties that ensure the punishment fits the crime. Without realistic punishment, there is little deterrent and the cycle goes merrily along, leaving behind the devastation of innocent victims, hard-working, law-abiding citizens who have been forgotten by a system that all too frequently appears to be soft on crime.

Whatever the divisiveness of the Criminal Justice (Amendment) Bill (2009) on gangland crime, which allows for covert surveillance and non-jury trials, I feel on a personal level that these changes are necessary if we have any hope of reclaiming our streets and upholding the justice system. Had such covert surveillance measures not been allowed in the UK, the people responsible for killing eleven-year old Rhys Jones would most likely have escaped justice, free to kill again.

Asking innocent law-abiding citizens to give evidence in an open court, or to act as jurors without a guarantee of freedom from intimidation or repercussion against themselves or family members is unrealistic, given the gun-happy gangs that roam our streets. For these gangs life is cheap and if it means "taking out" someone to keep themselves out of prison, so what? There is no disincentive unless tough measures are introduced. We must grasp this nettle for the sake of our children's future, before it is too late.

As well as looking at how some of Ireland's most notorious crimes were solved by the heroes of the Garda Forensic Science Laboratory, *Dead Men Talk* spreads its net further afield to outline some of the best known international cases, such as those of serial killers like Harold "Dr Death" Shipman, Ted Bundy and the Yorkshire Ripper.

These Irish and international cases are interspersed with chapters on the technical aspects of the science of forensics, which covers a vast range of areas including pathology and the cause of death, trace evidence, biometrics (fingerprinting, retinal scanning, etc.), DNA, ballistics, computer forensics, document analysis, even forensic entomology – the study of insect activity on a dead body. You might need a strong stomach for some of the details!

I have always had a fascination with forensics, ever since I studied physics and chemistry in my early days. When I later became involved in the field of investigation, I was (and still am) a member of the Forensic Science Society in the UK, an august professional body of forensic scientists, which is associated with government, police, university and commercial organisations around the world. The constantly evolving developments in areas such as DNA, stem cell and general forensic technology are exciting.

There is little glory for the forensic scientist. They are rarely the "front room" boys or girls and usually only appear in public when giving expert evidence in criminal trials. Generally they remain in the background, beavering away, the unsung heroes and heroines of the modern judicial system. Without their crucial evidence, the streets would be less safe, more ruthless and many deadly criminals would, literally, get away with murder.

The men and women in our own Forensic Science Laboratory at Garda HQ in the Phoenix Park have worked under difficult conditions and circumstances since its inception in 1975. Dr Jim Donovan, the lab's first Director, is testimony to that, both in the workload he had and in the personal price he paid. Initially Jim

Donovan *was* the Forensic Science Lab, the only employee in the newly formed State laboratory, having worked as a toxicologist in the chemistry department of the State lab since 1971.

He paid dearly for his dedication, with several attempts on his life, as criminals feared the testimony of his forensic evidence. The notorious Martin "The General" Cahill made a number of attempts on his life. The first was around Christmas 1981, when a car bomb forced his car off the road. He was lucky to escape alive. Weeks later, on 6 January 1982, came the incident that would change his life forever. Jim was driving in the Clondalkin area of Dublin when, as he tells it, he remembers a flash, and then the car rearing up. He still can feel the searing heat and hear the terrible noise – the boom of the explosion, as the bomb went off. He could barely move. His clothes were blown off and his legs were shattered. He reached down to find broken bones, his flesh and tissue ripped apart. His face and eyes were cut and he had extensive damage to his right hand, which was stuck to the steering wheel, frozen to the spot. Crucial nerves in his hand had been damaged, and he was unable to move it; it was locked in place on the wheel. The mental trauma is untold.

Speaking to him again about his ordeal, almost twenty-eight years after that attempt on his life, he still suffers horrendous pain, needing constant medication and hospital visits, and daily physiotherapy. He has abdominal problems as a result of the injuries and his wounds still ulcerate and bleed. He can no longer feel his foot, or what's left of it, and he has the daily gruesome grind of self-examination, to make sure it is not gangrenous, as oozing can be a problem. He still needs the help of a pain reliever – a spinal cord implant, which makes his day just about manageable. The suffering of Jim's wife, Mary, watching his pain, worrying about him, when he insisted on returning to work, is not something you sign up for when you speak the words "for better or for worse".

If this is making you feel ill, think of twenty-eight years of daily pain, a lifetime of suffering, all because of what is, sometimes, a thankless job. Would *you* do it? Not many would swap places with the men and women of the Forensic Science Lab. Safe behind closed doors, in their lab coats, they are exposed every single day to the swamp of human frailty, the most heinous crimes imaginable, and the mindless criminals who have no regard for life. They are exposed to the dangers of telling the truth of their findings in a court of law, knowing what happened to their former Director.

With the realisation of the enormous value forensics has to offer, the laboratory slowly grew in numbers and capabilities but, then as now, they remain overworked, understaffed and underfunded. Even through the wealthy Celtic Tiger years, despite an increase in serious crimes and a growth in population, there was no extra money to develop the service. It takes years to become a highly experienced forensic scientist, in whatever area of practice, be it chemistry, physics, biology, botany or in the newer specialities such as DNA. There is no substitute for experience, and the constant pressure and stress of coming up with results for the ever-increasing workload is a worry.

Forensic scientists are a fundamental and crucial part of our security; our crime detection and prevention, our safety lies in their hands. We need to respect and value them, giving them the tools they need to protect us. If we have any hope of making the streets safer, we need tough laws, strong police enforcement and as a final deterrent, a well supported, better funded, forensic science unit, with more qualified staff to share the load.

We are lucky to have many of the best forensic scientists in the world working at the State laboratory, but that may change, such are the demands of that pressurised environment, if we neglect what we have. Whenever the Forensic Science unit is written about, it inevitably refers to the horrors suffered by Dr Jim Donovan, and rightly so, but it is often overlooked that the existing staff have not been without their security difficulties, just because they did their job and gave independent scientific evidence in court against a criminal. They too, have needed police protection at times; they too, have families, and it is an unenviable position to be in.

Most people go to work, get paid, go home. They don't need to be constantly on alert, looking over their shoulder. In the present climate of drug-fuelled gang warfare, there *is* no honour among criminals. They see anyone as fair game, even innocent bystanders. The forensic scientist, together with the gardaí, are our first line of defence. If, simply due a lack of resources, dangerous criminals walk free, Ireland will be a lawless State. It's a dirty job and someone has to do it, but for God's sake let's give them the tools, the protection and the manpower to share the load.

1

The Lowdown on Forensics

CSI, detective films and crime books may give the impression that forensics is done on the spot by police forces who come up with an instant result, bag the villain and get a conviction. Nothing could be further from the truth. The area of forensics is a vast one, requiring scientists from various disciplines and specialities, including chemistry, physics, pathology, ballistics and numerous other areas. They work in close co-operation with the police and provide scientific evidence and expert witness services to the courts and criminal justice system. They are not interested in or concerned with circumstantial evidence, unreliable testimony or even securing a conviction. They present the scientific evidence in hard facts, which may either convict or acquit an accused. It's all about teamwork, as no single scientist can do all the analysis in a case, which could include a mix of evidence from blood spatter, to trace evidence such as fibres, powder residue, cartridge cases from a shooting or bodily fluids in a rape case. The demands are many and varied and can include multitask disciplines to bring the elements in a case together.

The scenario goes something like this. A 999 call is made; depending on the nature of the call, the fire brigade, ambulance or police are directed to the scene; sometimes it can be all three. If the gardaí determine that it is a crime scene, the detective unit arrives and the crime scene investigation unit gets to work. The area is immediately cordoned off and remains so until gardaí are finished with it.

If somebody has died in suspicious circumstances, the State Pathologist, currently Dr Marie Cassidy, is called to examine the body on site. On call around the clock, she has the unenviable task of examining dead bodies, often under the most difficult circumstances, performing post mortems and determining the cause of death. She will also be called upon to give independent evidence in any subsequent court case or coroner's inquest. Dr Cassidy is assisted by the Deputy State Pathologist, Dr Michael Curtis, and on a part-time basis by Dr Margaret Bolster and Dr Declan Gilsenan.

According to official figures from the Department of Justice, there were 1,789 headline offences involving homicide, manslaughter and infanticide (not to mention attempted murder) in Ireland between 2000 and 2007, which averages almost 257 a year, or 4.9 per week, with 300 in 2007 alone. Given these figures, the workload for Dr Cassidy and her deputy, Dr Curtis, is incredibly demanding.

We often see crime scene teams on the news, carrying large brown bags marked "EVIDENCE". Maintaining the chain of evidence is crucial. Scene of crime officers (SOCOs), as they are known in the UK – the Technical Bureau's crime scene investigation unit in Ireland – are responsible for collecting and transporting the evidence. They must ensure that the integrity of the evidence is maintained and it has not been contaminated in any way. Each piece of evidence must be photographed, documented and sealed in a time-dated, signed, secure evidence bag and brought to the Forensic Science Laboratory as soon as possible.

The Technical Bureau's job includes photographing the crime scene, dusting for prints and collecting any other evidence available, forensic or otherwise. The forensic evidence is passed on to the Forensic Science Laboratory for examination, while the Technical Bureau deal with other matters such as fingerprints, ballistics, mapping and photography. The crime scene is mapped out, showing the layout of any buildings, where the body was found, perhaps showing an abandoned weapon, lost shoe, etc.

Unlike in television, forensic examination is not done from the back of a mobile evidence van, with instant results. Some areas can be painstakingly slow, despite modern technology. It can be a waiting game; whether it is in the area of toxicology, ballistics, DNA or entomology, "good" science takes time. It must stand up to the scrutiny of legal defence experts and there is no room for sloppy results. The evidence will speak for itself, as the maxim says.

In the meantime, an incident room is set up at the investigating garda station. The investigation is co-ordinated from there and all information from the Technical Bureau is collated and distributed to the investigating detectives, to allow them to follow up leads. A suspect list is drawn up, individuals are interviewed and investigations are undertaken; search warrants may be issued and a search of one or more premises may be made. Gardaí may then charge a suspect, who may plead guilty or not guilty.

A guilty plea allows a case to be prosecuted without the need for numerous witnesses and is therefore quicker. The court usually takes such a plea into consideration when imposing a more lenient sentence. Alternatively, a file may be prepared and sent to the DPP.

Where a defendant pleads not guilty, the prosecution must prove beyond reasonable doubt that the person committed the crime. Obviously, forensic evidence plays an enormous part at this stage. With the huge backlog of criminal cases involving killings, and with figures showing 300 such killings in 2007 alone, it is understandable that it can sometimes take two years or more to bring a case to trial and longer if there are problems, challenges or other reasons for delay.

It may seem quite difficult for twelve ordinary citizens of mixed background and educational standards to be expected to decide the fate of a person on trial for murder, manslaughter, rape or other serious crimes. Despite the vast array of witnesses and evidence paraded before them, and the efforts of both the prosecution and defence to persuade them for or against a conviction, they are also faced with complicated forensic evidence, which can sometimes be a lot to take in.

The jury can't allow themselves to be influenced by personal prejudices on anything such as creed, colour, ethnic origins or social background; nor can they be told if the defendant had form – previous convictions – not even if they had murdered or raped before. Each case must stand or fall on its own merits and each defendant appears before the court as innocent as a newborn baby, regardless of the facts of the case, be they minor or the most heinous of crimes.

How then, can complex forensic evidence be explained in a straightforward and meaningful way to members of the jury? Even those familiar with *CSI* may not have a good understanding of the principles of forensics, expecting miracles from the experts. A forensic scientist is not there to present a case that will convict or acquit a defendant. They simply present the facts, the science, as they have found it. The evidence tells its own story, for good or bad – it's up to the jury to decide if it is sufficient to convict a defendant.

So how do they make it simple, understandable and intelligible to your average juror? Firstly, it will be presented by what is referred to as an "expert witness", someone who knows their specific area like the back of their hand, has studied and worked in the field for years and has examined hundreds, if not thousands, of similar cases. The science is routine to them but it may be the first time ever that a juror has come face to face with a particular area of forensics. The area of expertise is vast – from DNA to ballistics including guns and ammunition, trace evidence, chemistry, physics, biology, fingerprinting, arson, forensic psychiatry, handwriting analysis, biometrics or forensic accounting. Remember that the expert witness is under oath and their professional integrity will be judged by their professionalism, expertise and impartiality in presenting their findings.

The KISS method is probably best – keep it simple, stupid. In presenting this evidence to a jury, an expert may use video, audio and other equipment to aid the explanation. For example, the presentation may include photographs of a crime scene – sometimes gory or graphic pictures of the victim – maps, documents or evidential material such as the murder weapon, be it a gun, knife or ligature. Fingerprints, evidence of mobile phone texts or conversations, blood-stained clothing, shoes that match shoe prints taken at the scene or even evidence from computer forensic examination can all be presented to the jury to consider. Given the wide-ranging evidence, it needs to be explained and interpreted in clear and understandable terms for a jury.

Experts often refer to "trace evidence" – but what exactly does this mean? Probably the easiest way to describe trace evidence is anything, however small, collected by scene of crime officers such as fibres, hair, broken glass, blood, shoes or clothing which may itself have trace evidence, including mud, sand or even the DNA from a perpetrator or victim's skin cells. The possibilities are vast and it is essential that such evidence is recovered and collected in such a way as to ensure it is not contaminated in any way by the officers of the crime scene investigation unit themselves. To make sure this doesn't happen, the CSIU will wear protective clothing such as plastic disposable jumpsuits covering their body, as well as protective footwear covers, gloves and a mask, to ensure there is no cross-contamination from their clothing fibres, skin or hair to the crime scene's potential evidence.

Additional trace evidence may be taken post mortem and can include anything – if, for example, a body is found in a building, soil samples may indicate that they were killed elsewhere. Fingernail scrapings, taken by a pathologist post mortem, may indicate that a victim struggled with their attacker, scraping them and perhaps picking up skin cells or hair clumps, which can later be matched to a suspect's DNA. Hair in particular not only can provide DNA evidence, but can identify chemicals used if the hair has been dyed or coloured, which in turn can be isolated to particular sales outlets or hairdressing salons in a given area.

Every contact leaves a trace, from fingerprints to footprints to DNA. Even the most careful criminal will usually leave something behind. It may be invisible to the naked eye but, nonetheless, it is usually there to be found with the help of chemicals and polarised light microscopy. Light normally vibrates in every direction, but by using a polarised light microscope, the light travels one way and, used in conjunction with a high magnification of anything from 1,000X to over 300,000X, it can be effectively used to examine bullets, firearms and a range of materials, which can identify a speck of blood or pick up minute skin cells, fibres or hair particles from a vacuum cleaner, where an after crime "clean-up" was attempted. These methods can also identify properties in a specimen (for example, duct tape) found at a crime scene, tracing it back to a particular manufacturer.

When dealing with substances such as drugs that have been seized, a gas chromatograph mass spectrometer (GC-MS), separates unknown substances into different components. It then counts the different fragment masses – for example, it can identify if a drug was mixed with starch or sugar. The results are plotted on a bar graph and the substance can then be identified from a known list of substances, thus identifying it as heroin, cocaine or just plain flour.

Some kind of getaway vehicle is used in many criminal activities – a motorbike, truck or car on stand-by to pick up an individual or gang after a robbery or murder. Like everything else in forensic science, tyres leave a trace, particularly if there is a fast getaway with screeching tyres and burning rubber. The marks left behind often clearly indicate the pattern of the tyre tread. Hit-and-run crimes can also be identified; sometimes victims may even have a tyre mark embedded on their clothing or skin.

If investigating detectives are lucky enough to have a tyre print, they can match it to a suspect vehicle. Given the multitude of cars, vans and other vehicles on the road and the range of manufacturers of both cars and tyres, the possible combinations are massive but computers can produce likely matches quite quickly. Like footwear, vehicles leave their own track marks and have their own peculiarities, depending on the car. The steering may pull to one side, or there may be damage or wearing on a particular tyre, which may be enough to identify its presence at a crime scene.

Tyre tracks can be left in a variety of surfaces, from muddy laneways to grassy fields. By tracking through certain terrain, they can pick up or deposit blood, glass, debris, stones and soil, which can all place a vehicle in a specific area. When combined with other damage to the car, such as flaking paint, this can put a car at the scene of a crime. (See the case of the Yorkshire Ripper, Chapter 32.)

With developments in forensic science, the odds are becoming increasingly stacked against the criminal "getting away" with their crime.

Good detective work and forensics go hand in hand (although not *all* forensics are necessarily done in a laboratory). Sometimes the simple approach – a process of investigation and elimination – can solve a crime, which was the case in the murder of Denise Flanagan back in the early 1980s.

It happened right in the middle of Dublin city, in the quiet area of Stoneybatter. The close-knit community woke up to learn that a woman had been found strangled in a laneway next to their homes. Elderly locals were afraid to leave their houses with a killer on the loose.

There was little to go on, but a search of the area by investigating detectives turned up a single lens from a pair of glasses. It could have been anyone's, just lost, or broken and thrown away. The case could have ended there, remaining unsolved, but for an astute detective, Martin Donnellan, and his fellow detective Frank Hand. Both men would later become legends within the gardaí. The pair followed through on their instincts and had the lens examined to find if it was a prescription lens, if the owner was long-sighted or short-sighted, and where the glasses had been bought. There were a huge number of opticians in Ireland at the time; the detectives had no indication as to where it had come from, but they had to start somewhere. The possibilities were endless, covering virtually everyone who wore glasses in the country. Establishing the prescription strength of the lens narrowed the possibilities down to a more manageable number – assuming the lens belonged to the killer in the first place. Checking every optician in the country, Donnellan and Hand pinpointed the very specific prescription to an optician in Dún Laoghaire, who identified a customer fitting the bill.

Following further investigations, they also managed to trace a taxi driver who recalled having picked up a fare that night. He remembered the dead woman, Denise Flanagan, and gave a good description of the man who shared the taxi with her. A forensic search of his taxi identified fibres on the passenger seats, some of which matched those found on Denise Flanagan's clothing.

Armed with this information, and the identifying details from the Dún Laoghaire optician, Donnellan and Hand arrested a Blanchardstown man for the murder of Denise Flanagan. Fibres from the taxi seat were also found on the man's jacket, together with other fibres from the dead girl's clothes. Following their gut instinct in the time-honoured tradition of all good detectives, they got their man, who was later convicted of murder.

Martin Donnellan went on to feature prominently in An Garda Síochána, rising to the rank of Assistant

Commissioner before his retirement. Twice commended for his courage, he also received the Scott Medal, awarded only for the "most exceptional bravery and heroism involving the risk of life in the execution of duty".

His partner in that investigation, Detective Frank Hand, was instrumental in capturing the notorious murderer Malcolm MacArthur in 1982, as he tried to slip out the back door of the apartment in Killiney belonging to the then Attorney General, Patrick Connolly. Gardaí turned out in force to arrest the deranged MacArthur, covering both the back and front doors. They eventually opted for the front, leaving the steadfast Frank Hand stubbornly sticking with the back door. Had he not done so, MacArthur might well have slipped away into the night and murdered again.

Frank Hand continued to give his all in taking on the worst of the worst criminals, eventually paying dearly for it. In 1984, aged twenty-seven, he was gunned down by heavily armed raiders who robbed the local post office of around £200,000, two miles outside Dunshaughlin in County Meath. The IRA gang sprayed the detective's car with machine-gun fire, killing Detective Hand instantly.

2

Carnage on the Beach:
Lord Mountbatten

It was 1979 and Northern Ireland was in the throes of the Troubles. Killing was the currency of the day as every dawn brought another death on either side of the political divide. Ironically, it was the year that Pope John Paul II visited Ireland to preach a message of peace and tolerance. Yet just a month before his arrival, one of the country's most horrific murders took place in Sligo.

On a bright August day a little group set out on a day trip from Mullaghmore Harbour in Sligo. The party included seventy-nine-year-old Lord Henry Mountbatten, who was Prince Philip's uncle, Mountbatten's daughter Patricia, her mother-in-law, Lady Barbourne and Patricia's film-director husband John Knatchbull, along with their fourteen-year-old twin sons Nicholas and Timothy, and fifteen-year-old Paul Maxwell, a lad from Enniskillen holidaying with his family at their nearby cottage, who was acting as boat boy.

20

At around 11.30 a.m. the little group boarded the twenty-eight foot green and white boat, *Shadow V* and set off from the fishing village of Mullaghmore to collect lobster pots and do some fishing. Lord Mountbatten never felt the need for a bodyguard during his annual August holiday in Ireland. Instead the group was tracked by a garda car that drove along the sea road, keeping them in their sights. Sixteen minutes after they set sail, there was a loud explosion that echoed across the bay two miles away. The *Shadow V* had been blown to smithereens.

Boats in the vicinity raced to the scene and managed to pick up Mountbatten's daughter Patricia and her husband, and one of their sons. All were very badly injured. There was no hope for the rest. The wreckage strewn across the water told the tale. All that remained of the boat floated in matchsticks on the sea. The best they could do was to recover the bodies, or what was left of them. Lord Mountbatten's legs had been blown off. Barely alive, he was rescued, but died from his injuries a short time later. Nicholas and his eighty-two-year-old grandmother, together with the boat boy Paul Maxwell, were dead.

The awful carnage shocked the entire country; even those who silently supported the IRA were horrified that the IRA was prepared to kill the elderly and children.

The police and forensic investigators had their work cut out to piece together the evidence. Reports estimated that around fifty pounds of gelignite had been used in the explosion, although that was later contradicted by forensic reports from garda ballistics expert Detective Sergeant

Michael Niland, who put it closer to five pounds (others claimed fifteen pounds). It was both a difficult and harrowing task for the team, given the devastation that lay before them. Six garda subaqua divers had the grisly job of recovering body parts and debris, including the boat's engine, which was submerged thirty feet below the surface.

Dr Jim Donovan of the Garda Forensic Science Laboratory in Dublin had the grim task of working the case. The first and longest-serving Director of the lab – which had been in existence for just four years at the time – Jim, who was known for his courage and tenacity, was to become the leading scientist in many high-profile cases, and was later to feature himself as both a victim and an expert witness.

It was a harrowing job for all involved, as what remained of the victims and the vessel were forensically examined for any evidence that might lead to the culprits. The cause of death was beyond question; the nature of the injuries, the way the skin and flesh had been torn apart, could only have been as a result of the bomb blast. Sand, timber, paint flecks and fabric from what was left of the clothing and any other trace evidence could be found was collected and minutely examined for clues. The remains of cushions and parts of fishing rods were all examined for any trace of explosives and other forensic evidence. Despite the fact that they had been immersed in the briny waters, Dr Donovan found that what was left of the victims' clothes was contaminated by nitro-glycerine, one of the main ingredients of gelignite. Examining the bodies, he also found slivers of paint flakes imbedded in the victims' skin.

Dr Donovan ordered that samples of the sand along the coastline from Bundoran in Donegal to Wicklow should be taken for comparison purposes. Particles as minute as sand can be tested with electron microscopes and microprobes to establish their origin and history, known as provenance. This can indicate the source of the sand grains, whether they have come from igneous or sedimentary rock, whether they were transported by running water, or other valuable information. They can even identify the presence or absence of unusual minerals or certain microfossils which can limit the sand specimen to a small geographic area. This can either place a suspect at a crime scene or even support their alibi. Used more frequently in forensic geology, it also makes a major contribution to criminal forensics. When the sand particles along the coast were tested, not one of over 100 samples was found to match the sand on Mullaghmore beach. This was later to prove crucial to the case.

Detectives investigating the atrocity established that the *Shadow V* had been moored unguarded in the public dock at Mullaghmore, and even strangers would have had no difficulty accessing the boat. Mullaghmore was just twelve miles from an IRA enclave over the border in Northern Ireland. Strangely, despite the volatile political situation and given the public knowledge of Mountbatten's annual visits there, from a security standpoint, it was not deemed to be at risk.

The IRA admitted responsibility for the Mountbatten bombing in a statement released immediately afterwards, which said: "This operation is one of the discriminate ways we can bring to the attention of the English people the continuing occupation of our country."

Meanwhile, gardaí at Granard in County Longford had detained two men in a stolen Ford Escort car a short time before the bomb went off. A passenger in the stolen car, Thomas McMahon, was a well-known member of the IRA. Detectives were still questioning him and the driver of the car, who gave a false name, when the bomb went off. (The IRA later admitted they had detonated it by remote control from the cliff top.) A detective recognised the driver as Francis McGirl, the nephew of John Joe McGirl, former Chief of Staff of the IRA. It seemed too much of a coincidence.

Thomas McMahon claimed he had just hitched a lift from the driver but said he knew nothing about him. He told gardaí he was going to meet a married woman but refused to divulge her identity or where she lived to "protect" her. When the stolen red Ford Escort was closely examined, forensic investigators noticed sand on the car mats and tiny slivers of green paint on the back and front seats and in and around the gear stick. When forensically tested at the Garda State Laboratory, sand found in the stolen car and on both men's shoes, socks and clothes were found to be an exact match to the sea sand on the slipway leading to Mountbatten's boat at Mullaghmore.

When examined by the lab's Director Jim Donovan, both McMahon's and McGirl's clothing showed up traces of nitro-glycerine. It was a major breakthrough in the case. Smears of four different paints were found on the

24

toe of McMahon's boot and on his anorak, and on McGirl's boots and clothes. When Dr Sheila Willis forensically examined the boots and clothing, they matched the green and white paint layer samples taken from what remained of the *Shadow V*. The same paint was found on the bodies of each of the victims, and inside the abdomen of one victim who had been blown in two.

The cause of the explosion on board the *Shadow V* was identified as gelignite. The bomb had been placed under the wheel. As soon as Lord Mountbatten took the helm, it was detonated by remote control, causing his legs to be severed. The evidence was stacking up against McMahon and McGirl. Both men were arrested and charged with the murder of Lord Mountbatten and the other members of his party.

When the case opened in the Special Criminal Court, Dr Jim Donovan gave detailed forensic evidence over three gruelling days in the witness box, while cross-examined by the defence. He produced items recovered from the blast, including the blood-soaked clothing worn by Mountbatten; pieces of the boat with the name *Shadow V* still emblazoned on a piece of timber; the control panel; and even slivers of timber removed from the dead bodies. Detailed evidence of the paint used on the boat, Interlux yacht paint, was given by locals who had worked on it over a number of years. The manufacturer's information on the technical components of the paint mix added to the forensic information. Jim Donovan produced evidence showing that the specialist yacht paint matched the paint found on both defendants' shoes and clothing and in the stolen car. McMahon's jacket had paint smears from the *Shadow V* and nitro-glycerine was found on his jacket and trousers, while McGirl had similar trace evidence on his clothing.

Dr Sheila Willis, then a young, well-qualified forensic scientist, now head of the Forensic Science Unit herself, conducted tests on the paint from the boat and said the odds against the same paint being found on "unrelated" individuals were 250,000 to one. In other words, statistically, it was proved beyond reasonable doubt. There was no question that the paint found on the defendants identically matched that of the *Shadow V*.

Despite the defence counsel's efforts to discount evidence that the paint "smudged" the defendants' clothing while they were planting the bomb, Dr Willis readily demonstrated to the court just how it happened. She produced a slide containing a sample of the paint to Mr Justice Hamilton, the presiding Judge, who wiped it on his robe, showing how easily the paint smudged and transferred to clothing.

Evidence was also given relating to the sand embedded in the defendants' shoes, which when forensically analysed, proved to be local to Mullaghmore. Sand is quickly shed and lost as we move around, yet there remained a substantial amount of sand on the men's socks and footwear and in the car, indicating that they had very recently been in contact with it.

A local man had made a statement to gardaí saying he saw McMahon and McGirl, who was known to him, swap cars outside his house. He said he noticed a strange yellow Ford Cortina parked outside his home. When he looked out the following morning it was gone. As he went outside, he saw the two men pulling up and parking the yellow Cortina. They then got into a red Ford Escort and drove away.

When the abandoned yellow Cortina was examined, it was also found to have traces of green paint and sand, which when forensically examined also matched the samples found on McGirl and McMahon and the *Shadow V*.

When the case came to court the man denied having made the statement voluntarily. He was deemed to be a hostile witness. The man now denied having seen Francis McGirl in the car outside his home.

McGirl's defence immediately moved for an acquittal. Mr Justice Hamilton refused. He said the evidence against McGirl, though circumstantial, was substantial enough to put him at Mullaghmore shortly before his arrest, and that he had driven away from there with McMahon; and he had nitro-glycerine and ammonium nitrate, two components of gelignite, on his clothes. McGirl had also made a statement to gardaí in Granard, County Longford, saying that he "put no bomb on the boat", before gardaí had ever mentioned the Mullaghmore bombing, indicating that McGirl was aware of the bomb, even if he himself had not transferred it to the boat. On that basis, Mr Justice Hamilton said McGirl was not entitled to an acquittal at that stage.

Thomas McMahon sat quietly waiting for the decision of the court. He smiled as he was found guilty of murdering all four victims, then turned and gave a clenched-fist salute to the gallery, which was packed with Republican sympathisers. McMahon was imprisoned for life. He spent thirteen years in Portlaoise Prison, where most of the IRA prisoners were kept. Somewhat surprisingly, he was found not guilty of membership of the IRA.

In 1985 McMahon was one of a group of eleven prisoners who made an unsuccessful attempt to escape from jail, using fake prison officer uniforms, guns and explosives. In 1988, while in a holding cell at the Four Courts in Dublin awaiting a High Court case he was taking against the State, in relation to an assault claim against a prison officer, he pulled out a Browning pistol he'd smuggled into the Courts and fired a shot in an attempt to escape. The escape failed and the case went ahead, with McMahon being awarded £4,000 in damages against the prison officer.

Considered one of the most active members of the IRA during the 1970s, he was one of the first to be released during the first IRA ceasefire. Just before Christmas 1997, Thomas McMahon, one of the longest servicing prisoners, was released from the training unit at Mountjoy Prison under the terms of the Good Friday Agreement.

Francis McGirl, the driver of the stolen car and believed to be the person who planted the bomb, was acquitted of murder. He was also found not guilty of membership of the IRA, having sworn on oath that he was not a member. He later died in a tractor accident on his farm in 1994.

3

The Hit Girls: Helen Golay and Olga Rutterschmidt

They say money is the root of all evil. It was certainly proved true when two elderly women hatched the most bizarre get-rich-quick plan of all time, literally out of Hollywood.

Helen Golay (77) and her seventy-five-year-old friend Olga Rutterschmidt hatched a conspiracy that, if successful, would have let them live out their lives in luxury. The elderly ladies had lived in Los Angeles since the 1950s and had known each other for over twenty years, having first met at a health spa. Both loners, surprisingly they had become good friends. They had led lonely childhoods and found comfort in each other. Helen – née Sinclair, who was originally from Texas – confessed her utter distress at the loss of her father in a car crash, something later to prove ironic. Shuttled among various family members and friends, she ended up in a foster home. Eventually moving to California, she married and had two daughters but the marriage broke up. A second relationship lasted less than a year, leaving her with a baby daughter.

It was then she realised she could make easy money suing people. Her first attempt was so successful, she bought an apartment with the money.

Her next move was into real estate, where she worked with an older man, Artie Aaron. When he died, Helen Golay used a power of attorney agreement signed to protect the business, to transfer his properties, worth millions, into her own name, leaving his daughter penniless.

Her Hungarian friend Olga was injured in bombings during the Second World War and fled to America. Olga and Helen made strange bedfellows, though they had much in common. Both had failed marriages and were short of money, which they made no secret of. Together, they thought up schemes to boost their finances, and tried everything from small-time frauds, including thefts of wallets and handbags from health clubs, to making bogus claims on a variety of people, hoping to get a quick payout. When asked what she worked at, Olga said she sued people for a living. In fact, Olga and Helen often gave "evidence" on each other's behalf during such claims, sharing the proceeds.

During their early friendship, they hung out together in Beverly Hills hotels and other "hot spots", trying to scam money. Helen Golay was well toned and tanned, wore short skirts and had the figure to go with them. Her friend Olga intrigued people with her Zsa Zsa Gabor accent. Pretending to be hotel guests, they would lounge around the pool on the lookout for a good target, a wealthy guest happy to throw money at them. They indulged in petty theft from the guys' wallets whenever possible. They moved onto bigger scams, taking out numerous credit cards in false names and paying one off with another, until they finally ran out of steam, leaving the card company high and dry.

But Golay was interested in higher stakes. She boasted to her hairdresser how easy it was to marry an older man, take out life insurance on him, and then bump him off by secretly putting daily doses of Viagra in his food, until he had a heart attack. She even delightedly described herself as "evil".

Their latest scam would certainly have a big payout. The two women sought out and befriended destitute and homeless men from a local Hollywood church. In a wonderful act of charity, they rented out apartments for them and supported them financially for two years, until they got on their feet. Lauded by the community as "angels of mercy", after their two years of financial support from the women, the "rehabilitated" men returned to the community to start a new and independent life, while the women continued their work with the revolving door of homeless men, all ready and anxious to get a place on the amazing programme.

Paul Vados was one of the first "lucky" ones to get on the programme. The seventy-three-year-old had no family and had been living rough for some time. The two women befriended him and gave him something to live for. He loved his new apartment and had everything he needed – a warm bed, good food and their friendship. Vados died in a hit-and-run incident in Hollywood in 1999.

Ken McDavid was only fifty, so it meant a real chance of a new start in life for him. He could get his life back and he really appreciated everything the two women did for him. They were just two of the many homeless "down-and-outs" the ladies befriended.

The two years went by quickly, and it wasn't long before the men "left" their new home to make their own way in the world, as the ladies told the Hollywood church members. There was no news as to where they went or what happened to their lives after they left the sheltered accommodation; after all, they were on their own now and could provide for themselves.

When the FBI arrived one day to arrest the old ladies, it came as a complete shock to the church leaders. It transpired that, for these two, charity began at home. They had perfected a plan to ensure that they made millions of dollars from the destitute people they had befriended. They specifically targeted the loners, the forgotten, those without friends or family and set them up with their new lives. After the two-year period, the men, now smartly dressed and respectable members of the community, were ready to make their way in the world. Their apartments were to be handed over to new "worthy causes".

The "girls" took them for a celebratory meal, drugging their food from their stockpile of medications prescribed for their own invented conditions. They took their protégés for a little ride while the drugs kicked in, dumping them in an alleyway late at night. Checking that the coast was clear, they drove over the comatose men with their car, making it look like a hit-and-run. The underside of the car was just six inches from the ground at the lowest point, crushing the men as it drove over their bodies.

Some were killed in Hollywood, others like Ken McDavid in West Los Angeles. After they killed off the "forgotten" men, already written off by any family they had, the women collected from various insurance companies. The killer sisters-in-crime claimed to be the men's elderly relatives, collecting a massive payout from insurance companies. The women made almost $2.8 million on Vados and McDavid alone and they stood to make a whole lot more if their plan succeeded. They had plenty more policies lined up, just waiting to be collected. When an insurance company raised a query on the Vados claim for $600,000, the pair sued. Under LA law, after two years in existence, a policy cannot be queried or contested. The company promptly paid up.

Police were investigating a spate of suspicious hit-and-runs. All the victims appeared to be middle-aged or old men without family or former down-and-outs. All had been crushed to death by a vehicle, late at night in an alleyway. There were never any witnesses to the "accidents" and the unidentified men carried no identification; they were just another "John Doe".

Further detailed postmortem examinations confirmed the initial findings that the victims had died as a result of crush injuries sustained from a moving vehicle, but strangely there was a new twist to the cases. Each victim had varying amounts of the same drugs in their system. When the men were eventually identified, it transpired that there was no record that they had been prescribed the drugs, nor did they appear to have any medical conditions relating to the substances. It was unlikely that they were all junkies, all killed in alleyways in separate hit-and-run incidents.

Their last victim, Ken McDavid, was found dead by a passing patrol car on 21 June 2005. His body had been crushed, his shirt was covered in grease marks, clumps of hair had been torn from his head and part of his flesh had been ripped off by the vehicle. Detailed forensic tests found paint flakes and tyre marks left on McDavid's body. Paint flakes can be tested with a light microscope, a scanning electron microscope or even a stereomicroscope, which revealed the paint layers, to find a jigsaw-like match between the paint flakes and paint chips on a car. Additional forensic tests used pyrolysis gas chromatography, which identifies the make and source, mix and age of paint. While such tests became better known for identifying fake Vermeer paintings, on this occasion it led investigators to the Ford Motor Company.

Independently, other forensic scientists identified the tyre marks found on the body as having come from a 1999 Ford Mercury Sable station wagon. Ford had changed the tyre makes in 1999 and these new tyre tracks were clearly visible on the victim's body. Detectives confirmed that the 1999 model Ford Mercury Sable came in silver, the exact match of the paint flakes found on the dead man. They had their murder weapon. They knew the make and colour of vehicle involved in the latest hit-and-run but they still had to track down the car and the culprits.

Police became suspicious when the same two women claimed the bodies of Vados and McDavid. There was no evidence that either woman was related to either victim, despite their claim to be a cousin and fiancée in each case. When detectives contacted insurance companies checking on possible insurance payouts, they discovered that both Helen Golay and Olga Rutterschmidt had policies with a number of companies. They found more than twenty-three policies on McDavid and a further twelve on Paul Vados.

CCTV was recovered from the surrounding streets and shops close to where McDavid's body was found. After hours of trawling through the footage, a Ford Mercury Sable was identified on three separate cameras. When the footage was enhanced, it showed a silver Ford Mercury Sable station wagon as it turned into a Westwood alleyway, just before midnight on 21 June 2005, the night Ken McDavid's body was found in the same alleyway by a passing patrol car.

CCTV from the petrol station showed Golay and Rutterschmidt on a public phone in the petrol station that night and telephone records showed that a call had been made from the coin box to the Automobile Club at the same time the two women were captured on CCTV. Detectives contacted the Automobile Club and discovered that on the same night, a woman had called the club from the station, asking for her car to be towed, as she had broken down close to the Westwood alleyway. She gave her Automobile Club membership number and details, identifying herself as Helen Golay. On her instructions, an Automobile Club truck driver towed the car to a street next to Golay's home, an hour before McDavid's body was discovered.

Investigations revealed that two elderly women had bought a 1999 Mercury Sable wagon from a dealership using a driver's licence in the name of Hilary Adler, with an address in Encino, California, and the ownership had been registered in that name. When police contacted Ms Adler it transpired that her handbag had been stolen from a Santa Monica health club frequented by Helen Golay and Olga Rutterschmidt. The women fitted the description given by the car dealer, one of whom had used Adler's identity to buy the Mercury Sable station wagon. He later identified Rutterschmidt as the woman who signed the purchase documentation.

Despite having the car towed close to home, the women abandoned the car in the next street. It accumulated numerous parking tickets and was eventually impounded. When it wasn't reclaimed, the pound sold it on to recover their costs.

Detectives quickly located the new owner and recovered the car before any evidence was destroyed. Forensic examination found evidence of blood and tissue on the underside of the car, matching Ken McDavid's DNA. The ripped tissue matched the injuries on his body. DNA was found in three places on the car including the impact area, and his fatal injuries were consistent with having been hit at speed by that specific vehicle.

Fingerprints found on the driving wheel and dashboard area of the car were identified as belonging to the two women, while McDavid and Vados's fingerprints and DNA were found in the back of the car, despite having being "taken for a ride" several years apart.

A forensic examination of the car also found that the passenger underside had been distorted and pushed up over an inch by the impact. Grease and dirt from part of the underside had been wiped clean, suggesting that the car had run over something. The grease and dirt found on McDavid's shirt exactly matched that on the rest of the car, when examined under forensic conditions. Further forensic evidence showed red paint splatter on one wheel of the station wagon. This was matched with red paint found outside Golay's home. Police had also received complaints about vandalism in the area, and they had taken photographs of the paint damage to substantiate Golay's insurance claim for vandalism. The vehicle was also identified as having been used in the hit-and-run on Paul Vados.

Investigating officers discovered that Golay and Rutterschmidt had filed insurance claims worth more than $4 million and were awaiting a further payout of almost $2 million. Golay owned dozens of properties and lived in property worth millions. She drove a Mercedes SUV and spent a fortune on plastic surgery, while her friend appeared to have a significantly less-well-off lifestyle.

The FBI decided to maintain surveillance on the women. They watched as the pair apparently groomed yet another victim for murder. They saw Olga pulling up beside an old man. She spoke to him for a while before inviting him into her car. They had apparently been "grooming" this man for some time. FBI watched as she took him to the bank, where she helped him to fill in forms.

Police recovered papers she'd thrown into the trash on the way out – "reply" envelopes to a bank and a life insurance company. Dropping him off, she went to an internet café and attempted to open a credit card account in the old man's name. Following through on the discarded envelopes, the FBI had enough information to arrest and charge the women with the credit card and insurance fraud.

Golay's home was raided by police, who took away items for forensic examination, including a diary and planner, which had a partly torn page. Forensic handwriting analysis identified part of a car registration number and a vehicle identification number belonging to the Ford Mercury used to murder the victims. The handwriting was matched to Helen Golay.

They also found numerous incriminating documents, including Hilary Adler's driving license, earlier reported stolen from the health club and later used to purchase the Mercury Sable car, as well as dozens of rubber stamps with the signatures of various men, included the already-dead Ken McDavid. After getting the men to sign insurance documents, the women made copies of the signatures and used them to make numerous applications for life polices through various companies, without the men's knowledge.

Both women were arrested and charged with two counts of murder and murder for financial gain, as well as multiple murder and conspiracy to commit murder.

When the case finally came to court the glamorous grannies took on different personae. Gone were the "blood-red talons", as described in news reports, bleached blonde hair, red lips and short skirts. Now they looked like two demure old ladies in a "butter wouldn't melt" moment. But it was not to last, as prosecutors produced the array of forensic evidence against them. The Ford Mercury murder weapon was brought to a basement beneath the court, where forensic specialists explained their findings in painstaking detail to the jury. Finally, prosecutors played a videotaped conversation secretly taken while they were in jail awaiting trial. The two women were heard arguing like alley cats, each blaming the other for their predicament. Olga accused Helen of being responsible for their downfall, accusing her of being "too greedy", taking out too many insurance policies and drawing attention to themselves. The sisters of mercy knew their end was nigh.

The former friends sat stony-faced as a Los Angeles Superior Court Judge handed down two life sentences, each without the possibility of parole. The judge said he would have imposed the death penalty but for their advanced age.

4

The Cause of Death: Forensic Pathology

One phrase that you'll hear often on news reports is: "The cause of death was . . ." Every murder, every suspicious death or even certain accidents require an investigation to determine the cause of death. A coroner may be asked to hold an inquest into the cause of death in an individual; on occasion, the coroner's court is adjourned, pending the outcome of a police investigation.

Forensic pathology involves the study of death and how the person died – the *how*, *why*, *where*, *what* and *when* of death. The forensic pathologist is just like a journalist following a story trail. In the case of murder when these questions have been answered, it's time for the investigating detectives to find the *who* – the person behind the murder and, on occasion, the identity of the victim, which brings it back to forensics, DNA, fingerprinting and odontology (forensic dentistry), amongst other disciplines. Assume nothing; "trust but verify" is the motto.

The cause of death is determined in a number of ways. Obviously, where the body was found and in what circumstances is of great importance. Are there visible injuries that could not have occurred naturally? Are there any signs of an attack, knife or gunshot wounds, strangulation or poison? Each and every possibility has to be examined and identified or eliminated. Could it have been a suicide? If this is a possibility, was there a history of depression, mental illness, a life-changing event, had medication been prescribed? These are all factors to be considered before a final decision is made.

The main "proof" lies in the postmortem examination, which can readily show the cause of death as a result of an attack with a knife, gun or blunt instrument, for example. It can show if a knife attack is likely to have come from a left- or right-handed attacker, whether they were taller than the victim or smaller, depending on the area and angle of attack – all valuable clues for investigating detectives.

For example, did the victim die from strangulation? Was there evidence of rope marks or ligatures on the body, resulting in asphyxiation? Asphyxiation – a lack of oxygen causing death by choking – is not always a result of strangulation but can also happen through smoke inhalation in a fire, which of itself could have been malicious or set after death to cover up a murder. Similarly, what appears to be suicide may not be the case. Just because a body is found hanging does not prove it was suicide. A crush injury which causes broken ribs can also result in asphyxiation; this is often seen in people trapped under a heavy object. A lack of oxygen to the brain can cause a build-up of carbon dioxide in the victim's tissues, which can be determined in a postmortem.

Blunt force trauma, often reported in murders, results from injuries inflicted with a heavy object such as a hammer, a baseball, a piece of wood or metal, the butt of a gun or other such objects. It can also arise from impact injuries, such as in car accidents. Blunt force trauma injuries are not always visible, as internal injuries can camouflage them, until eventually the victim collapses due to internal bleeding. Indications may be bruising, cuts and abrasions from being beaten.

Signs of defensive wounds are a good indicator that the person was attacked or, on occasion, was the attacker, as they may have wounds on their arms and hands, which they instinctively hold up to defend themselves. Often, in an effort to save themselves, a victim can scratch an attacker or pull hair, which may leave DNA evidence under the victim's fingernails, which can later identify the attacker.

A person might die as a result of a heart attack brought on by an injury. UK law works on the "thin skull" principle; if you punch someone and they die as a result, because they have a predisposed condition you weren't aware of, you are still guilty of murder. You take your victim as you find them. A punch to the stomach can rupture the spleen, which can cause death if left untreated. One recent example where this may have happened was at the G20 protests in London. An incident was caught on camera in which a man, who was not involved in the protests but was on his way home from work, was hit by a policeman. The man fell to the ground and died a short time later. Postmortem results have led to an investigation into his death.

While the vast majority of drownings are accidental, there are some occasions when a victim has been intentionally drowned, whether in a bath, a swimming pool or at sea. Rarely, a case of "dry drowning" will be seen. This is where water enters the throat and the larynx goes into spasm, forming a seal and blocking entry to the lungs. While this stops more water getting in, it won't allow the initial intake of water back out.

Drowning may be considered but is not always the primary cause of death if the victim was found in unusual circumstances. Was the body weighted down with rocks or wrapped in a sheet or plastic? Perhaps their hands and feet were tied up, stopping them from swimming to the surface? Often these victims have fought their murderers and will retain DNA evidence of their attackers. If the body is found at sea or in other salt water conditions, but only fresh water is found in their lungs, it can be assumed that they were dead before they were dumped at sea. It may be that the victim was killed elsewhere and then dumped in the water to hide the body, as in the Melissa Mahon killing, where Ronnie Dunbar (aka McManus) was convicted of manslaughter, having dumped the dead girl's body in a lake in Sligo.

As well as the cause, the location and time of death can often be determined through a postmortem. Postmortem lividity – livor mortis, as opposed to rigor mortis – usually develops within an hour of death, depending on the location of the body. It continues to develop for a couple of hours until the blood settles in the part of the body nearest the ground. For example, in a body lying on its back, the blood will pool in the back, while a hanging body will appear to be bruised, with the blood settling in the lower arms and legs. In the past this was used as a reference to the time of death but as scientific knowledge increased, it was realised that when a body is moved within a short time after death, the blood hasn't coagulated and would resettle elsewhere, in the lowest new position.

If a hanging body is cut down and put lying on the floor shortly after death, the blood would change position, although the obvious ligature marks would indicate that the person was either hanged or had committed suicide. If rigor mortis has already set in and the hanging body is then moved – for example, dumped in a ditch – it will be apparent that the body was moved after death. The time it takes rigor mortis to set in depends on several factors: e.g. whether the weather is hot or cold; if the heating is on in the house or the body is in a freezer; if the person is very young or very old (due to the lack of muscular development in the very young and the degenerative effect of wasted muscle in the old); and so on.

Certain types of poison can change the appearance of postmortem lividity, from its natural dark rose colour to a purplish blue, as seen in carbon monoxide poisoning, which shows up more as a cherry colour.

In certain instances the manner of death can cause what appears to be rigor mortis but in fact has been associated with terror in a victim, or in some cases even in a suicide. A muscular spasm of the face, known as *risus sardonicus*, which looks like a manic grin, or a spasm in the hands, which appear "locked", similar to a stroke victim, can manifest itself just before death and can sometimes be an indication of a terrifying death, perhaps at the hands of a murderer.

The stages of decay or decomposition falls into two categories. The first, known as autolysis, is a process within the body where the cells' enzymes start to shut down postmortem. The rate of autolysis can vary due to extremes of temperature, slowing down in extreme cold and speeding up in hot conditions. Putrefaction occurs when bacteria is released from the intestinal tract into the body after death, which breaks down the body and "melts" the body fats. All this can be an indication of how long the victim has been dead.

The FBI has studied the effects of the elements on dead bodies at their specialist facility known as "The Farm", set in 386 acres of woodland in Quantico, Virginia, forty miles from Washington. It is a city within a city and even includes a "rough" part of town, known as "Hogan's Alley", which was set up in 1986 after two FBI agents died in a shoot out. It gives agents ongoing practice in working the streets to tackle gun crime. It includes a bank, post office, theatre, courthouse and shops, just like any small town. It even provides its own "cast" of actors who are "mean criminals", ready to take out anyone getting in their way. With no set programme, it keeps the FBI agents on their toes, as they never know what might happen.

Quantico also houses a state-of-the-art Forensic Science Research and Training Centre, psychological profiling, the Violent Criminal Apprehension Programme (ViCAP), Drug Enforcement Agency (DEA) training, and FATS, a Firearms Automated Training system, which hones the firing skills and reaction time of agents. Quantico also provides training for many international police forces. Members of the Garda have attended courses there.

Some specific causes of death are looked at in later chapters, especially those that indicate murder. For example, Chapter 5 looks at asphyxiation while Chapter 8 delves into the ancient world of poisoning.

5

Leaving Me Breathless: Asphyxiation

We often hear of people dying of asphyxiation; but what exactly does that mean, and is it always murder? It can mean a lot of different things and, yes, it can be murder, but not always. The term "asphyxiation", although derived from a Greek word for "no pulse", simply means that a person's airway is blocked and they stop breathing; unless they are revived, the person will usually die. In murder cases, it can mean anything from strangulation to smothering with a pillow or suffocation with a plastic bag. Women are more likely to be the victims of strangulation, as it takes a lot of strength to strangle a victim, who is likely to be fighting off the attacker. Even if they survive the attack, they may suffer severe damage to the trachea and the oesophagus, not to mention bloodshot eyes and a severe headache or even brain damage.

If the victim dies, however, asphyxiation may not immediately be recognisable to the untrained eye; but it can be readily identified in a postmortem, often by bloodshot eyes and tiny ruptured blood vessels on the eyelids and facial skin, giving a speckled look much like tiny red freckles; these are known as petechiae. Ligature or rope marks may be seen around the neck; or if the killer used his hands, the bruised area may be larger and more irregular, particularly if the victim struggled and the attacker's grip moved. If the victim was tied up, wrists or other areas of restraint may also have marks and bruising.

In certain cases, death may not have been the intention. This is the case with an act known as autoerotic asphyxiation, which is designed to heighten sexual passion. It is a dangerous practice that can and does kill or has long-term effects, including brain damage or even brain death, because the brain has been starved of oxygen. Other injuries can include damage to the trachea, oesophagus or vocal cords.

For the purpose of a criminal investigation, a postmortem can identify any build-up of carbon dioxide in the victim's tissues caused by oxygen deprivation. This will also apply in cases of suicide by hanging, which can be differentiated from a murder situation by a medical examiner.

Of course, a lack of oxygen can come from other sources, such as the all-too-frequent death of a child who has swallowed a bead or other small object, which has got struck in their throat, accidentally cutting off their air supply, or adults who choke on food. Some victims have been found to have smothered to death, suffocated by a pillow, a piece of clothing, plastic bags or even a pair of tights.

Whether it is suicide or murder, ligature marks can tell the story to a forensic scientist. A ligature mark can provide evidence of the type of material or fabric used by an attacker, which can be linked back to its source. The marks may be made by rope, cord, silk, nylon or some other product that can withstand the strain of strangulation. Not every strangler uses these methods, as brute force and strength can literally crush the life out of a smaller or weaker victim, but this too can be identified and a postmortem examination will show sustained pressure on the windpipe. The pathologist will also check if the tongue and larynx are enlarged, if strangulation is suspected. Other signs of damage can include obstruction of the carotid arteries and the thyroid arteries, which can indicate the amount of pressure used by the attacker.

Frequently the victim will have an imprint on their neck, just as a tyre mark leaves a track in soft ground. Even the width of the item used can be established from the ligature mark. Ligature marks in a suicide differ in direction and type of imprint, which can help the pathologist differentiate between a staged suicide or a genuine one. Even when a victim is strangled with an attacker's bare hands, the fingermarks can be present in the size and shape of the attacker's hands.

6

Tragedy in Galway:
Manuela Riedo

The dream of a two-week stay in Ireland ended in tragedy for seventeen-year-old Manuela Riedo. The beautiful Swiss student had been in Galway for just a couple of days when her life was cruelly taken away by an evil beast.

The only child of Arlette and Hans-Pieter Riedo, Manuela had come to Ireland to do an English course with her schoolmates, a group of forty-odd students and two teachers from her school in Berne. The school had come to Ireland for the third year in a row to do the intensive course, and Manuela's parents were happy to let her join them. They believed Ireland was the safest country for their child. Seventy-two hours later, she was dead.

Manuela's semi-naked body was found on waste ground at Lough Atalia in the heart of Galway on 9 October 2007. A trail of her clothing led from the footpath to the waste ground where she lay, strewn there by her killer. Her body, partly hidden by bushes, naked from the waist down, was covered with her jacket, held down by a rock. It seemed she never had a chance to defend herself.

Chief State Pathologist Dr Marie Cassidy examined Manuela's body and concluded she had died from asphyxiation. She was most probably attacked from behind; her attacker had overpowered the teenager, dragging her to the ground. There were no telltale signs of a struggle, no scratch marks, no skin or hair under her fingernails, which would have indicated that she had fought off her attacker. She didn't stand a chance. The attacker used huge force, putting such pressure on her neck that the gold crosses on a chain around her neck were embedded into her skin like a tattoo. Her attacker had badly beaten the young teenager in a frenzied attack, before finally raping her. She suffered several injuries to her head and, strangely, her killer had cut a small patch of skin from her groin.

In a detailed search of the area, scene of crime officers scoured for any evidence of her attacker. They found a used condom hanging on a nearby bush. It was to prove a crucial link in identifying Manuela's killer. That, and the telltale "souvenir" of skin cut from Manuela's groin.

Gardaí immediately suspected the involvement of local man, twenty-nine-year-old Gerald Barry, from Rosan Glas, Rahoon in Galway. Well known to police, he was a career criminal with a violent history. Barry, an outrageous liar, initially denied having anything to do with Manuela's murder. Barry, who was living in his sister's apartment, claimed he had gotten up between 3.00 and 4.00 p.m. on the day in question. He told gardaí he hadn't been anywhere near Galway town that night, claiming that he drove around with his brother, Kevin Barry, and brother-in-law Dennis Ward, for most of the evening, before going to Ward's house to watch television. He said that he got a lift back home and was in bed by 11.30 p.m. He claimed he'd never heard of nor seen Manuela Riedo. He also said he hadn't been anywhere near the Lough Atalia area, known locally as "the line", for over three weeks, the last time being in September, when he'd gone to visit his mother in Mervue.

Meanwhile, gardaí and forensic scientists were working away in the background. Technical investigation on Barry's mobile phone proved he'd sent a text message to Melissa Curran, the mother of one of his three children, around 7.00 p.m. on the evening of Manuela's murder. Despite having denied being in Galway city that evening, Barry made a second call at 7.20 p.m., which was transmitted through the mast at Lough Atalia, where Manuela's body was found. An hour later, when he again phoned Melissa Curran, he was still in the area, and again the call was transmitted through the Lough Atalia mast. Another call to Dennis Ward, Barry's brother-in-law, was later confirmed by Ward himself. He told gardaí that Barry had phoned him and arranged to meet him later that night outside Supermacs in Shop Street, in the heart of Galway city.

Gardaí already knew that on the night Manuela was murdered, she had left the home of her host family, the Tierneys, between 7.00 and 8.00 p.m., on her way to meet friends. Despite having been just hours in Galway, the girls had already discovered a short cut into town along the railway line. Mr Tierney had warned Manuela not to take the short route, especially at night. It was October and it was dark early. It wasn't a safe place to be, but all the girls used the route, and it saved Manuela a long walk.

Gardaí discovered that, just a week after Manuela's death, on Wednesday 17 October, Barry had sold a Sony Ericsson mobile phone to his sister's boyfriend, Mark Kealy. Manuela's phone was missing. It was a Sony Ericsson. Barry had deleted the telephone numbers on the phone, in the belief that it wouldn't be identified. Forensic analysis retrieved and identified texts in the memory; they were all in German. The last one was sent on Monday 8 October, just hours before Manuela's murder. Poignantly, it read in German: *"Hi Mum, All going well in Galway. It's raining but I have the right clothes for the rain, so don't worry everything is OK all my love Manuela."*

Following a search of Gerald Barry's home, gardaí found Manuela's digital camera under the mattress in his bedroom. It still contained some of the photos she'd taken. It was a strange move for a man not known to be stupid – unless he wanted to be caught.

There was no way out for Gerald Barry, who was arrested and charged with Manuela's murder. He denied everything, saying he knew nothing about the murder or the girl.

When forensic investigation saw his lies unravelling, Barry eventually admitted to having had consensual sex with the teenager. He later said she had died accidentally, when he "hugged" her too tightly, claiming that when he realised she was dead, he covered her with her coat "out of respect". He admitted he'd used a condom, saying he had thrown it away afterwards. It was to prove his downfall. Forensic scientists identified Manuela's DNA from the condom found close to her body in nearby bushes. More importantly, they also identified Gerald Barry's DNA from the condom. Barry thought he had beaten the rap by admitting to consensual sex with Manuela. There was never any doubt that there was nothing consensual about it, as the forensic evidence had shown. Manuela wasn't that kind of girl and, with Barry's history, things were beginning to add up.

Gerald Barry was well known to gardaí. He had form – a lot of form. He had been in and out of trouble all his life. In 1997, he was sentenced to five years for violent disorder, following a vicious, unprovoked attack in 1996 on a seventeen-year-old Tipperary youth, Colm Phelan, in Eyre Square in Galway. The innocent teenager died as a result of his injuries. Barry didn't serve five years. A year later, in 1998, he was jailed for two years after attacking an old man in his home. The pensioner was blind in one eye, and following Barry's vicious assault, the elderly man lost the sight in the other eye. Barry also had previous convictions for sexual assault, including an assault on a former girlfriend and other offences. He was the prime suspect in the oral and anal rape of a twenty-one-year-old French woman on 16 August, two months before he killed Manuela, as forensics had recovered the attacker's DNA – that, and his modus operandi (MO) of taking a "souvenir" of the victim – but of course none of that

could be made public before he had his day in court.
Barry was out on bail for breaching a protection order
when he killed the Swiss teenager. Following his
conviction for the rape and murder of Manuela, Barry
pleaded guilty to two counts of rape of the young
Frenchwoman, having attacked her on a GAA pitch at
Mervue in Galway.

Manuela's distraught parents watched in silence as the
jury found Barry, described by Manuela's father as "the
devil", guilty of murder. He was jailed for life. Mr Justice
Carney ordered that Barry be put on the sex offenders
register. In July 2009, Barry was also sentenced to two life
sentences for the rape of the Frenchwoman. It is unlikely
we have heard the last of Gerry Barry.

7

When a Stranger Calls:
Sharon Coughlin

When Sharon Coughlin's ten-year-old daughter came home from swimming around 7.00 p.m. on 15 September 2007, the front door was locked. She tried phoning her mother's mobile, but couldn't get hold of her. She phoned her aunt Caren and she and her sisters Orla and Brenda tried to find Sharon, but they too drew a blank. It was completely out of character for thirty-seven-year-old Sharon, who had her phone on day and night and was never unavailable.

Sharon's son was almost five and was with relatives for the day while Sharon took time off from her job as a barmaid in the Market Bar in Ballymahon Street in Longford, where she had worked since she was a teenager. The popular, hard-working mum was bringing up her two children alone.

It was not like her to leave her children for so long. She usually picked up her daughter from swimming, yet she had made no contact to say she was delayed or to ask any family member to do it for her. The worried family contacted the gardaí.

Having dropped off her daughter at swimming classes in the town, Sharon had headed to Tesco to do her weekly shopping. Investigating gardaí checked out the CCTV footage at the local Tesco store and identified her in the car park at around 4.30 p.m. on the Saturday afternoon. She was then seen walking in the direction of home. It was the last time she was seen alive.

With the investigation ongoing, gardaí were contacted by the owner of a vacant house, just yards from Sharon's home. The property had been empty for over two months and was in the process of being renovated. When the owner went to the house around nine o'clock on Saturday night, he found the body of a young woman in the bathroom and immediately phoned the police. Scene of crime officers from the Technical Bureau examined the house. The woman, who was partially clothed, had been covered up and hidden under a new bath that had recently been installed. The body was identified as Sharon Coughlin. Clumps of hair and blood were also found in the house and sent for forensic analysis. Fingerprints were found around the house and on the covering that concealed the body.

The investigation considered several angles, including the possibility that Sharon might have known her killer. Was it possible that her killer had been a customer of the Market Bar and perhaps knew her, or she knew him?

A postmortem by the Deputy State Pathologist Dr Michael Curtis at the Midlands Hospital in Mullingar reported that Sharon Coughlin had died of asphyxiation due to pressure on the neck. Her face bore the telltale petechiae marks found in some cases of strangulation, which are caused when the capillaries, the smallest blood vessels in the body, are ruptured. There was no doubt that Sharon had been strangled to death.

But before her murderer killed her, he'd raped her. Forensic examination of the body fluids revealed the presence of semen. DNA was extracted and held as evidence against possible suspects.

Sharon's bag and clothes lay strewn around the empty house. Her money and mobile phone were missing, as were two packets of Mayfair cigarettes she'd bought on her visit to Tesco. The mobile phone was monitored and, forty-eight hours later, gardaí discovered it was being used with a different number. Someone had switched SIM cards but the signal was still being bounced off local masts. Analysing the signals in the triangulation method, which cross-references the location of the masts bouncing the signal from the user to the person they are calling, detectives could home in on the stolen phone and identify the location where it was being used.

It was enough to lead them to David Brozovsky, a Czech national who was living at Grian Ard, Ard na Casa, in Longford. Unknown to them, Brozovsky had given the phone to someone as part-payment for a debt. That person immediately changed the SIM card and began using it, not realising that either the phone or Brozovsky were connected to Sharon Coughlin's murder. They told investigators what they knew.

David Brozovsky, a nineteen-year-old father of one, had moved to the area following his arrival in Ireland a year earlier, in 2006. He had been living alone since splitting from his girlfriend and child. Detectives quickly established that Brozovsky was no stranger to crime. In co-operation with Interpol, the world's largest international criminal police organisation, which serves 187 member countries, providing information and assistance on international crime and criminals, detectives discovered Brozovsky had twenty-five previous convictions in the Czech Republic for various offences, including aggravated theft and extortion. From there he had moved to Belgium, where he had two further convictions for aggravated theft, before he arrived in Ireland. At nineteen, he was already a career criminal. Now, he was a murderer as well.

Detectives working the case established that, after the rape and murder, Brozovsky rifled through Sharon's belongings, stealing her cigarettes, money and anything else he could find. He subsequently went to Western Union and sent €60 to his girlfriend and child, part of the €100 he'd stolen from the dead woman.

Brozovsky was arrested. His prints matched those found on the covering concealing the body, and the DNA from the semen sample taken post mortem from Sharon Coughlin matched his DNA. There was also trace evidence – clumps of hair and blood were found at the crime scene and forensic analysis identified that some of the hair had come from the attacker, as Sharon tried to fight him off. Sharon's stolen phone had been passed on to another party and was tracked back to Brozovsky, who used it to pay off a debt. CCTV at the Western Union office and his payment sent to his girlfriend immediately after the murder, together with all the other evidence, put Brozovsky in the frame.

He confessed to the rape and murder of Sharon. He told detectives that he'd broken into the vacant house to "do drugs". He'd seen Sharon Coughlin walk by on her way to Tesco and waited for her to return, intending to steal her bag. When she passed, he dragged her into the house and raped her. He said that, as she tried to fight him off, she was crying and shouting, "Why are you doing this?" Afterwards, he strangled her and dragged her upstairs, where he hid the body wrapped in a covering under a newly installed bath.

Brozovsky pleaded guilty to the charges. Mr Justice Liam McKechnie said: "It was a mindless, utterly barbaric, savage attack and I really have no words of comfort to say to the grieving family." By all accounts Sharon Coughlin was "a kind, generous person and hardworking, and her death . . . was an absolute tragedy". David Brozovsky was given a mandatory life sentence by Justice McKechnie, with a further thirteen years for the rape of Sharon Coughlin. The sentences were to be served concurrently.

Sharon's two children, her ten-year-old daughter and her five-year-old son, were completely traumatised at their loss. Already a one-parent family, they were now without their mother. The ten-year-old suffers from nightmares, and her little brother can't understand why his mother is not coming home, asking friends to help him find his mammy.

8

Toxicology:
The Poisoned Chalice

Toxicology or the science of poisons has been around forever. Poisons were the tools of kingmakers, disposing of many a monarch; from the time of Socrates, who was despatched with a dose of hemlock, to the Roman emperors and the ancient Egyptians, who used antimony, opium or even arsenic to sort out their rivals. In more recent history, Hitler took cyanide to escape capture by the Allies.

In Victorian times it was common to dispose of an enemy, a discarded spouse or a wealthy relative, by poisoning them with toxins such as deadly nightshade. Many of these dangerous poisons were readily available over the counter from the local chemist or bought from ironmonger shops.

Fortunately, modern forensic toxicology can usually identify cause of death by poisoning, or in the case of serious illness, if caught in time, it may even save a life.

Good investigators and forensic scientists can unearth evidence to show means, motive and opportunity as well as the forensic evidence to prove what really happened.

The FBI profiling unit have established the profile of a typical poisoner to be a white male, average to above-average intelligence, an underachiever, inadequate personality; non-athletic, cowardly, neat and orderly, a loner; meticulous, a careful planner, non-confrontational physically or psychologically. Strangely, they didn't include women in their profile.

Generally, money, power or revenge are at the root of such horrific acts, as was the case of American Ronald O'Brien, who murdered his own child, poisoning him and claiming the insurance. In some instances, it is as simple as giving a "loved one" a dose of something they are severely allergic to, sending them into anaphylactic shock – a "tragic accident" and an easy way out for the grieving spouse, who believes they can avoid the expense of a divorce and collect the insurance to boot. L Adelson, a respected American forensic toxicology pathologist, said: "Most signs and symptoms associated with natural disease can be produced by a poison and practically every sign and symptom observed in poisoning can be mimicked by those associated with natural diseases."

Morphine

The notorious Dr Harold Shipman from the UK was convicted of killing fifteen patients and is believed to have killed at least 186 other patients after he qualified as a doctor in 1970. He administered high doses of morphine, having first ensured that they had "signed over" their assets to him in recently changed wills, many of which failed to stand up to the scrutiny of handwriting analysis and proved to be forgeries. (See Chapter 9.)

Polonium

The most recent high-profile murder by toxins was that of Russian dissident Alexander Litvinenko, who died as a result of radiation poisoning by Polonium-210 in London in 2006.

A specialist in the intelligence service, investigating corruption by renegade former KGB officers and the Russian mafia, Litvinenko angered Vladimir Putin after he exposed an FSB plot to assassinate Boris Berezovsky, a powerful tycoon who fled to the UK. (The FSB are the Russian Federal Security Service, formerly known as the KGB.) Putin had Litvinenko arrested and he spent almost a year in prison.

There had been several other attempts on his life in the UK, before the November 2006 attack. Then, following a night out with his wife at a London restaurant, Litvinenko became really ill and went to the local hospital. "Simple" food poisoning was ruled out, as his wife had eaten the same meal. Poisoning was suspected, as he suddenly began losing his hair. Forensic analysis of his hair for the suspected poison thallium revealed only minute trace elements, ruling it out as the cause of his illness. Haematological, immunological and biochemical tests showed that Litvinenko was riddled with radioactive contamination, yet he was not known to have had any contact with radioactive materials. Forensic investigators found further radioactive contamination at his home and in his car. The car was so dangerously contaminated it had to be destroyed. Everywhere Litvinenko had visited over the preceding days, including two hospitals, were checked out. He had met two men – one a former KGB agent – at London's Millennium Hotel and two occasions and at the Itsu Sushi restaurant. All these locations were found to be contaminated.

Forensic investigators from specialist radiation research units were convinced it was radiation poisoning, but they still had no idea what type of radioactive material was involved. Despite tests, they could not pick up gamma rays, usually found in radioactive material. In desperation, they tested Litvinenko for alpha particle emissions, expecting to find nothing, as alpha particles only cause damage if they are ingested or inhaled. It came as a shock when the test was positive. Litvinenko was emitting alpha particles, which later proved to be Polonium-210. Polonium-210 radiation poisoning had never been known outside of nuclear projects. Litvinenko had more than 200 times the lethal dose.

Forensic scientists at the UK Atomic Weapons Establishment tracked the radionuclide Polonium-210 back to Russia, where almost ninety-eight per cent of Polonium-210 is made. Following the trail, forensic investigators found traces of Polonium-210 on two British Airways planes flying to and from Moscow, used by the former KGB agent when he travelled to London to meet Litvinenko. The man was also identified in Litvinenko's company by British intelligence agents, from CCTV footage.

The ex-KGB "friend" of Litvinenko used a fax machine in the London office of a Russian businessman, which also bore traces of Polonium-210. It was established that the Russian men meeting Litvinenko had handled the deadly toxin, but only Litvinkeno ingested it in a cup of tea served to him by a "waiter" believed to have been a Russian agent. Despite knowing the identity of these men, and having established a great deal of forensic evidence, the British authorities' request for extradition from Russia was refused. Although no one was brought to justice due to diplomatic difficulties, the Litvinenko affair was a sign to the public that political espionage is still prevalent. Russia's embarrassing problem was solved by Litvinenko's death.

Ricin

Georgi Markov, a Bulgarian dissident, was famously assassinated in London in 1978 while waiting for a bus. In a typical "James Bond" scenario, he was jabbed with the tip of an umbrella in the back of his thigh. When he turned around, a man apologised in a foreign accent and jumped into a passing taxi. Markov thought nothing of it and went to work – he was a journalist in the BBC – but became ill with a fever and vomiting. The following day he was admitted to hospital but he died four days later.

Following a postmortem examination, the skin around the puncture wound in his thigh was sent for specialist forensic toxicology examination to what was then the Chemical Defence Establishment, now called the Defence Science and Technology Laboratory, at Porton Down in

Wiltshire. They managed to extract a tiny pellet, no more than 1.5mm in diameter, from the skin sample. Under close examination they noticed two microscopic holes which could hold infinitesimally small amounts of deadly poison. The holes were now empty, having discharged their deadly cargo of ricin.

Ricin is produced from the castor oil plant and has been widely used as a poison since the sixth century. The multicoloured seeds of the castor oil plant from which ricin is made look innocent, but Mexican workers who made necklaces from these seeds frequently died just from handling the highly toxic seeds or from holding the "beads" in their mouths while stringing them onto the necklace chain.

Death by ricin poisoning can be excruciating. It can take between two and twenty-four hours to develop the abdominal pain, vomiting and diarrhoea. The toxin causes haemorrhages in the intestines, as well as acute liver, kidney and heart failure. Even a small dose can immobilise the victim within days, with severe dehydration, burning throat, intense headache, exhaustion and cramp. The victim dies a horrific death from hypovolemic shock, when the heart can no longer supply blood to the body. Ricin is twice as toxic as cobra venom, if administered by injection, and it is considered the most toxic substance in the plant kingdom.

This was the poison of choice of Sharon Collins's would-be hit man, Essam Eid. Collins was convicted of trying to hire a hit man to murder her millionaire lover, PJ Howard, and his two sons so that she could inherit his wealth. (See Chapter 29.)

Ricin is the stuff of James Bond, spymasters and terrorists. Most would-be poisoners look to simpler solutions.

Anaphylactic Shock Inducers

Peter Mere Latham, a nineteenth-century medical tutor, said: "Poisons and medicines are often times the same substance given with different intent." Disposing of a spouse by "dosing" them with a substance or product to which they are extremely allergic, such as peanuts, or a medication known to cause anaphylactic shock, such as sulphonamides, has been known. The "poor unfortunate" husband or wife finds their spouse dead, supposedly the victim of a tragic accident or suicide. There may be little evidence to suggest that it was self-administered; it could have been given in a generic and unmarked product by a "caring" spouse and innocently taken by the victim. With no one left to tell the truth, the killer may well get away with it, unless diligent detectives and pathologists look beyond what appears to be the obvious.

Even prescribed products such as an antibiotic can kill, if the victim is seriously allergic to it. For example, some people are susceptible to sulphonamides, once a common ingredient in antibiotics, now seldom used. It can cause anaphylactic shock, where the body system "shuts down", causing major breathing difficulties, a severe drop in blood pressure, loss of consciousness and eventually heart failure. It is not unknown for some would-be killers to administer small doses over a period of time, suggesting that the person had been ill for a long time and eventually died from "natural causes".

Cyanide

In Washington State in 1986, Stella Nickell's husband Bruce died of emphysema and the grieving widow picked up the life insurance money. They'd had the policy for some time but Stella didn't realise that when the death was due to natural causes, it paid less than the $175,000 she was expecting.

Elsewhere in Washington, another young woman died after taking an over-the-counter painkiller. She was found dead on her bathroom floor. A postmortem showed she had died from cyanide poisoning. An inspection of her home revealed a bottle of brand-name painkillers in her medicine cabinet. The pills were forensically examined and found to have been laced with cyanide. The manufacturing company recalled their product and a public warning went out in the media, which brought a response from Stella Nickell. She said she believed that her husband's recent death could have been as a result of the poisoned pills. Bruce Nickell's body was exhumed and it too was found to have traces of cyanide, enough to have brought about his death.

Stella was delighted; she was about to come into a lot more from the insurance company. However, investigators were suspicious and decided to dig a bit further. They spoke to members of Bruce's family and a different picture emerged. Detectives painstakingly went through every possible angle to prove that Bruce had been killed. Finally it paid off as they found Stella's fingerprints all over a book on poisons and toxicology at the local library. She had spent time there examining the books before her husband's death. Judging from the fingerprints, she was particularly interested in the chapters on cyanide poisoning and its lethal effects. There was also the small matter of two pill bottles in her home – the ones she'd claimed to have bought for her husband. She told investigators she believed they came from the contaminated batch. She was right; the pills were contaminated. They too contained cyanide.

A forensic investigation of the pill bottles found both in Stella Nickell's home and in the home of the other victim, Susan Snow, revealed evidence of minute particles of green algae. The grieving widow's home had several fish tanks. Samples of the algae from the tanks were forensically examined and found to match the algae particles found in the contaminated pills. Stella Nickell was charged and convicted of the double murder of her husband and of the random victim, Susan Snow. She got life imprisonment.

Arsenic

Arsenic was a common poison for centuries. It was famously used by the Borgias to dispatch their enemies, of which they had many. Napoleon's excruciating death was also believed to have possibly been a result of arsenic. More recently, it featured regularly in films and was much beloved of the notorious Nannie Doss, a serial bride and infamous poisoner, who disposed of five husbands and several other family members with doses of arsenic.

Arsenic is a deadly toxin, but is in less common use today as it can be readily detected with modern forensics. In 1998, it caused the deaths of four people at a food festival in Japan, while many others suffered severe poisoning. The food was found to have been deliberately contaminated with arsenic. Today, it can be found in certain insecticides and weed killers, but its use and availability is restricted in many countries.

Strychnine

Seen in many "who done it" movies of the fifties, strychnine was commonly used in pesticides to kill rats and other vermin. In humans, it affects the central nervous system, causing strange arching convulsions, where the victim's body bends backwards in an arch on the ground. A vicious toxin, it also causes a contraction of the facial muscles, known as *risus sardonicus*, which resembles the maniacal grin of the Joker in *Batman*. It causes severe pain and respiratory failure.

Organophosphates replaced many of the older products such as DDT in pesticides, but these are equally lethal to humans. Products such as herbicides can also have serious effects. Paraquat is the best known; it was often the poison of choice in murders or suicide, resulting in a prolonged and painful death.

Other poisons are less subtle and vary from country to country.

Ethylene Glycol

Ethylene glycol, as used in solvents, brake fluid or antifreeze, has been readily available for over fifty years, yet it can be one of the most toxic substances if ingested. Brake fluid has been used to dispatch "insignificant" others, love rivals or even in suicide bids. It's cheap and terminally toxic. Without commercial additives, it is a sweet-tasting liquid but is colourless and odourless and has been known to be mixed with food as a fatal poison. It has been intentionally used as a poison by killers to horrific effect, causing a collapse of the central nervous system, kidney failure, hallucinations and heart problems.

Initially, the victim may appear to be intoxicated or suffering from the effects of a drug overdose, before collapsing into a coma. If caught in time, it can usually be treated, provided the dosage is not too high.

There have been many instances of poisoning by ethylene glycol in the US and several female killers have disposed of up to six husbands, collecting the insurance money, until eventually caught. Shirley Allen was finally caught following the disposal of her third husband, who had been complaining of a strange taste in his drinks. Shirley's daughter noticed her mother putting something into a drink; it looked like antifreeze. She reported her to the police, but by then it was too late and Lloyd Allen had died. Her hopes of collecting a big insurance payout faded when toxicology tests proved he'd been poisoned. She's currently doing life in a US prison.

In a recent case in the US, a man was rushed to hospital by his work colleagues in a bowling alley. After a sudden onset of nausea, vomiting and abdominal pain, they assumed he had food poisoning or appendicitis. He later became lethargic and unresponsive. Extensive blood, urine, spinal fluid tests and cat scans were all normal but additional tests showed up a high level of glycolic acid, which usually causes renal failure if untreated. After extensive treatment in an intensive care unit, the patient was released from hospital but required long-term care. Investigation showed there had been no attempted suicide. A criminal investigation was then launched, which proved that the twenty-three-year-old had been poisoned by a co-worker. He was not the intended victim, as the would-be murderer had planned to poison another staff member, but put the toxic substance in the wrong man's drink.

In a suspicious death, the presence of ethylene glycol is identified by the presence of calcium oxalate crystals, which usually appear in the shape of a "folded envelope" in the urine and can be identified by forensic analysis. Other techniques used to identify the toxin include ultraviolet light, which makes it appear as a green-coloured glow both on the clothing and in the contaminated urine, which will test fluoresced.

Insulin

In the UK, thirty-five-year-old ward sister Deborah (Dee) Winzar, from Kettering General Hospital, was convicted of killing her thirty-four-year-old husband Nick McCarthy by injecting him with a lethal dose of insulin. McCarthy had been awarded major damages as a result of a road traffic accident that had left him in a wheelchair. The couple had a three-year-old son, Tadhg, and Nick McCarthy, who worked as a departmental manager in a nearby centre for the disabled, took care of the boy when his wife was on night duty. Having given her husband a massive dose of insulin, injecting it into his lower body where he couldn't feel the jab, McCarthy's wife went to a party and stayed overnight with a friend.

The following morning, she rang her son's kindergarten to check that her husband had dropped him off. When she was told he hadn't, she surprisingly asked the kindergarten manager to call to her house to check on her family. The kindergarten manager found the toddler playing in the hall as his father lay in a coma. Paramedics rushed to the house, initially believing McCarthy had pneumonia, because of his breathing difficulties. It was only later in hospital that tests showed he was suffering from hypoglycaemia, only seen in diabetics. As he had no history of diabetes, this was extremely unusual.

Just forty-eight hours later, while in intensive care, he was visited by his wife. Shortly after her departure, it was noticed that his IV medication tube had been disconnected. Two days later, with McCarthy still fighting for his life, his loving wife Dee visited him again. After her departure, staff noticed that McCarthy's drip tube, supplying vital drugs to keep him alive, had been interfered with. It had a large air bubble, a potential killer if left unnoticed. The alarm, designed to alert staff to any problem, had not gone off as it should have done. A technical inspection showed no fault in the machinery, which was working properly.

Despite the best efforts of the nursing staff, after nine days fighting for his life, Nick McCarthy died. His wife, Dee Winzar, was charged with his murder. She had the means, motive and opportunity, as well as her medical knowledge, and access to insulin as a nurse had put her in the frame. The promise of an inheritance was too tempting for the evil nurse. Independent experts gave evidence of the lethal dose of insulin that had killed him.

Despite her protestations of innocence, claiming it was the work of an intruder, she was found guilty by Birmingham Crown Court and sentenced to life imprisonment. The judge hearing the evidence said her crime was "as evil and calculated as can be envisaged". Winzar, who'd kept her maiden name after her marriage, appealed against her conviction but the Court of Appeal found that the nurse had murdered her paralysed husband, leaving their young son without a father or a mother.

Toxic Gases

Sometimes an unfortunate gas explosion will demolish a house or even kill the occupants. This is usually due to a gas leak, a broken main or some accidental source. However, there have been incidents of murder by toxic gas – just another cause of death for the pathologist to uncover.

Television adverts warn of the dangers of carbon monoxide poisoning. Carbon monoxide is a colourless, odourless gas that deprives a person of oxygen without any warning, as it insidiously envelops their home. It is sometimes used in suicide bids, such as when the person connects a hose to their car exhaust, starts the engine and pumps the noxious gas into the car.

Carbon monoxide (CO) detectors are readily available, changing colour at the first sign of a leak, but are unfortunately not in common use. There are many other gases used in industry and found in nature that can be toxic, but CO is the poison of choice for many, in the belief that it can be covered up as an accident.

9

Patient Men: Colin Norris and Harold Shipman

Every couple of years a shocking case will hit the headlines: a serial killer is finally caught, years after the murders have taken place. Sometimes it comes about by accident or luck, the killer making a mistake or being in the wrong place at the right time. Frequently it is through the dogged persistence of the investigating team – the cold case unit who revisit the evidence – or through new forensics developments such as DNA profiling, which make criminal convictions possible.

Not all serial killers are readily identifiable within the community. Many are well-respected members of society, until they get caught. Cases such as those of Colin Norris or Dr Harold Shipman in the UK in recent years show examples of "pillars of the community" who became killers.

A number of deaths of elderly female patients occurred in Ward 36 at Leeds Hospital. The women were often in poor health and their deaths were not entirely unexpected. Ninety-year-old Vera Wilby, recovering from a hip operation, was about to return home when she was found semi-conscious after a sudden hypoglycaemic attack, despite not having diabetes. Due to quick medical intervention by Dr Emma Ward, a diabetic specialist, she survived, and was able to tell doctors that a male nurse, Colin Norris, had given her an injection just before she felt unwell. A blood test revealed that she had been given unprescribed doses of morphine and insulin.

Several other patients in the same ward had died unexpectedly, and in 2002, following a Coroner's Order, police began an investigation into the deaths of eighty-six-year-old Edith Hall, Doris Ludlum (80), Irene Crooks (79) and Bridget Bourke, an eighty-eight-year-old from Mayo, who had all died at the hospital while successfully recovering from hip operations.

Bridget Bourke's body was exhumed a year after her death and a forensic examination showed that she had not died from complications following her hip surgery. Similar results emerged from the other women, all of whom had died as a result of insulin overdoses, causing a diabetic coma from which they had never recovered. None of the women were diabetic and despite their advanced years, none had terminal diseases. It was now a murder hunt.

In a two-year investigation, detectives took over 7,000 statements and seized 3,000 exhibits, tracing back the murders to Colin Norris. It was a difficult case, as many of the dead women had been cremated, which accelerates the degradation of insulin, unlike with other toxins, giving forensics no chance to identify the toxin. In the case of other "intact" bodies exhumed, pathologists found levels of over 1,000 units of insulin, whereas a diabetic would normally take fifty units. Extensive forensic neuropathology, pathology, pharmacology, endocrinology and toxicology tests were done and the combined forensic evidence from experts, including experts in diabetes, established the causal link between the deaths and Norris's unauthorised administration of high doses of insulin with malicious intent.

Investigators analysed complex shift patterns, time frames, hospital procedures and security as well as access to drugs cupboards, withdrawal of drugs and syringes. Working back through break times, sick days and related data, they established that all the deaths had taken place when Colin Norris was on duty on Ward 36. All occurred at 5.15 a.m., while Norris was alone and the ward was quiet. Unnoticed at the time, Norris had withdrawn large amounts of insulin which could not be legitimately explained and didn't write them up into the records or on patients' charts.

Police discovered that Norris had been violent to his gay boyfriends and had also killed their pets with insulin overdoses. He hated his elderly female patients and arrogantly "predicted" their deaths when on duty, saying he didn't "like the look of them". Inevitably, he was right, as the patient usually died during the night. He told colleagues in what was described as "an attitude of detached amusement" that it was his luck that patients "always died" on his shifts. When he "found" Bridget Bourke unconscious, he "showed no urgency in trying to revive" her. She died twenty-four hours later.

In 2008, Norris was found guilty of four sample counts of murder and one count of attempted murder at Newcastle Crown Court. Mr Justice Griffith Williams said: "You are a thoroughly evil and dangerous man, arrogant and manipulative with a real dislike of elderly patients." Norris was given four life sentences, with a further twenty years in respect of the attempted murder, with a minimum term of not less than thirty years.

Harold Shipman's case was even more notorious for the sheer number of patients he killed. Shipman, or "Dr Death" as he became known, murdered hundreds of patients over a career spanning several decades. Manchester Coroner John Pollard suggested, "We might be looking at 1,000."

The story emerged after Alan Massey, a local undertaker in Hyde, Greater Manchester, had become concerned at what he considered "an unusual coincidence" in the deaths of a large number of Shipman's elderly patients. He noticed that the vast majority of them died fully clothed, either sitting up or lying on a couch. He said: "There was something that didn't quite fit." He tackled Shipman, who reassured him that everything was in order. He even showed him his death certificate book.

Massey's daughter was not so easily reassured and confided her suspicions to Dr Susan Booth, who was from a different practice. Under British law a doctor from an independent practice must countersign cremation forms issued by the original doctor, in this case Harold Shipman.

Dr Booth discussed the matter with her practice colleagues and they decided to pass on their concerns to the coroner, John Pollard, who immediately contacted the police.

Despite an investigation, the police found nothing against Shipman, unaware that he had rewritten the records of the patients he'd killed to match their treatment. A forensic examination of the handwritten documents would clearly have shown that all the "records" had been written at the same time. The ink, paper and indentations did not match other documentation held in the surgery, which spanned back over many years. Computer records could have been identified by a forensic computer expert after forensic examination of the hard drive, identifying and extracting the permanent records and details of any alterations made, but at that time, the investigating officers took the matter at face value and were reluctant to call the doctor's character into question.

The Shipman Inquiry later questioned the quality of this investigation, and said lives could have been saved if the investigation had been more thorough. Police never checked if Shipman had a criminal record. Had they done so, they would have discovered that, in 1975, he had been thrown out of an earlier practice for forging prescriptions including pethidine, an opioid painkiller, which he later claimed, without any evidence, to have been taking himself. He was subsequently convicted of forging prescriptions and fined £600. He had also spent time in rehab but was back in general practice within two years.

It took the death of ex-Lady Mayoress Kathleen Grundy to catch the killer. Well known to everyone in

Hyde, the fit and active eighty-one-year-old was heavily involved in the local community and worked tirelessly for local charities, including meals-on-wheels and Age Concern. Kathleen never missed an appointment and was rarely ill; her timekeeping and reliability were renowned. When she failed to show up for an appointment, a check was made on her home. She was found fully dressed, lying on the sofa, dead. Distraught, her friends called her GP, Shipman, who pronounced her dead.

When Kathleen's daughter Angela Woodruff was contacted, she was concerned at her mother's sudden death. As a qualified solicitor, under the law, she expected a postmortem. Shipman was adamant – there was no need for a postmortem, as he had seen her mother earlier that day to take blood samples for a study on ageing. Angela took him at his word.

A few days after the funeral, Angela got a call which gravely concerned her. A firm of solicitors contacted her, claiming to have a copy of her mother's will. The strange thing was that her own practice had always dealt with her mother's affairs, including her original will, which was lodged in their safe. When the other solicitors, acting in good faith, showed Angela "their" copy, she immediately knew it was a fake. It was poorly worded in language not of her mother's meticulous style, badly typed and the signature was not her mother's usual neat signature; it was much too big. Tellingly, it left everything to Dr Harold Shipman, including a sum of £386,000. Angela Woodruff said: "The concept of Mum leaving anything to her doctor was unbelievable."

After interviewing the "witnesses" to the will, Angela was certain that Shipman had murdered her mother for the money. She reported her belief to the police. The Detective Chief Superintendent in charge of the investigation was equally suspicious and the finger of suspicion pointed directly at Shipman. He later told the Shipman Inquiry: "You don't have to have twenty years as a detective to know it's [the will] a fake. Maybe he thought he was being clever, an old lady . . . but everyone knew she was as sharp as a tack." Forensic investigation and handwriting analysis proved them right. There was zero chance that Kathleen Grundy had made that will.

But that wasn't enough to prove he'd murdered her; to do that, they would have to exhume the body for pathological examination. It is very unusual to have to apply for an Exhumation Order from a coroner and the Greater Manchester Police had never done it before, but that would soon change as they became experts in the area.

When Kathleen's Grundy's body was exhumed, pathologists took extensive samples of hair and tissue which were sent to different laboratories for examination. That way, the various labs could produce independent evidence for comparison. Mrs Grundy's fingerprints were also taken and a forensic "comparison" examination was made to the fingerprints found on the "new will" in favour of Harold Shipman. Some prints matched staff from the reputable firm of solicitors, who were innocent to the subterfuge, and these were eliminated from the enquiry. Fingerprint and document analysis experts identified three sets of relevant fingerprints on the will.

Two sets matched the innocent witnesses and the third was identified as being that of Harold Shipman. There was no evidence of any of Kathleen Grundy's fingerprints. Clearly, Mrs Grundy had never handled the document. Renowned handwriting and calligraphy expert, Mike Allen, who has worked on cases for me in the past, examined the "new will" and described the signatures as "crude forgeries".

Police raided Shipman's surgery and home before he had time to learn of the exhumation. Dr Shipman's response was aggressive and arrogant. He showed contempt for the police when they produced a search warrant and gave no indication that he knew his number was up. Among the items recovered was an old-fashioned Brother portable typewriter. It was subsequently forensically examined and the typeface, lettering and ribbon ink, together with areas of damage, were compared to the badly typed will made in favour of Shipman. It was a match. Shipman claimed that Mrs Grundy occasionally borrowed the typewriter. This improbable tale was later shot to pieces when forensic scientists proved that the same machine had been used by Shipman not only to draft the counterfeit will, but to produce other fraudulent documents and prescriptions.

When asked what had happened to the blood samples he'd claimed to have taken from Mrs Grundy for the study on ageing, Shipman said he'd sent them to the lab. When it was put to him that no such study existed, he tried to wriggle out of the dilemma, saying he had mislaid the samples under some paperwork and that by the time he'd found them, they were no longer of use, so he'd disposed of them.

Detectives who searched Shipman's home were shocked

at the state of his house, it was littered with possessions, ancient newspapers and a large collection of jewellery which didn't belong to his wife. Things were beginning to add up but police were overwhelmed at the sheer scale of what they were facing. A series of other questionable deaths would have to be investigated and that meant prioritising those most likely to yield positive results.

Greater Manchester police became adept at seeking exhumation orders, initially seeking orders for those where the body hadn't been cremated, before moving on to others. Shipman had always encouraged the families to have their dead relative cremated. As their attending doctor, he could certify the death without a need for an inquest or any further investigation, which he always put down to ill health and natural causes. Understandably, the families trusted him and frequently took his advice, despite the sometimes "unusual" causes of death on the death certificates, citing medical conditions which had never been mentioned during their lifetimes.

Things began to gain momentum when the first forensic toxicology report came in on Kathleen Grundy. Forensic toxicologist Dr Julie Evans found that Kathleen Grundy died as a result of a massive morphine overdose, her death occurring within three hours of getting the injection. Shipman never expected this outcome and later "reluctantly disclosed" that his patient Mrs Grundy was a "morphine junkie", addicted to painkillers. Anyone who knew the glamorous, intelligent lady knew she was anything but.

The net began to widen as police investigated any of Shipman's patients who had died following a visit by him.

An initial examination of Shipman's computerised patient records revealed no clues. The patients appeared to have had certain conditions, had been treated appropriately for them but, due to age and complicating factors, they had succumbed to the disease. In fact, on his last visit, he would often make sure to let the family or care home staff know how ill the patient was and to expect the worst.

It was not until the forensic computer investigation unit got involved that the depth of Shipman's conspiracy emerged. Within hours of a patient's death, Shipman would log on to his computer and change the records to match the outcome, altering his notes to suggest the sudden decline of the patient and the lack of response to treatment. In Kathleen Grundy's case notes, he had retrospectively altered her notes to suggest she was a morphine addict, and he made several entries over a period of years, suggesting he was treating her for the addiction. While it is not unknown for people of all ages and walks of life to become dependent on alcohol or drugs, Shipman lost the run of himself, making entries indicating that ex-Lady Mayoress was "stalking the streets seeking out drug dealers to feed her habit".

In some 495 cases reviewed, Shipman gave non-terminally ill patients injections of around 30mgs of morphine. Dr John Grenville, an expert on general practice, told the Shipman Inquiry that he had only given four 10mg diamorphine injections in twenty years, whereas Shipman had, for example, given 30mg doses to twelve different patients in three months, enough to instantly kill a very strong fit young man. Dr Grenville said: "I can't imagine any circumstances when you would give a single dose like that to so many people." There could be no doubt the injections were intended to kill the patients. Dr Grenville also said it was "extremely rare" for patients to die while the doctor was visiting them, or a very short time later.

Shipman, who claimed to be a computer expert, actually knew little about computers and even less about how they worked. He assumed that by deleting what he had already written – the genuine patient case notes – and replacing them after death with spurious ones to suit his purposes, he was home and dry. After all, the records were there, going back years for anyone to see. His hard drive proved his downfall, the silent witness to his murderous intent. It led forensic computer specialist Detective Sergeant John Ashley step-by-step through Shipman's every move in his effort to conceal the killings. The experts used a combination of systems including FRED (Forensic Recovery of Evidence Device) in combination with EnCase, which can locate both the original and the "new" file, identifying when they were originally created or written, when any changes were made and what records or data had been deleted. The forensic computer interrogation told them all they needed to know.

During questioning, Shipman was asked about a patient who had died at 3.00 p.m. on 11 May 1998. He had accessed his computer using his own name and password and changed an entry on the patient's file just hours *after* her death, indicating that she had complained of chest pains. He then backdated the file entry to 11 October 1997, eight months earlier. Shipman denied it, not believing for a moment that the detectives could possibly prove he had changed a computerised record.

Winnie Mellor was another victim of Dr Death. Planning a trip to the Holy Land, the active seventy-three-year-old died suddenly and unexpectedly following an unrequested visit by Shipman. Kathleen Mellor only learned of her mother's death following a phone call from Shipman. Bizarrely, he played a lengthy "guessing game" as to why he was calling. The strange conversation appeared to be leading nowhere. Kathleen asked Shipman if her mother was dead. He coldly replied: "I see you understand" and put down the phone.

It later emerged that Shipman had called on Mrs Mellor twice the day she died. The second time, he had knocked on a neighbour's door, saying he was calling to see Winnie, but could get no answer. He said he could see her sitting on a chair through the window and he thought she was dead. He already knew this, as he'd killed her with a morphine overdose on his earlier visit. When the neighbour told him she had seen him going into the house earlier, he got angry and said, "You stupid girl." The cold calculated killer was angry that his earlier visit had not gone unnoticed. The neighbour later gave police specific information about the timing and duration of his visits.

Forensic computer evidence showed he later altered Mrs Mellor's records to show that she had a history of chest pain and angina, which her family denied. EnCase and FRED extracted the original file, which showed no evidence of any such complaints or treatment during her time as Shipman's patient. In fact, she rarely attended him, such was her good health.

Shipman was charged on fifteen sample counts of murder. During the course of his lengthy trial, forensic evidence emerged that, over the course of many years, he had forged morphine prescriptions for at least twenty-eight patients. He had also "stolen" medication from the patients' homes immediately after their death, stockpiling it to kill others. He had prescribed morphine for people who had never required any pain relief. The prosecution case was that not one of the patients cited in the cases had terminal illnesses. All had died suddenly and unexpectedly.

In each case, Shipman had something to gain, not always monetary. It was like some sick kick for him to be able to control life and death. Some police officers had seen how cruel and calculating Dr Death actually was, even before the murders came to light. Following the death of sixty-two-year-old Ivy Lomas, for instance, police called to her GP, Dr Shipman, to help them find and notify her next of kin. Shipman was unsympathetic and sneered at them, saying he was thinking of getting a plaque with Ivy's name on it for his waiting room, to mark the spot where she had died waiting to see him. Shipman had left her there, despite knowing she was at death's door (having already injected her with a lethal dose of morphine). He had made no attempt to resuscitate her or send for an ambulance. Any normal medic would have dropped everything for such an ill patient, as Dr Grenville told the court.

UK government pathologist Dr John Rutherford gave detailed evidence of his analysis and collection of body tissues from many of the deceased. He said that none of the victims had died from disease or old age. The cause of death in every case had been morphine toxicity.

Bill Catlow, a friend of healthy and active seventy-seven-year-old Lizzie Adams called to see her, only to find Shipman examining her expensive collection of porcelain as Lizzie lay dying in an adjoining room. Bill felt Lizzie's pulse; she was still alive and warm and he called to the doctor to help. Shipman said it was too late, that he was cancelling the ambulance – in fact he had never called one, telling Mr Catlow it was only his own pulse he felt, and that he was just imagining his friend was still alive. Catlow was adamant that Lizzie was alive and could have been saved, but then he didn't know about the murderous morphine she'd just been given. Shipman was right; it was too late and Lizzie died. The porcelain was among the "treasures" later found in Shipman's home.

Others told of how Shipman had called to the homes of elderly relatives for routine visits. After being alone with them for some minutes, he would say they were seriously ill and that he'd called an ambulance for them. Evidence would later show that Shipman never called an ambulance for any his dying patients. Had he done so, difficult questions might have been asked by the hospital, inquests or postmortems carried out, and he would have been exposed as a killer. Nora Nuttall's son Tony slipped out for five minutes and was surprised to find Shipman leaving the house as he came back, saying he'd called an ambulance; yet he was leaving her alone. Shipman touched her neck and said, "She's gone." Family members called to Shipman's surgery demanding to see Mrs Nuttall's medical records, details of her death and why he'd called to see her. Shipman said the dead woman had phoned the surgery and asked him to call. Forensic examination of telephone records proved that no such call had been made from the Nuttall house, nor was there a log of the call by surgery staff.

The lengthy trial heard damning forensic evidence. Shipman was found guilty on all counts of the deaths of fifteen patients. They represented the hundreds he murdered during his lifetime. He was also found guilty of forging Kathleen Grundy's will.

Mr Justice Forbes said: "You murdered each and every one of your victims by a calculated and cold-blooded perversion of your medical skills, for your own evil and wicked purposes . . . I have little doubt that each of your victims smiled and thanked you, as she submitted to your deadly ministrations." Shipman was sentenced to fifteen life sentences for the murders and a further four years for forgery. In an unusual move, Justice Forbes said, "It is my recommendation that you will spend the remainder of your days in prison."

There were many unseen victims of Shipman. Renate Overton lingered for over a year in a coma after Shipman gave her a toxic morphine injection in 1994. Others were cremated, making a clear-cut case against Shipman virtually impossible. Many basic mistakes were made. Ineffectual investigation by detectives out of their depth; a fear of reprisal from patients or those with suspicions; and a fear of not being believed when outrageous suspicions were voiced against a professional: all conspired to protect Shipman from close scrutiny. But for the sterling work of a myriad of forensic scientists, Harold Shipman, Dr Death, would still be wielding the syringe of the grim reaper on his innocent patients.

His capture and imprisonment was too much for the serial killer and on 13 January 2004, four years after being sent to prison, Shipman took his last victim: fifty seven year-old Shipman committed suicide, hanging himself in his prison cell.

Emerging information following on the Shipman Inquiry's final report indicates that he may have been responsible for killing many more than the hundreds already believed. It appears that Shipman's first victim was probably sixty-seven-year-old Margaret Thompson, who died unexpectedly in 1971, while Shipman was with her. Fifty-four-year-old Tom Cullumbine and two other men, as well as four-year-old Susan Garfitt who suffered from cerebral palsy, were also possibly early victims. In October 1972, while working at Pontefract Hospital, Shipman told Mrs Garfitt that her daughter was going to die and that there was no point in prolonging her suffering. The distraught young mother went for a cup of tea and came back to find her daughter dead. The Inquiry found that Shipman had most likely given the child a lethal injection.

By 1975, he had already killed some fifteen patients. Reports from Pontefract Hospital where Shipman worked as a junior doctor, showed they had an unusually high mortality rate during his three years there.

Harold Shipman currently holds the unenviable title of Europe's most prolific serial killer.

10

Busted by Bugs: Maggots, Mystery and Murder

It might seem strange to imagine that bugs, flies, creepy-crawlies and maggots all have an important part to play in forensic science. Known as forensic entomology, the study of bugs, maggots and flies can provide "evidence", including an indication of the time of death. Bugs can multitask in numerous other areas of criminal investigation, from identifying the country of origin of illegal drugs, to tracking a criminal's movements.

Police forces and forensic scientists worldwide are constantly striving for new ways to detect drugs and other threats to security. Incredibly, recent developments have seen wasps and bees replacing tracker dogs in seeking out drugs and explosives. In New Mexico, scientists have "trained" bees to detect various types of illicit drug, homing in on them via their highly sensitive antennae, which contain hundreds of thousands of sensors. Incredibly, it takes just minutes to train in the bees and success rates have been excellent. They have even managed to train them to pick out explosives and potential terrorists by focusing on the vapours emitted.

How does entomology work in practice? It's a simple science at its best and, unlike television portrayals of some forensic "miracles", this one really does what it says on the tin. It all starts at the beginning of life – a bug's life, that is. It's strange to think that bugs, flies, worms and maggots can be the first-line "detectives" in pinpointing the time of death. Of course, many other factors come into play which can affect the calculations, such as where the body is found. In most instances, important evidence can be established about the time of death based on the body's location and other circumstances. Did the death take place in winter or summer? Did the victim die where the body was found or was it taken there? Was it found in the countryside or in a large city? The creepy-crawly "detectives" all leave their own clues for the forensic entomologist to find. By promptly collecting and examining the various species, the entomologist can estimate the time of death depending on the stages of development of the various specimens.

Very soon after death, and sometimes even while the heart is still beating, stab wounds, bullet entry or exit holes and even scratches will bleed, and the body will give off odours that attract insect life. In open ground, insects will even lay eggs in a moist open wound, attracted by the blood. Flies and bluebottles are usually the first to arrive, followed by various others species, depending on the location, as decomposition takes place. Each will take its place at the scene at various times, always in the same rotation, like diners booking a restaurant table. They will vary from country to country and climate to climate, but all will tell their own macabre tale as to the estimated time of death by their structured timetable of arrival on the body.

The rate at which they arrive and lay their eggs or leave their maggots can be fast, sometimes within minutes of death, depositing them in open wounds or in other orifices. Depending on the weather, they can take between seven days and six weeks to go through their life cycle from eggs to maggots and flies, which gives the forensic entomologist an indication of how long the body has been dead or *in situ*. If, for example, the body is found in a country field but exhibits signs of infestation seen only in a city, it is likely the killing took place in the city and the body was moved after death. In hotter climates, the decomposition rate is rapid if the body remains outside, as evidenced by the number of maggots present and their developmental stages.

Forensic scientists study the bodily changes and decay rate based on all these factors and, assuming the body has not been frozen, which can mask the natural decomposition, it will provide valuable evidence as to the most likely time of death. In general, some bugs and insects found in and around a dead body are necrophagous, in that they gorge on the dead body, laying eggs which can, with the aid of an electron microscope, help to identify the species involved and give a timeframe as to how long the body had been there. The absence of maggots or other flesh-eating insects on a body with obvious wounds suggests that the wounds were probably inflicted post mortem, either in the transportation of the body or as part of the killer's intention to mutilate it.

A forensic photographer will usually take photographs to record the various stages of entomological infestation, as the insects can continue to develop, even after the body is moved to the morgue for a postmortem. It is important to photograph the body as quickly as possible, to retain a record of the insect life on site.

In situations where the body has been submerged in water, localised tiny fish or crustaceans such as fresh water prawns may take up residence inside the body. This is a common occurrence in Ireland, where bodies found in areas such as Dublin Bay or even in canals have been found to have prawns and small species of fish inside, which was the case in the mutilated body of Farah Swaleh Noor, found in the Royal Canal in Dublin. (See Chapter 11.)

In the case of a potential murder, where evidence of bullet wounds, entry and exit points or knife wounds are found, necrophagous (flesh-eating) bugs, attracted by the blood, can destroy the wound site beyond recognition. They enter the body through the opening and wreak further havoc from within. Injuries caused after death, possibly when transporting a body, are less likely to bleed, depending on the time interval between the death and the moving of the body, and this too can show whether the death took place where the body was found or was moved there after death.

The type of insect found on a cadaver is also a good indicator of how long the victim had been dead, as each species of insect arrives at different stages of decomposition. This is known as insect sequencing. The first insects, flies – or rather, bluebottles – can arrive within minutes. Drawn to the moist areas of a body, they lay their eggs in the eyes, mouth and nose area. Maggots gorge on the moist flesh, before slithering away to the soil, to emerge a week later as fully grown bluebottles, restarting the cycle all over again.

Dermestid beetles are next in line. These flesh-eating beetles arrive in colonies and can quickly reduce a corpse to bone. They are used by taxidermists to "clean" animals of their flesh before they are preserved and stuffed. Bugs can help to prove or disprove if the victim was poisoned or was using drugs, as analysis can identify toxic chemicals ingested by the bugs from the victim's body, even where the body may have already decomposed.

11

The Canal Corpse and
the Scissor Sisters

When a headless corpse was seen floating in the Royal Canal in Dublin, passers-by couldn't believe their eyes. Initially they had thought it was a mannequin, a broken shop dummy discarded by someone. It wasn't unusual to see rubbish floating in the canal; people discarded all sorts of things.

A few people had spotted a black plastic sack floating in the canal, but thought nothing of it. As the days went by, more body parts floated to the surface and people really began to worry. It was definitely something sinister. There were a number of calls to Tara Street Fire Brigade station, the command-and-control centre for Dublin, and they relayed the message to North Strand station, situated two or three minutes from the canal. Callers thought someone had fallen into the canal. It now sounded like a drowning, but when the fire brigade arrived on the scene, they weren't too sure. They could see an arm and then a leg with a sock on. Worried it might be a hoax call, they dragged the canal and to their horror, pulled in what was obviously the remains of a human arm. It was decomposed and had a strong odour of rotting flesh. Once out of the water it began to disintegrate even further, what was left of the flesh falling away like overcooked meat. The experienced fire crew put the arm back into the water to prevent any further damage and sealed off the area. It was now a crime scene. Soon the area was crawling with cops. They had to work fast, as darkness was falling and the investigation team needed to examine the area as soon as possible.

Anything can disturb forensic evidence – heavy rain, for example, can wash away evidence – but in this case, everything seemed to be under water anyway. As soon as the news broke, every newsroom in Ireland was carrying the story, sending journalists, news teams and photographers to the scene.

Garda subaqua divers had the gruesome task of retrieving the body parts, while mapping out the underwater area and marking the location of what body part was found where – an arm here, a leg there. The divers ensured that what remained of the body was preserved as well as possible, securing the parts in specialist plastic bags underwater, before eventually bringing them to the surface for forensic examination. This was a horrific murder – the body had obviously been dismembered. The torso, arms and legs were present, but there was no head.

Initial media reports suggested it might be a ritual killing. There had been one in London some time previously (see Chapter 17), and with the influx of foreign nationals from some countries, where juju and black magic still hold sway, it couldn't be ruled out. Some tribes believe that by slaughtering a human being they can gain special powers, increase their knowledge or cure ills. It seemed far-fetched in a country not used to such beliefs, but was well known within Interpol and other crime forces. Nothing could be ruled in or out at this stage.

The first major problem in any murder case is to identify the victim. If the victim is known, it provides a start in the investigation, a process of eliminating or identifying a possible killer. The method of killing, motive and means can all help to fill in gaps in the puzzle. Without victim identification, it is difficult to know if it is a gangland hit, the murder of a spouse or a killing during a robbery.

In this case, there were wide possibilities and everything had to be investigated. Without a head, it wasn't going to be an easy task. Yet another difficulty was the extensive decomposition of the body parts, making it difficult to establish the victim's race. The remains looked white, but between the blood loss, the postmortem marbling and the length of time in the water, the gardaí couldn't be sure. It's not very often that a headless body is found in Ireland and few garda detectives could recall such a case. The only one that came to mind was a couple of years earlier when the headless body of a twenty-five-year-old mother of two from Malawi was found in a stream in Kilkenny. It too was initially believed to have been a ritual killing.

Over forty years earlier, there had been a similar case in Dublin, when Hazel Mullen was killed and dismembered by her boyfriend Shan Mohangi, a medical student studying in Dublin. Mohangi had befriended the family and was readily accepted by them, even though Hazel was just sixteen years old.

It was a traumatic relationship which ended tragically, with Mohangi killing the teenager and dismembering her body, which he then boiled up in the basement kitchen of the Green Tureen restaurant in Harcourt Street, where he had a part-time job. Gardaí were baffled for a long time. A well-known journalist, Jimmy Cantwell, asked his friend, my father Bill Kavanagh who was a private investigator, to help him investigate the whereabouts of the missing Hazel. They visited the basement of the restaurant and both were convinced that the young girl met her death there and relayed their information to investigating gardaí. They were later proved right, much to the horror of the Irish public at the time.

Now, almost half a century later, it had happened again. A dismembered body had been seen floating in the Royal Canal, in sight of Croke Park.

The postmortem was carried out by Deputy State Pathologist Dr Michael Curtis. Given the discoloration of the body, the victim could be identified in a number of ways. Fingerprinting is the main form of identification but, as it is not done in Ireland unless you have a criminal conviction or, since 2001, are applying for asylum, it is of little value if the victim has not come to police attention. Similarly, DNA is the most effective form of identification, but unless a comparison sample is available from the victim having been tested previously (say, for example, in a criminal investigation for sexual assault), identification may not be possible unless investigators have some idea as to the possible identity of the victim and can compare it to the DNA of parents, siblings or children of the person concerned. You may have the haystack, but no needle.

In cases such as the body in the canal, a body could normally also be identified from dental records, as the teeth are preserved, even where the body has completely decomposed, but without a head, there were no teeth and what was left of the body was of little forensic use without something to compare it to. Gardaí had nothing to go on; they weren't even sure of the nationality or race of the victim. The Forensic Science Laboratory at Garda HQ called on the expertise of their colleagues in the Forensic Science Agency Lab in Carrickfergus in Northern Ireland. Their isotope analysis expert Dr Augenstin examined the torso to try to establish the possible origins of the victim. Isotope analysis, a relatively new forensic development, which was also used in the "Adam" case in London (see Chapter 11), can identify the person's diet from the nitrogen, oxygen and carbon found in the bones, along with strontium and lead, which in turn can be an indication of their nationality based on their diet over a number of years. The isotopic ratios of these elements vary depending on the region a person lives in, affecting the isotopic "signature" of body tissues. When analysed by a mass spectrometer, this can point to the person's geographical origins as the isotopic oxygen is absorbed by tissue, teeth, fingernails, hair and bones. This is best done through analysis of the teeth, but without a head, that was impossible.

The idea that this had been a ritual killing began to take hold. There appeared to be several similarities with known ritual killings abroad, including the fact that the head and the penis were missing. Contact was made with a specialist unit in Pretoria, South Africa, who advised on the evidence usually seen in ritual murders. Eventually the idea of a ritual killing was ruled out. While isotopic analysis would indicate that the man's origins were Kenyan, his diet proved he had lived in Ireland for some considerable time.

Gardaí sought the help of the media to publicise the crime in the hope of identifying the body. They issued pictures of the Ireland football jersey found on the torso and they contacted immigrant communities and newspapers in an effort to identify the body.

The real breakthrough came when friends of the victim became concerned that they had not seen him for some time. A number of people recalled that their friend, a Kenyan man known as Farah Swaleh Noor, had been wearing an Ireland jersey when they last saw him on St Patrick's Day. Despite efforts to make contact with him, they had neither seen nor heard from him in the two months since. The investigating detectives were sure they'd found their man. One man in particular recalled meeting Noor in the company of his girlfriend, a much older woman he called "Katherine".

Gardaí discovered that Noor had already come to their attention in the past, although mainly for minor offences. He was also a suspect in the Raonaid Murray murder and had been interviewed and formally interrogated by the team investigating her killing. Something else emerged from the police files that would be crucial to identifying the body in the canal. A former girlfriend of Noor had made a complaint to gardaí when Noor threatened her and their child. At last they had something with which to compare the DNA of the body to a known relative – his son – if in fact the body was that of Noor. Either way, it would identify or eliminate him from the investigation.

Dr Dorothy Ramsbottom of the Garda Forensic Laboratory in Garda HQ, Phoenix Park, examined the DNA sample from Noor's son. It was a match for what remained of the body in the canal. There was no doubt now that the body was that of Farah Swaleh Noor, or rather, Sheilila Salim, which was his real name. Finding his child by a former girlfriend had been crucial in determining the victim's identity.

The investigation got into full swing. Concerned friends of Noor had identified his girlfriend's name as "Katherine". It turned out that her name was in fact

Kathleen, but now at least they had an address and detectives lost no time in checking it out. By the time the team descended on Noor and Kathleen's address – Flat 1 at 17 Richmond Cottages – Kathleen had moved out. Nonetheless, with the co-operation of the new tenant, the forensic team moved in. If Noor had been murdered there – and there was no evidence of that as yet – forensic evidence would be found.

Given that the body was dismembered, his head cut off and his arms and legs hacked off, as well as his penis, the crime scene must have been awash with blood. An adult male has around six litres of blood in his body, and there is no doubt that Noor lost most of that where he was killed. Between the blood loss and the hacking with knives and frenzied hammer blows to disintegrate the major bones in the body, there had to be traces of tissue and bone fragments which were overlooked by the killers. Despite the huge efforts to disguise the crime scene, every contact still leaves a trace. This time was no different.

The new tenant certainly hadn't noticed anything that disturbed her – no blood splatter, no sign of a struggle. The place was clean and tidy when she took over the flat – but for one rather unusual thing. When she had rearranged the furniture she noticed that there was no carpet under the bed. It looked like a piece had been cut away. The carpet close to the door and window had ragged edges, as if it had been well torn or ripped away.

The forensic team examined the area and found blood particles, invisible to the naked eye, caught between the cracks on the floorboard and on the base of the bed. It is often a case that murderers clean and scour the floor and walls to wash away blood splatter, not realising that a residue is often left between the cracks in floorboards and other areas, which shows up under specialised chemicals such as Luminol, which can readily highlight blood where the naked eye can't. Fresh blood is bright red, but with time, it will dry to a dark brown or black and may be invisible on timber floors. Blood spatter – as opposed to blood splatter – can show the direction from which the victim received a blow, resulting in a particular pattern or random dispersal of blood drops in a specific direction. Evidence of blood is often found in the drains of showers, baths or sinks, despite Trojan efforts to clean up and wash it away, it is virtually impossible to cover all the traces.

The blood spattering and splattering found in the flat at Richmond Cottages were analysed by Dr Brid McBride of the Garda Forensic Laboratory. It was a match for Farah Swaleh Noor. Gardaí had established that Noor had entered Ireland in late December 1996; in January 1997 he had applied for asylum, giving false information as to his identity and background, claiming to have been born in Mogadishu in Somalia, when in fact he was from Kenya and named Sheilila Salim.

Having spoken to friends of the dead man and learned more about his relationship with "Katherine", now identified at Kathleen Mulhall and her daughters Linda and Charlotte, investigating gardaí built up a picture of a dysfunctional and violent relationship. Their follow-up investigation at

Richmond Cottages and the forensic evidence found there convinced them that they'd identified the crime scene and the Mulhalls were in the frame as possible killers, having been the last people to be seen with him on the day he disappeared.

With ongoing intelligence and investigation progressing the case, the family's mobile phone communications were monitored. This appeared to implicate John Mulhall, Kathleen's ex-husband and father of Linda and Charlotte, with the crime scene, if not the crime. The girls certainly spoke to their father soon after Noor's murder, and later information suggested that John Mulhall had called to Richmond Cottages after the fact, but had fled in shock and horror. He was not suspected of having been involved in the killing; he was a decent man by all accounts, but as a father, he may have tried to protect his daughters and was worried about Linda's four children.

Four and a half months after the dismembered body in the canal was found, the gardaí had their killers. But this was just the beginning. There was a lot more to come and the case had to be proved beyond all reasonable doubt to a jury of twelve citizens. The case against them had to be watertight.

Following a conference of the investigation officers, it was decided to arrest the Mulhalls for the murder of Farah Swaleh Noor. The sisters, Linda and Charlotte (known as Charlie), were arrested at different locations and taken, along with their mother Kathleen, to various garda stations in Dublin for questioning. John Mulhall was also arrested and taken in for questioning. They all denied any knowledge of the murder of Noor. Kathleen, for her part, insisted he was still alive and laid out how she had being trying to find him. After twelve hours in detention, they were released without charge.

Gardaí were playing a waiting game. They knew John Mulhall in particular was traumatised by the whole event. He couldn't come to terms with what he knew his daughters had done, however much he loved them. Eventually the strain became too much for him and he made a call to try and put things right. He phoned the investigating gardaí and asked for a meeting. It was what the gardaí had been hoping for. A nervous John Mulhall told gardaí that his daughter Linda knew where the victim's missing head was and, with a little gentle persuasion, he was sure she would be relieved to talk. They arranged to meet up later that night at the family home but Linda never showed up and her phone was switched off. It subsequently transpired that Linda had tried to commit suicide by slitting her wrists, and was in hospital.

By arrangement, gardaí met up with Linda as soon as she was out of hospital, but at that time, she was beyond talking. Some time later Linda rang Detective Inspector Christy Mangan, who headed up the investigating team, and asked to speak to him. Mangan had spoken to Linda and other family members on several occasions and Linda respected his kindness and professionalism. When they met, Linda, who was in a distraught state, blurted out that she and Charlotte had killed Farah Swaleh Noor.

Linda made a full and frank confession, even going so far as to take DI Mangan to where she'd hidden Noor's head. She also told him where, in a local lake, they had disposed of the hammer and the knives used to dismember Noor. The garda subaqua team subsequently recovered the murder weapons from the lake.

On 14 September 2005, Linda Mulhall was formally charged with the murder of Noor. She appeared before the District Court and was remanded in custody. As yet, her sister had not confessed to gardaí. Subsequently arrested on unrelated charges, she continued to deny Noor's murder when questioned about it, yet surprisingly admitted to knowing Noor's dismembered body lay in three sports bags around the flat and said she had helped carry them to the Royal Canal. She also said she had used his ATM card to take money out of his account but denied that either she or her sister Linda had killed him. When asked about the missing head, she claimed she didn't know where it was, saying "me ma had it", and went on to claim her mother had hit Noor with a hammer and then cut him up with a knife.

After further questioning and denials, Charlotte shocked the detectives by finally confessing, saying, "Everything that Linda says happened." She went on to admit that, following a bout of drugs and drinking, Noor had tried to force himself on Linda, despite her protests and her efforts to push him away. In an effort to help her sister, Charlotte said she had stabbed Noor in the neck and Linda had hit him with a hammer. They stripped him of his trousers, leaving only his Ireland shirt on the torso and cut him up before eventually putting the body parts into sports bags. She claimed they'd left his head in a park beside The Square shopping centre in Tallaght. Charlotte Mulhall was later charged with murder on the direction of the DPP and, following an appearance at the District Court, she too was remanded in custody.

Just before Christmas, John Mulhall hanged himself, no longer able to live with the nightmare. He had admitted to detectives that while he had nothing to do with the murder, he had received a call from his daughters on the night Noor was killed. He couldn't believe what he was being told and rushed over to Richmond Cottages to see what had happened for himself. When he went in, he looked around for Noor, but there was no sign of him. He had hoped that, at worst, Noor had been injured by the women, and initially, not seeing him, thought he had gone out, until they told him what had happened and showed him the dismembered body parts in bin liners. He was horrified and incredulous, but scared for his daughters. He had repeatedly tried to persuade them to confess, yet couldn't bring himself to turn them in. When they finally confessed and the gory details were exposed in the media, the strain was too much to bear, and he took his own life.

Linda was allowed out on bail pending the trial, but Charlotte, who failed to comply with her bail conditions by signing on at a garda station, was returned to Mountjoy to await her trial. Their mother, Kathleen Mulhall, fled the jurisdiction and was not around to support her daughters in their ordeal. The tables were to turn as, when the trial commenced before Mr Justice Paul Carney in the Central Criminal Court, Linda was nowhere to be found, and only Charlotte was in the dock, taken there from prison. A bench warrant was issued for Linda's arrest. When gardaí eventually located her, she was in a very poor state, both mentally and physically. Taken to Mountjoy jail overnight, she appeared in court the following day but her barrister, Senior Counsel Brendan Grehan, asked the court that she be referred for examination by a forensic psychiatrist.

When the trial eventually got underway, the sisters pleaded not guilty. As the gory details of the killing were laid out for the jury and the assembled media and general public, there was a horrified silence at the viciousness of the murder. The Mulhall sisters did not give evidence.

After a protracted trial, the jury's deliberations were lengthy. They returned to court on several occasions to advise that they could not come to a verdict and were deadlocked, only to be urged by Mr Justice Paul Carney to resume their deliberations. They eventually came to a decision. Linda Mulhall was found guilty of manslaughter by a majority of 11–1, while her sister Charlotte was found guilty of murder by 10–2.

Mr Justice Carney described the case as "the most grotesque case of killing that has occurred within my professional lifetime". In October 2006, he sentenced Charlotte, who'd recently had a baby boy, to mandatory life imprisonment, while Linda was given fifteen years.

Kathleen Mulhall, who had gone on the run, voluntarily returned from the UK and in May 2009 she pleaded guilty to aiding and abetting her daughters to clean up the mess from the killing, the day after the sisters had killed and dismembered her boyfriend. She was sentenced to five years' imprisonment, backdated to early 2008.

12

Criminal Connections: DNA and Forensics

The discovery of DNA, the basic genetic material found in the body's cells, was like finding the Holy Grail for many scientists, unlocking the mystery of life. Described as the blueprint of life, DNA (deoxyribonucleic acid) carries our genetic code and is handed down through generations of families. It is our genetic inheritance; it makes us what we are.

DNA is the one constant in our lives. People change with age but our DNA remains the same. The chemical structure is different in every individual. The odds against finding someone else with the same DNA as you are 1 in 65 billion against, except in the case of identical twins; they are not distinguishable by DNA, as they are the result of the same single egg splitting after conception. (However, the fingerprints of identical twins still separate their biometric identity from their DNA or genetic fingerprinting.)

First discovered over twenty-five years ago by Professor Alec Jeffreys, a Lister Institute Research Fellow at Leicester University, "DNA fingerprinting" (also known as DNA profiling) has remained the single most important medical breakthrough in genetic coding. The simplest way to describe DNA coding is to compare it to supermarket bar codes. Each is unique to its own product or the individual person, the only common DNA being identical twins, much like two tins of beans of the same size and brand that carry the same bar code.

In 1987 the Lister Institute of Preventative Medicine gave Cellmark Diagnostics, an ICI company, exclusive worldwide rights to the technology, and today, Cellmark continues to provide international access to individuals, government bodies and organisations around the world in the many applications of DNA identification.

Cellmark's services are best known for paternity testing. Before Jeffreys' discovery, there was no way of proving who the father was in any disputed case. Today, paternity testing is used in many applications, from medical requirements to match donors, to criminal investigations and in family law custody, divorce and inheritance cases. It is the foolproof way of telling who is, or is not, the daddy.

It is also used in immigration issues, where DNA relationship testing is done to identify genuine family members applying to join their relatives in the UK, Australia or other countries having such entry requirements.

Testing DNA has become routine, simple and very quick. The most common method, as seen in *CSI* and other forensic or medical programmes, is usually a mouth swab, where a cotton bud is rubbed on the inside of the cheek to gather the saliva. But unlike television images, the saliva itself doesn't contain DNA and this method is only successful if you manage to get enough buccal skin cells from inside the cheeks or mouth to allow a reliable result.

DNA analysis can be extracted from semen, buccal cell saliva, tissue, blood, bone, muscle, hair, faeces or urine among others. The results of such analysis can identify or eliminate possible suspects. Red blood cells carry no DNA, but the white cells in the blood provide a good source of DNA. Some rapists and sexual attackers are under the misapprehension that they can't be caught by DNA testing if they've had a vasectomy. Aside from the array of collectible DNA samples from a victim, DNA is readily extracted from the body fluids of men who've had vasectomies.

DNA has vast potential and can lead to the identification of criminals through numerous means. A discarded handkerchief, condoms, sweat stains, skin, hair or dandruff can all bear witness to the perpetrator.

In an early case in the UK in 2003, fifty-three-year-old truck driver Michael Little died after a brick was thrown through the windscreen of his lorry from a footbridge. The brick hit him in the chest, causing a heart attack from which he died. Investigating officers attending the attempted theft of a Renault Clio close to the footbridge believed the incidents might have been connected. They recovered the brick for examination. Forensics were able to extract DNA from the brick and, following their instinct, scene of crime officers took DNA samples from the nearby car incident, believing the perpetrator had tried to steal it to make his getaway. The DNA from the car and the brick matched, but neither was listed on the DNA profiles database. Determined to do justice to the victim, they searched the database for a close match, in the hope of finding a relative of the attacker. Amazingly, this produced a close relative, which led to the identification of nineteen-year-old Craig Harman, who was convicted of the motorway manslaughter in 2004. It was the first case where a DNA database threw up a close relative resulting in identification of the criminal.

DNA can be used to identify victims of murder, arson, catastrophic accidents, plane crashes or road traffic accidents; it can also be used for "cold cases" or where bodies are found buried and in situations where the body is otherwise unrecognisable. By using comparison DNA with living relatives, the identity of the victim can be established.

In the case of badly decomposed or burnt bodies, mitochondrial DNA (mtDNA) can be used to establish their identity. mtDNA contains hundreds of thousands of copies of mtDNA per cell, like backup copies on a computer. mtDNA comes from the mother's side; while the father has mitochondria in his sperm, it is not preserved in the egg and therefore not passed on to his children. Thus it is easier to identify brothers and sisters in a family from the maternal mitochondrial DNA. They will all share the same mtDNA as their mother, assuming they are all her natural children. This can be genetically linked right through the maternal line from the mother for thousands of years, with little change seen.

This has been used to investigate claims of the female lineages of the Romanovs, the last of the Russian royal family executed by the Bolsheviks in 1918. The Tsar, his wife and five children were dragged from their beds, told to dress and were then executed. The children survived the initial gunfire, as diamonds hidden in their clothes deflected the bullets, but they were eventually killed off. Legend had it that one girl survived, and hence the mystery of a possible relative emerged.

DNA evidence finally ruled out claims by an elderly lady who maintained for over sixty years that she was the Grand Duchess Anastasia of Russia, a direct descendent of the Romanovs. Before DNA profiling, this could neither be proved nor disproved, but she had thousands of followers who believed passionately in her story, and not without reason. She bore identical scars and birthmarks and knew enough fine detail about the princess as a child to convince people who had actually known her. But for the discovery of DNA, her legend might have lived on.

DNA can also provide indication of race and gender. While a mother will pass on her mtDNA to her sons, their children will not inherit it, as they will take their mtDNA only from their mother's maternal lineage. DNA profiling, although still being developed, was used for the first time to determine the genetic mother of a young boy due for deportation by the UK Home Office. Lawyers acting for his British mother contacted Alec Jeffreys. He agreed to help but said, "It was like a jigsaw with most of the bits missing." The boy's father had left Britain and couldn't be contacted. Jeffreys took samples from the mother, her three daughters and the disputed son. He said "the results blew me away". The results showed every genetic character in the boy was present in the women or her daughters. The mother had passed on the mtDNA to all her children, including her son. The Home Office dropped the case and the child stayed with his mother.

DNA profiling is undoubtedly the single biggest forensic tool in the fight against crime and has been responsible for bringing numerous criminals to justice who otherwise might have "beaten the rap". A good example are cases of sexual assaults on women and children, which remained unresolved until the advent of DNA profiling.

13

The Missing Link:
Colin Jacklin

Police in the UK were worried when a series of indecent assaults and rapes were carried out in Newcastle and the surrounding area in the early 1990s. In each case a middle-aged man had grabbed the victim in broad daylight as they walked close to a footbridge, dragging them into the undergrowth, where he indecently assaulted or raped them. One thirteen-year-old girl told of her terror as the attacker asked her how old she was, before forcing her to take off her clothes and indecently assaulting her. She said, "I told him I was only eleven because I thought he might leave me alone." A fifteen-year-old was dragged away and raped in similar circumstances, by a man using the same *modus operandi*.

In another part of the country, a twenty-four-year-old was raped on her way to work in a nearby pub. The method was the same: an unseen man grabbed her in a headlock and held her down so she couldn't see his face. She pleaded with him not to hurt her, certain she was going to be killed.

There appeared to be a serial rapist on the loose, possibly someone who travelled in his work – a sales rep, a truck driver . . . it could have been anyone. None of the victims could identify their attacker. In the rape cases, semen samples were obtained from the women, but, as yet, there was no suspect to compare them to. The DNA extracted from the semen samples in each of the other cases came from the same source. Police now knew for certain they were dealing with the one man. Despite their best efforts, there was nothing to link the perpetrator to the attacks and the trail went cold.

Ten years after the last known attack, police stopped a man suspected of drink-driving; they breathalysed him and took a swab – a saliva sample – from his cheek. They couldn't believe their luck when the samples matched the serial rapist.

The man, fifty-one-year-old Colin Jacklin, the father of at least seventeen children, had previously served time for sexual offences against children, but at the time DNA analysis wasn't available. Jacklin, caught by genetic fingerprinting, was arrested and charged with a series of rapes and sexual assaults. Forensic experts confirmed that DNA testing showed that Colin Jacklin's semen and saliva matched the samples taken from the victims at the time of the attacks. The odds against it being anyone else were said to be a 1 in 60 billion chance.

Newcastle Crown Court took just forty-five minutes to find Colin Jacklin guilty of the vicious attacks on the young children and the barmaid. Judge Helen Paling adjourned the sentencing for psychological reports but warned Jacklin that he faced "an indeterminate sentence". Jacklin got life behind bars. An appeal against his conviction was turned down. His forty-year-old fourth wife Julie, mother to four of his children, refused to believe her husband was a rapist, despite his previous jail time, and promised to stand by him. She said her husband was innocent; "We intend to fight on and prove the truth." The fact that in the intervening period while he was in prison, there were no further rapes matching his MO or DNA, was lost on her.

14

Death Comes Like a Thief in the Night: Grace Moore

When thirty-eight-year old Grace Moore's daughter ran screaming from their home at Erris Grove in Belfast, neighbours thought it was just a teenage tantrum. What was to unfold shocked even the most hardened detectives, as sixteen-year-old Lori told her horrifying story.

The teenager had spent the night at a friend's house and was rushing home to tell her mother all about it. As she let herself into the flat in November 2006 she called out but got no response. Walking into the kitchen, she saw a scene straight from a horror movie. Grace Moore lay dead, spread-eagled in a pool of blood on the kitchen floor. The terrified Lori ran screaming to her grandparents' house nearby, banging on the door and screaming hysterically. When they let her in, she was so distraught her grandparents had difficulty understanding her, but they knew something was seriously wrong and called the police.

When detectives arrived on the scene, they couldn't believe their eyes. Even the most experienced, hard-bitten of them were deeply shocked at what they saw. Lori's mother Grace had been repeatedly stabbed in a frenzied, brutal sexual attack. She had also been bitten extensively before being strangled. After killing her, the murderer coolly plundered her home, methodically going through every room, taking anything of value from the small ground floor flat, leaving it ransacked and in turmoil, with fittings pulled from the walls and discarded items strewn around the floor. The cool killer even went through her make-up drawer, stealing her perfume and jewellery.

Police had no idea who or what they were dealing with. Was it the act of a psychopath or a frenzied drug-fuelled murder? Only time would tell. The scene of crime officers got to work examining the crime scene. A postmortem revealed that Grace had been stabbed multiple times before being raped. They identified that at least one stab wound had severed the carotid artery. Her throat had been slit from ear to ear, resulting in massive haemorrhaging. The pathology report confirmed that Grace had also been strangled, severe bruising to the neck and specks of blood that dotted her eyelids like tiny freckles telling the tale.

Grace's bloody handbag lay forlornly close by her body, empty of all it contained. Bloody fingerprints were found inside and outside the bag, evidence that the killer had rifled through it after he'd killed her. A bloody fingerprint was also found on the kitchen wall and another on a torn envelope. The blood on the floor was identified as Grace's but the bloody prints could only belong to her killer.

Forensic examiners found a wealth of evidence in the flat. On checking the bathroom, they recovered spit, still clinging to the toilet bowl. Forensic testing of the sputum provided a detailed DNA profile of the murderer. Semen was also found under Grace's body, where she lay on the kitchen floor, and swab analysis showed up more internal semen, where she had been brutally sexually assaulted. Unsurprisingly, it matched the DNA extracted from the toilet spit.

Investigating officers were deeply concerned. Detective Chief Inspector David Cunningham said: "I've been a police officer for twenty years and have dealt with a lot of tragic cases in that time, but this is the most disturbing case. Because of the vulnerability of Grace, the vicious nature of the attack on her, and the fact that she was found by her sixteen-year-old daughter, made it a particularly difficult case for all those involved".

Worried that it was some form of deviant sexual or ritual killing, Belfast police contacted the FBI for assistance. The FBI's centre for the Analysis of Violent Crime, in Quantico, Virginia were experts in such crimes. They believed that Grace's killing was "a sexually motivated homicide". The killer got his kicks by raping and then killing his victim. Their behavioural science unit examined the evidence and formed the opinion that the killer was cool and calculated. He had methodically gone through the flat after he'd brutally butchered and raped Grace. He wasn't in a panic, anxious to flee the scene, nor had he any fear of someone walking in on the scene, or of being caught.

On the other hand, ritual killings, if that's what it was, still take place in some African countries. DNA tests can now be used to identify the ethnicity of an individual. By testing the mtDNA from the female line, the ethnic origins can be identified. They usually fall into groups known as haplogroups, which are divided up into various genealogical groups, such as American Indian, European, Asian and African. By checking for a specific group such as "L" haplogroups, it is possible to establish whether the killer had African origins or not.

Worried that he would kill again, police launched a full-scale manhunt. The forensic evidence was stacking up, but they needed a suspect to match it to. Detectives checked out all the CCTV cameras in local shops, garages and on the streets. They put out media appeals for any information that could help to find the vicious killer. Local people were shocked at the grisly murder in their midst and were quick to respond.

A female friend of the victim told police that the night before Grace was found butchered, they had had a rare night out together in Belfast. They had been to the Pink concert at the Odyssey, where they got a free voucher for the Skye nightclub. Deciding to make a night of it, they went to the club and, while there, they were joined by four men. At closing time, they shared a taxi to the Ormeau Road. Twenty minutes later Grace got out of the taxi accompanied by one of the men. They tried unsuccessfully to get a late-night carry-out from the side door of a pub, but while they were there the taxi drove off without them. Grace's friend and the other men continued on in the taxi. Police believed Grace may then have invited the man back for coffee, but she never got a chance to make it.

Now having information on Grace's movements on the night, the CCTV footage examination was extended. People who had seen them in the nightclub also came forward to help the police investigation, following the broadcast of the footage on *Crimewatch*. It led them to identify a Nigerian man named Alauya. The investigation picked up speed as detectives spotted the man fitting Alauya's description on CCTV at a garage close to Grace's flat. He was calmly walking around the food section at a local garage. He paid for a burger and rice, and was about to leave the shop when he turned back and bought a bar of chocolate.

Police digitally enhanced the CCTV and captured a clear enough picture to identify the suspect. He was seen on the CCTV footage wearing a distinctive light and dark blue striped T-shirt. The shirt was covered in blood, which probably happened when he slit Grace's throat. It didn't appear to worry him. As soon as the police released the CCTV footage to television news, calls began coming in hard and fast as several more people identified the suspect. One man told police that Alauya had called to his house in a taxi and left a suitcase, asking him to look after it for a few days.

Detectives immediately called to this man's house accompanied by the SOCO team, who fingerprinted the case and examined its contents. It was found to contain items of clothing obviously belonging to Alauya, but also

Grace's DVD player and speakers. The case was also stuffed with jewellery and other personal items later identified as belonging to Grace, including documents and her chequebook, now bloodied by the killer's handling. In no hurry after the brutal killing, Alauya had spent time going through the flat, assessing the valuable items and discarding the rest. The killer's fingerprints were found on all of the items.

The clothes in the suitcase gave police a good idea of the suspect's height and build, and even the style of clothes he wore, but more importantly, detectives found a light and dark blue T-shirt – the one Alauya was wearing when caught on CCTV in the garage shop. It was covered in dried blood. A forensic examination identified the blood as Grace Moore's. The sweat-laden shirt matched the DNA found in the killer's semen.

Detective checked Grace's bank account and found that the killer had used her Ulster Bank card on at least two occasions. Forensics clearly followed the trail of these transactions back to Alauya. He even used Grace's card in different locations a short time after the murder to buy "top-up" phone credit, which was traced directly to Alauya's mobile phone.

Following the appeal on *Crimewatch*, a second taxi driver came forward. He remembered dropping Alauya to a house the day after the murder. A few days later, while cleaning out his taxi, he found documents with Grace Moore's name on them stuffed down the back seat.

They had their man; now all they had to do was find him. It wasn't long before police in Belfast picked Alauya up.

Detective Chief Inspector Cunningham credited the public response in helping to catch the killer. He said people who knew Alauya, including members of the local Nigerian community, quickly identified him and provided information on his habits. As a result, Kristoff Emmanuel Alauya was arrested at the Skye Nightclub. He had returned to the very place he'd met Grace the night of her death – possibly on the prowl for his next victim.

Liaising with the gardaí, PSNI investigations showed that Alauya had previously been living in the Republic. He had arrived in Ireland in 2002, claiming to be just seventeen and alone in the world, and applied for asylum. Within two years, while his claim was still being processed and the outcome not looking good, he married an Irish woman and had a child with her. With his status under review, he fled the south and headed for Belfast, expecting to be extradited. Within forty-eight hours of arriving in Belfast, he had met and murdered Grace Moore.

Alauya was charged with her murder and the theft of her belongings. Despite all the evidence, he denied the charges. The case came before Belfast Crown Court in November 2008. Police showed the CCTV evidence of the killer wearing bloody clothes, walking away from Grace's flat after the murder. A taxi driver gave evidence of having picked up Alauya close to the flat. He told the court that he had noticed his passenger's blood-stained clothes, and said the man had told him to stop at Creighton's garage, as he was "hungry".

This evidence was substantiated by additional CCTV,

which showed Aluaya flagging down the passing taxi at around 4.20 on the Saturday morning; later, the taxi was caught on CCTV pulling into Creighton's garage. The taxi driver waited outside while Alauya went into the shop, and minutes later CCTV showed him getting into the taxi carrying his food.

Forensic evidence was given of the blood-stained T-shirt, identified as the victim's blood, which was found in his suitcase. Forensic experts told the court that semen found under and in the body matched Alauya's DNA, as did the spit in the toilet bowl, while bloody fingerprints on the stolen property were identified as belonging to Alauya.

The prosecution had a watertight case, added to which was the additional information provided by gardaí. Alauya had a history of violence and had attacked before. Gardaí told the court that he had robbed two taxi drivers at gunpoint on two consecutive days. He had pleaded guilty to those charges, but he had absconded from a Kildare court before sentence could be passed. He fled the jurisdiction and turned up in Belfast. The court was told of Alauya's asylum claim and that, despite his marriage, he had fathered at least four children with four different women.

With the overwhelming evidence stacked against him, just two days into the case, Aluaya changed his plea to guilty, in the hope of a more lenient sentence. The twenty-five-year-old was found guilty on all counts.

In passing sentence Mr Justice Weir said he found "no evidence of remorse or contrition" adding that it appeared Alauya "felt more sorry for himself than he did for the victim or her family". The judge found it "impossible to comprehend" that after raping and brutally murdering the young woman, he had coolly ransacked her belongings, stepping over the bloody body. He added: "No one who has seen the police photographs could be anything but appalled at the callous manner in which her body had been left spread-eagled, lying on the kitchen floor."

He sentenced Alauya to life imprisonment, with a minimum term of twenty-two years. On the count of rape, he sentenced him to a ten-year term, with a further two years for theft, to be served concurrently. He also made an order that Alauya should be put on the police sexual offenders register for the rest of his life.

Police officers working on the case described it as by far the most distressing they'd come across. But for the Trojan work of the police and forensic scientists in the Forensic Science Agency Northern Ireland (FSANI), Alauya would, if the FBI profilers were right, most probably have killed his next victim within days. The fact that he had returned to the very nightclub where he had met Grace Moore within hours of her killing, does indeed suggest that he was already lining up his next victim.

15

Murder Most Foul: Bettina Poeschel

Bettina Poeschel was looking forward to her first visit to Ireland. The highlight would be the visit she planned to the world-famous historic site at Newgrange. Working as a journalist in Germany, she wrote about culture and history and Newgrange was just what she wanted to see.

The twenty-eight-year-old journalist had travelled extensively in South America and in other countries considered dangerous for a lone woman traveller, so Ireland posed no threat, especially as she was staying with an old friend from Germany, who was living in Dublin. She had so much to see and do on her six-day trip, and she was looking forward to the warm welcome she'd heard so much about, saving the special Newgrange trip for her last day in Ireland.

On the morning of 25 September 2001, she set off from Dublin and caught a train to Drogheda. When Bettina didn't return to Dublin that night, her friend was worried. It wasn't like Bettina, who was always so organised. Her flight the following day was an early one; she was booked on the Aer Lingus flight to Munich, which left Dublin at 7.30 a.m. Her friend contacted the gardaí about his concerns and an extensive search operation was launched.

The tall German blonde was spotted on CCTV boarding the Belfast train in Dublin and, again, leaving the train station in Drogheda. She was also picked up by CCTV walking around Drogheda and standing outside a shop in Donore village, wearing a Gortex jacket against the rain.

She was spotted again around 11.35 a.m., walking alone on the Donore road, heading in the direction of Newgrange. That was the last time Bettina Poeschel was seen alive.

Three weeks later, on 17 October, in a follow-up search of the area, Garda Pat Kelly found Bettina's badly decomposed body in dense undergrowth. She was naked from the waist down, but for a pair of black pants around her knees. A postmortem examination of the body showed she had been dead for some time, most likely before she ever reached Newgrange. It was clear she had been the victim of a frenzied and vicious assault. Lying face down, her head was detached from her body; her spinal cord was also detached and her feet, the palms of her hands and her calves were in an advanced state of decomposition. She had also been sexually assaulted.

Further searches of the area turned up a handbag, glasses and a purse which had been dumped in a nearby ditch. Gardaí also uncovered a pair of red shoes, mud-stained trousers and socks, together with a mobile phone – the same make and model used by Bettina – all hidden in a nearby skip in a graveyard in Donore, close to Portakabins used by road workers who were working on the nearby motorway. Forensic tests showed the glasses to be the same prescription lenses as worn by Bettina, and were later identified by her family as being hers. The shoes proved to be the same size as Bettina Poeschel's.

The mobile phone found in the skip revealed Bettina's last poignant text message to her younger sister Cornelia, sent two days before her disappearance, telling her she was on a beach and that everything was fine, she was having a good time.

The then Chief State Pathologist, Dr John Harbison, conducted the postmortem, which confirmed that Bettina been sexually assaulted. Forensic investigation confirmed the presence of semen. Dr Maureen Smyth, head of the DNA unit at the Forensic Laboratory in Garda HQ, extracted a DNA profile from Bettina Poeschel's leg muscle tissue. Vaginal swabs taken from the body identified sperm cells, which were then used to extract the DNA of her attacker. It would later prove to be a crucial breakthrough in identifying her killer.

In a follow-up investigation, detectives questioned the road workers, who included a number of Latvian workers, in the hope of a breakthrough. One of the Latvian men told gardaí that a fellow worker, Michael Murphy from Rathmullen Park in Drogheda, who was paid by their employer to pick them up and take them to work each day, hadn't turned up for his usual 10.00 a.m.

and lunchtime breaks on the day Bettina went missing. It was out of character, and they believed it could be connected with the murdered woman. Yet another worker recalled that Murphy told him he would be "gone for an hour" as he had to visit his doctor, and he later saw him heading off in the direction of Newgrange the day the German woman disappeared. Other road workers said that Murphy appeared very agitated and that he disappeared from the work site several times on the day Bettina went missing.

As the investigation progressed, other workers remembered seeing Murphy emerge from the toilet block, carrying a white plastic bag which appeared to hold Jeyes Fluid. Murphy claimed it was "bleach", saying he wanted to clean his dog kennels. Detectives were aware that the pathology reports had identified Bettina's clothes, especially her underwear and Gortex jacket, as having a strong smell of Jeyes Fluid. Subsequent forensic testing confirmed that the pathology report was right. There was strong evidence that the substance on the clothing was in fact Jeyes Fluid.

The circumstantial evidence against Murphy was beginning to stack up. Garda investigation established that Murphy, had not gone to the doctor on the day Bettina went missing, as he'd claimed. Detectives visited Drogheda GP, Dr Michael O'Brien, to check out this alibi. Dr O'Brien confirmed that Murphy had attended his surgery complaining he'd hurt his back bending down to tie his shoes. There was one major flaw in his story – the surgery visit had been on the day *after* Bettina Poeschel disappeared. Could the back injury have been due to a struggle or from dragging her body into the undergrowth? Whatever it was, why did he lie about the date unless he had something to hide? Murphy's alibi was blown wide open and gardaí had other reasons to put him in the frame.

Shocked at the horrific murder in their quiet little village, residents of Donore took every opportunity to help gardaí with their enquiries. One girl recalled that while sitting on a wall with two friends on the evening of the day Bettina went missing, she noticed a black Honda Civic pull up. A man got out and ran up the nearby laneway. A little while later, he drove off in the direction of Donore. It was getting dark and, while they couldn't identify the man, who was caught in the headlights of an oncoming lorry, they were certain it was a black Honda Civic. It seemed unusual at the time, and when Bettina's body was later discovered close by, they told gardaí about the incident.

It was time to talk to Murphy. Detectives paid him an early morning visit on 27 October, arresting him just ten days after Bettina's decomposed body had been found. They questioned him throughout the day, now certain that they had their man. When gardaí showed Murphy photographs of Bettina Poeschel, he denied ever having seen her before. By then, it had already been all over the news.

Asked to account for his movements on the day Bettina Poeschel went missing, he refused to explain where he'd been, before eventually saying, "I can't talk about it, just charge me with it." The gardaí obliged and, at around 7.00 p.m., Michael Murphy was formally charged with the murder of Bettina Poeschel. Murphy denied the murder and would plead not guilty at his trial.

In the background, the Forensic Science unit at Garda headquarters was steadily working away. They extracted Murphy's DNA profile from a hair sample and matched it with the DNA profile of the sperm cells of the attacker, found in the body fluids extracted from Bettina Poeschel. It was a match. Dr Maureen Smyth, head of the DNA unit at the State Laboratory in Garda HQ, said that there was "less than one chance in a thousand million" that someone else could share the same DNA profile as Michael Murphy. It was a damning indictment of Murphy.

When the case came to trial, Murphy resolutely pleaded his innocence. This was despite the fact that, as prosecuting counsel Mr Denis Vaughan Buckley, SC, reminded the jury, when arrested for the murder on 27 October 2001, he'd said to detectives, "Just tell the girl's parents I'm sorry for taking her life and for what I did to her. I'm so, so sorry." Also, during questioning, realising the game was up, Murphy said to detectives: "Look, I went back to the body two or three days later. I took the red shoes and the trousers and hid them in the skip at Donore graveyard. Have you found them yet?"

At the end of a four-week trial, the jury unanimously found forty-two-year-old Michael Murphy guilty of the murder of Bettina Poeschel. Appearing unfazed, Murphy sat passively, chewing gum, as he was handed down a life sentence. What the jury didn't know then was that

Murphy was no stranger to prison, or indeed to killing. In 1984, he had been convicted of killing elderly widow Catherine "Kitty" Carroll in October 1983, having strangled the sixty-four-year-old to death as she made her way home from a whist drive. He was convicted of manslaughter and got a twelve-year jail term but was released in 1992 after serving just eight years. Murphy had been well known to gardaí and had a long history of convictions for serious offences, including sexual assaults and armed robberies, alongside numerous other convictions which landed him in prison.

Research shows that lenient sentences cause great distress to the public and rightly so. Murphy was no sooner back on the streets in 1992 when he attacked again. After his release for the murder of Catherine "Kitty" Carroll, he attacked two girls on their way home from a disco, grabbing them by the neck and dragging them to the ground. They were lucky to get away with their lives. He was charged and convicted but got just six months for those attacks. Six months for a convicted killer was obviously no deterrent, as he went on to kill again, brutally raping and murdering Bettina Poeschel, before dumping her body in the undergrowth.

None of the information on his previous convictions could be revealed to the court or the media before the jury had handed down their decision, and perhaps that is something that should be reviewed. The law says that even recidivist murderers must have their day in court without their case being prejudiced by their history of violence or murder. Each case must be examined on its own merits, without the influence of previous convictions for murder or manslaughter, however gruesome, and many convicted killers are allowed out on bail awaiting their trial, innocent until proved guilty on this occasion. Given that most sentences are handed down concurrently, they have little to lose if they are going to spend a long time behind bars – as the saying goes, they might as well be hung for a sheep as a lamb, and some take the opportunity to commit other crimes while they are still free, or admit to other crimes, which are taken into consideration. That way, they get the benefit of serving all their time together. Once released from jail, they have a clean slate and nothing left outstanding that they can be charged with.

Gardaí knew they had their man; they just hoped and prayed that the members of the jury would see Murphy for the vicious murderer he was, and with the wealth of damning forensic evidence against him, they too were left in no doubt.

16

Buried in the Garden: Brian McGrath

When forty-three-year-old Brian McGrath went missing from his home at Coole in Castlepollard, County Westmeath in 1987, gardaí had little to go on. It was believed locally that McGrath, who worked as a general handyman, had gone to Holland. Although his wife and four children never heard from him again, there was little the gardaí could do.

It seemed an unfair end to what had already been a difficult and traumatic life for Brian McGrath. Life had never been kind to him. Abandoned as a baby, he was found on the side of a road between Meath and Monaghan, wrapped in a tablecloth. He was sent to the nuns in Dundalk before being passed on to the notorious industrial school at Artane in Dublin. He never knew his real name, just the name given to him by the nuns.

Twenty-three years after he was abandoned, he met and married his wife Vera. The young couple lived in

England for a while before finally settling in Coole, where Brian worked the land and hired himself out as a handyman, before coming to his untimely end. Six years after his disappearance, gardaí got a tip-off that Brian McGrath had never gone to Holland, or anywhere else for that matter. It confirmed he had been killed and his body had been disposed of locally. From information received in November 1993, it seemed that Mr McGrath had been beaten to death and hurriedly buried in a field close to his home in Coole. A few weeks after the murder, the killer had dug up the body, smashed it to smithereens and set it alight, before reburying it in the side garden of Brian McGrath's house, close to the Abbeylara road.

Following garda investigations in 1993 a man admitted to the murder and told gardaí he'd do it again if he had to. Gardaí attempted to bring charges against him, confident that, given the facts and the man's confession, it would be an open-and-shut case. They were dismayed to find that the DPP felt the case might not succeed if they could not confirm Brian McGrath's identity, which they were unable to do at that time.

Six years after he'd gone missing, a woman in Navan was questioned about the matter, and it is believed that she confessed to her part and that of another party in the crime and she showed them where they could find the body. Gardaí also travelled to the UK to interview a man about the killing, but the case never went any further at that time for various reasons. There were plenty of people with information to give and statements to make when Brian first disappeared, and again in 1993.

Despite the discovery of DNA profiling in the mid-1980s, it was still early days in developing its use in such cases, and if the confession was withdrawn, the gardaí would have had little chance of securing a conviction. The file was never closed; it just became a cold case. But years later, in 2008, it was reopened by the Garda Serious Crime Unit. They still had the bone samples from the remains found in 1993. They also exhumed the remains, which had been reburied in an unmarked grave at Whitehall cemetery, adjoining Mr McGrath's former home in Coole, watched over by some members of Mr McGrath's family. His wife, Vera McGrath, was not present. She no longer lived in the area, having moved some considerable time ago.

The remains were taken to the City Morgue in Marino, Dublin, for forensic DNA examination. Gardaí from the Technical Bureau were out in force, with five separate units assisting the team from the Forensic Lab and the various other experts on hand, including an anthropologist and soil surveyor especially retained by the gardaí to work both on the sites and at the City Morgue. An anthropologist is required where a body has been undiscovered for a long time. The organs and soft tissue are no longer available and hence any wounds to the skin are no longer visible. A forensic anthropologist can examine the bones and skeletal remains to establish the damage from cuts, blows, a hammer or gunshot wound, or even a high-speed crash. Dental records can be compared to the skull to help identify the person and the date of death can be narrowed down to within months of the death.

Brian McGrath's family home, where some members of the family still live, had become a crime scene. The Technical Bureau mapped, photographed and examined the interior and exterior of the crime scene with forensic detail, assisted by several forensic scientists and the serious crime squad.

All they could do now was sit and wait for the results that would put an end to the mystery. They came back positive. DNA from his children proved beyond doubt, that the remains were those of Brian McGrath, who'd been missing for twenty-one years.

By 2008, with the case now on a firm footing and with the DNA results in, gardaí arrested Vera McGrath, a woman in her sixties in November 2008 and took her to Mullingar garda station for questioning. She was later released without charge and a file was sent to the DPP. On the instructions of the DPP she was charged with the murder of her husband Brian McGrath on a date between 16 March and 18 April 1987 and was remanded in custody. Gardaí also travelled to Liverpool to interview a man in his forties about the murder. In February 2009, a man was arrested at Dublin Airport as he tried to board a flight to the UK. Forty-six-year-old Colin Pinder, who suffers from epilepsy, was charged with the murder of Brian McGrath. He was remanded in custody to Cloverhill Prison and was subsequently released on bail.

DNA, the unbiased scientific blueprint of life, was the silent witness to Brian McGrath's death.

17

Ritual Killings and
Plain Murder

Ireland's Celtic Tiger years fostered a huge growth in the population, with an influx of people from Europe and other countries seeking work. Combined with a huge upsurge in those seeking asylum in Ireland, this has brought about a vibrant, cosmopolitan community with diverse cultures and customs. In some cases, we have also "imported" criminal elements, either fleeing other jurisdictions or looking for new pickings, just as we have "exported" many of Ireland's notorious criminals and drug dealers, trying to escape the watchful eye of the gardaí, CAB, the Revenue Commissioners and even rival gang members who have put a price on their heads.

It was with this in mind that the initial investigation of the Farah Swaleh Noor murder was thought to have been a ritual killing, the dismembered body, minus the head, having been disposed of in the Royal Canal in Dublin (see Chapter 11). There were echoes of a similar murder in

London a few years earlier, when a young boy's dismembered and headless body was found in the River Thames. When no one came forward to report him missing or to identify the body, police named the child "Adam". He was estimated to be about five years old. No one was ever charged with his murder and, five years later, he was buried in a small blue coffin adorned with teddy bears, his only mourners being the police who investigated his horrific murder. Detective Chief Inspector Will O'Reilly read a eulogy for the child.

The funeral is over but the case is not closed. Over a million pounds has been spent investigating this complex crime, which has taken police across Europe and into Africa, including liaison with South African detectives in Pretoria where "muti" or ritual killings are commonplace. Detectives there pointed investigators in the direction of West Africa, where the ritual killings of very young children is practised. While initial analysis of Adam's DNA proved he had West African ancestors, his more recent origins were crucial if they were to establish what had happened.

When Adam's little body was first recovered, the postmortem revealed that the child had been beaten. He had suffered severe trauma to his neck and his head and limbs had been hacked away after his death. Later, forensic botanists examined Adam's intestines and stomach contents. A portion of a Calabar bean was found in his lower intestine. The poisonous Calabar bean leaves a victim conscious but paralysed. The ritual killers prefer to sacrifice young children, keeping them conscious to the point of death, as they believe their screams will wake their ancestors and empower them, before killing the victim and drinking their blood. In what remained of Adam's body, ground-breaking forensics also identified a mixture of clay pellets, particles of rough gold, quartz and bone, often used in muti or ritual killings.

Part of the investigation into Adam's death also involved advanced forensic examinations, including isotopic analysis to establish his ethnic origins, which showed that Adam's chemical bone makeup closely resembled that of the indigenous Nigerian population. Radioactive isotopes can identify the rock and soil formations in a given area, which are absorbed into the chemistry of bone structure of the natives. All of this evidence led investigators to conclude that the child had been transported from Nigeria to Britain, just days before he was murdered in a sacrificial ritual killing.

Adam's bone had led them to Nigeria, but a vast area of the country and neighbouring countries have similar rock and soil structures, which meant it was a marathon task to narrow the area down without any geographical soil maps in existence. Determined to do their best for the poor child, detectives set about mapping out the areas and taking their own samples. They had a come a long way and they weren't going to let the little boy down now. Their dedication and determination paid off and allowed scientists to narrow it down to an area covering fifty square miles between Ibadan and Benin City. In December 2004, a taxi driver in Ibadan was convicted of killing his own fourteen-month-old baby to provide the local witch doctor with a human head, which he needed to make up a "magic potion" that he claimed would bring the taxi driver riches.

It was a clear breakthrough for the detectives to narrow Adam's origins to the area, and it would become a marker for future cases. Scotland Yard now maintain a presence in Lagos, the capital of Nigeria, where such crimes are commonplace. It makes good intelligence to be on top of this as, with the influx of foreign immigrants, their quasi-religious, cult or criminal activities may travel with them. Of course, there is an issue of freedom of religion, but when that religion includes sacrificial killings of human beings, it is murder and is subject to the laws of civilised society.

The forensic breakthrough narrowed the area down, but investigating detectives still had no idea who the child was. They had his DNA profile and used it to source possible relatives through a DNA database, which is often used when there are unidentified victims of massacres, fire or aviation accidents. It is also increasingly used to narrow down suspects in murders, rapes and serious crimes. Identifying relatives of an unknown person by comparing DNA found at the scene with a database can assist in eliminating or identifying suspects.

While still working on this aspect of the case to identify Adam, investigations were ongoing both in Nigeria and the UK. In Nigeria, the Inspector General of Police, Tafa Balogun, said that over thirty "priests" and their "chief priest" had been arrested and would be prosecuted for ritual killings. Forensic experts were assisting them to identify the victims from skulls found in "deities shrines" following a raid by over 500 police on a number of villages. During the raid, police found over twenty skulls and fifty corpses in varying stages of decomposition. Inspector General Balogun described the practices as "barbaric" and said the "priests" would be charged with murder under the criminal code of the Nigerian constitution, which deals with secret cults and the possession of dead bodies.

Meanwhile, police raided several premises in London and arrested more than twenty people believed to be involved in human trafficking from Nigeria, including one man, Kingsley Ojo (35), who also went by the name of Mousa Kamara. Ojo admitted two charges of smuggling illegal immigrants into the UK from Nigeria.

Ojo is a native of Benin City, where Adam was from. Detective Chief Inspector Will O'Reilly, who headed up the murder case, said: "This man was discovered during the course of the Adam investigation, operating a trafficking enterprise between Nigeria, Europe and the UK. He is from the same city as Adam and is associated with one of our suspects, so we would like to speak to him again. We still suspect he may have had something to do with trafficking the child into the country." When police officers searched Ojo's flat they discovered a video of a mock ritual killing and a video of what appeared to be a human head in a basin. They also found voodoo artefacts, including the skull of a dead rat, pierced with a metal spike and bound in black threads. Ojo was also in possession of false passports and driving licences.

Ojo had arrived in Britain in 1979 posing as an asylum seeker from Sierra Leone. Given leave to "remain", which restricted him from travelling abroad, he still managed to bring numerous illegal immigrants in from abroad, providing them with false documentation. Despite his travel restrictions, he frequently flew to Naples with easyJet to bring back the illegal immigrants and "walk" them through the system – all for a price, of course. An unsavoury character, Ojo even stole his own dead son's birth certificate from his former girlfriend, Barbara Bourne, after he found out the child had died shortly after birth. He used it to get a false passport. Ojo was convicted of people-trafficking and sentenced to four-and-a-half years in jail. It is believed he trafficked hundreds of adults and children into Britain to work in the sex trade, claim benefit fraud for him or work as domestic slaves.

Meanwhile, police in Glasgow arrested a Nigerian woman, Joyce Osagiede from Benin City, and questioned her about Adam's murder. She subsequently returned to Nigeria. Her husband, Sam Onojhighovie, had been convicted of people-trafficking in Germany, but fled to Dublin. He was questioned by detectives in Dublin about Adam's murder. When the child's dismembered body was found, he was wearing a pair of orange-coloured shorts identified as having been sold only by Woolworths in Germany. The washing instructions were also in German. Police believed that Sam Onojhighovie was Adam's natural father and German police authorities initiated extradition proceedings against him.

Commander Andy Baker of Scotland Yard said that there was "a very strong link" between the traffickers and

Adam, who was also believed to be linked to two people arrested in Dublin and Glasgow. DI Will O'Reilly said, "We are pretty confident that we have the group of individuals who would have trafficked Adam into the country." They found the traffickers, but they never found the killers.

Through Adam's case, many others have been solved, including cases in Germany and Italy, as well as assisting in the more recent Irish cases of the murders of Farah Swaleh Noor and Paiche Unyolo Onyemaechi (25), whose headless body was found fifteen miles from her home, wrapped in bin sacks, close to the river at Pilltown, County Kilkenny, two weeks after she'd been reported missing by her husband, thirty-one-year-old Chika Onyemaechi. The woman worked as a lap dancer and a prostitute in both Limerick and Dublin. Chika Onyemaechi disappeared soon after reporting his wife missing, leaving no forwarding address. He was subsequently spotted in Lagos, Nigeria, by Interpol. Gardaí are anxious to speak to him but he is unlikely to return to Ireland, despite the fact that he left his two young sons behind.

Paiche Unyolo Onyemaechi was originally from Malawi, where her father is the Chief Justice, Leonard Unyolo. Paiche was buried in Waterford and her father, Mr Unyolo, and family members including Paiche's sister Lucy and brother Leon, attended the funeral, alongside the woman's two infant boys, Andrew, aged eighteen months, and three-year-old Andrew, who were taken into the care of their grandfather.

In April 2007, thirty-one-year-old Chijioke Ezekwem, then living in Donegal, was charged with failing to disclose information in relation to the murder. This was the second time Mr Ezekwen had been arrested and on this occasion he was remanded in custody, as it was feared he would flee the country, having lost a High Court application against a Deportation Order.

To date, Paiche's head has still not been found.

18

Fingerprints, Footprints and Biometrics

For centuries, fingerprints have been used to identify individuals in countries like China, Japan and ancient Egypt. They were even used to seal business deals in ancient Babylon. In fourteenth-century Persia, now called Iran, a doctor, who was also a government official, noticed that no two fingerprints were alike. Five hundred years later, a Scottish surgeon working in a Japanese hospital, Dr Henry Faulds, made a study of fingerprints as a means of identification, much to the regret of one of his students. Faulds thought his laboratory alcohol was disappearing very fast and decided to investigate. He found a glass stained with greasy fingerprints and quickly identified the student responsible by comparing fingerprints. It was the first recorded "crime" solved by fingerprint identification.

Even today, countries such as Ghana, parts of South America or rural China still use inked thumbprints to identify people, particularly for the purpose of voting. Of all incriminating evidence unwittingly supplied by criminals, fingerprints are the ultimate form of identification. Unique to every individual, even identical twins have different fingerprints, despite sharing the same DNA. While other characteristics may change with age or ill-health, fingerprints never really change; they can grow fainter or become scarred, but they remain with us from before birth until after death, to the extent that the Malaysian government are now fingerprinting all newborn babies in an effort to combat crime in the future.

From the ancient to the modern, fingerprinting and biometric technology are changing the way people are identified. With the development and evolution of fingerprinting, analysis can now be done by computers, which can scan hundreds of thousands of records and identify and digitally locate a match.

For example, the EURODAC programme uses biometric fingerprinting to process asylum seekers. A Norwegian company, Steria AS, designed the highly secure privacy programme, the central data system of which is based in Brussels. No names or personal details are entered into the system, as fingerprints are sufficient to fully identify applicants or those seeking to make multiple applications in other EU member states.

With the dramatic increase of non-nationals in Ireland's population over a short period, now put at twelve per cent of the overall population, the State is checking how many non-EU nationals are genuine asylum seekers by using fingerprint systems. The successful EURODAC system revealed as fraudulent the claims of many of the people who were seeking asylum in Ireland. On average, some ninety per cent of claims turn out to be unfounded.

But of course, we primarily think of fingerprinting in terms of crime scene forensics. Photographing fingerprints at a crime scene creates a chain of evidence, documenting where they were found and in what circumstances. This can later prove crucial in a criminal trial. Forensic photography of prints is also used for comparison purposes, identifying possible suspects who may already be in the system by scanning the crime scene prints into such databases as the NAFIS, the UK's National Automated Fingerprint Identification System; or the IAFIS – the FBI's Integrated Automated Fingerprint Identification System.

The FBI currently stores over 55 million fingerprints, palm prints and facial identification records, which it plans to expand even further. The current system gets in excess of 100,000 "hits" a day, and these figures don't include the 1.5 million fingerprint, retina/iris and facial ID records of Afghan, Iraqi and other people who have been stopped or detained at some time, as well as all those entering American military bases or stopped at borders for criminal activities.

The new system, tagged as Next Generation Identification, will gather a wide range of forensics and personal identification information and makes the stuff of science fiction movies into reality. Police officers, customs officials and passport authorities will be able to scan individuals on the spot with state-of-the-art biometric scanners, identifying anyone from the guy with an outstanding parking fine to the terrorist. Increasingly, countries are introducing new security measures into their passports, with biometric information, including finger-prints, becoming standard, making for the immediate identification of all travellers.

Fingerprint database programmes are now used worldwide by most police enforcement agencies and Ireland is no less effective in this area. In criminal matters, finger-prints of suspects are usually taken at a police station, but the latest technology allows for handheld scanners to scan fingerprints on-site, much like handheld supermarket product scanners. They can then access the database to identify or eliminate possible suspects.

Fingerprints are not just used in criminal identification, they are also widely used in commercial situations or for security reasons; for example, allowing employees access to certain restricted areas. Electronic checking of their fingerprints against a database of registered employees is a more secure means of identification and guards against the use of stolen ID cards, pin numbers or codes, which could allow access to unauthorised personnel. Some television programmes and films have suggested that fingerprints can be "imported" onto certain materials that could be falsely identified by scanning machines.

In the US, the FBI can, with the permission of an employer, keep the records of anyone whose background is checked as a condition of employment. If, at some stage in the future, that person is ever arrested or charged with a crime, but not necessarily convicted, the FBI can inform their employer about it. A "big brother" scenario if ever there was one.

Fingerprint Patterns

Think of a fingerprint as a "negative", like an old photograph negative; it is actually the reverse of the real thing. If you rub your hands with oil or ink, you can make an impression on a wall or paper and see exactly what *your* fingerprints look like.

But what *are* fingerprints? Humans have a rough surface on their hands and fingers as well as on their feet and toes. Known as friction ridge skin, it shows a pattern of ridges, whorls and lines designed to provide grip. Fingerprint patterns consist of three main common features: bifurcation; ridge lines; and an "island". Repeated patterns of ridge lines run back and forth on the skin, forming areas known as arches, loops and whorls, depending on how the ridges grow. When a ridge divides into two lines, it is known as bifurcation. A small section of a ridge, set between two continuous ridges, is called an island, for obvious reasons, while a triangular shaped area is known as a delta.

It may sound complicated initially, but like anything else, recognising such patterns becomes easy with practice. Modern scanners can now "read" fingerprints quickly and efficiently, making a tedious job easier for fingerprint experts. A suspect's fingerprints are matched to a crime scene by comparing points of identification, based on the number of repeat patterns of the arches, loops and whorls. Each of these makes up one point of identification, and they are individual to each person. It is considered a match when twelve points are found on a set of prints that exactly match those of the suspect.

The various patterns can be subdivided, as follows:

• *Arches*: Arches, which make up five per cent of the population's prints, can be plain or tented. A plain arch does what it says on the tin – it goes evenly from one side to the other, rising in the centre, whereas the tented arch is more inclined to rise steeply upwards at an angle. An arch has no delta or core.

• *Whorls*: Whorls are seen in approximately thirty per cent of all fingerprints, where one ridge starts at one side, crosses the finger and loops back in a circuit. Whorls patterns are usually circular and will generally have two or more deltas. They come in four types: plain, double, central pocket and accidental, depending on the type of circuit.

• *Loops*: Loops make up between sixty and seventy per cent of fingerprint patterns. A loop will enter on either side of the finger; touching or crossing over another ridge line, it crosses or loops back, normally in the direction of entry. There can be plain loops, double loops or central pocket loops and can be divided in ulnar and radial loops depending on the direction of the ridges.

This will not make you an expert on fingerprints, but should give a brief insight into the complicated but defining piece of evidence in many criminal cases. To imagine that no two sets of fingerprints are alike in the entire population of the world, which at the time of writing is around seven billion, is incredible, and it puts into perspective how significant fingerprint evidence really is.

Prints may get a little fainter in old age or by the nature of a person's work, so the ridges may become thin or worn, but they are still readily identifiable. Prints taken in old age or when damaged need very little ink. A technique known as "milking the fingers", to squeeze the blood flow into the fingers, is often done if prints are faint. Certain medical conditions such as psoriasis, although more likely to affect the arms and scalp, can occasionally leave marks on the fingers. The damage can actually make a fingerprint even more distinguishable, which also applies to any scar damage on fingertips.

Fingerprint Forensics

Fingerprinting is an important part of even the most basic police work, from the SOCOs' (scene of crime officers') identification of the small-time burglar to a murder investigation, where it is crucial to ensure that any possible fingerprints are carefully "lifted" from the crime scene, the weapon, if it is available, or from other areas such as doorframes, windows or other items – including the victim's body.

Since the early days of fingerprint identification, stories have been told of the lengths some criminals will go to ensure their "prints" can't identify them. In the 1930s, gangster John Dillinger had surgery to remove his prints. When it didn't work, he dipped his fingers in acid, killing off the tissue and with it his fingerprints. But it was only a temporary solution; the skin grew back and the fingerprints "reappeared". Many other drastic attempts by criminals to remove their fingerprints also ended in failure.

In the 1930s, fingerprints were developed with the use of silver nitrate, a caustic substance. It is now used more in medical situations to burn off warts or granuloma, the leftover bit from a baby's umbilical cord. From there, police moved on to using ninhydrin in the 1950s, which is still used today in various applications, including developing prints on porous surfaces like paper or wood. In the 1970s, lasers were introduced, highlighting latent prints. Now cyanoacrylate, the magic all-purpose superglue which is used in medical skin repairs and for household use, as well as in forensics, is used to bring up prints on non-porous surfaces. This is usually done in a fuming chamber in a laboratory.

Because fingerprints have natural ridges, infinitesimal though they are, they can excrete sweat or pick up moisture or oil from parts of the body or from other substances. Of course, the skin also has its own natural oils, invisible to the naked eye, which can leave a trace on numerous surfaces such as glass, wood or metal, and these too can be developed with powders and fluoroscopy, which make the prints glow in the dark.

Crime scene fingerprints fall into certain categories: latent, plastic and visible latent prints. Latent prints, made by natural oil or sweat, are usually but not always invisible to the naked eye but can be "brought up" or highlighted by dusting the area with special powder or SG fuming (i.e. using cyanoacrylate). Plastic prints are prints "impressed" in a soft substance like clay or putty, much like a child's fingerprints can be seen in PlayDoh. Visible latent or patent prints can be clearly seen in ink, blood or similar substances, such as the bloody fingerprint found at the crime scene in the Grace Moore murder (see Chapter 14).

Latent prints on newspapers, wallpaper and other porous substances can be picked up with the use of ninhydrin, which is sprayed onto the surface, showing up as a purplish-coloured print. Bi-chromatic latent print powder, a two-colour powder which shows up on any colour surface, can show up as grey, red or black on light-coloured surfaces and silver on dark surfaces.

Prints can also be brought up by powders such as magnetic jet black, Swedish black, silver special or magnetic silver; or the previously mentioned cyanoacrylate ("superglue") fuming or ruthenium. Powders are used to bring up latent prints on glass, tiles, mirrors, car bodies and other non-porous surfaces. Latent prints may also be picked up with laser light, where the prints appear luminous. Many of these products are commercially available to private detective agencies and security organisations providing independent investigation services.

Much like old-style photography, when developing a film, latent prints on non-porous surfaces can also be "developed" or brought out using superglue fuming. When exposed to the suspected surface, chemicals in the glue adhere to any oil in fingerprints, making it visible to the naked eye. Gentian violet is commonly used to bring out prints on certain substances such as latex, which stains the prints a deep purple, and was previously used by doctors as a prescription for oral thrush in infants. It is now a crime-fighting forensic weapon and is especially good on "gaffer tape", which is often used on the arms and legs to restrain a victim, or around the mouth to silence them.

The colour and chemical reactions of the powders vary according to the substances treated. There are a vast range of powders and colours, each doing its own job, and they are usually applied with a brush. A camel-haired brush was formerly used, but in more recent times there are various synthetic brushes that are better suited to the application.

It is only in recent years that fingerprints have been successfully lifted from human tissue, as it was previously believed that fingerprints would generally not leave a trace on human flesh, or if they did, they would be very difficult, if not impossible, to retrieve. Following extensive research by the FBI Laboratory's Fingerprint Department, in conjunction with police and medical personnel in Tennessee, USA, it was found that good quality fingerprints can be obtained from the skin of murder or sexual assault victims, which has led to the arrest of the perpetrator.

In many abductions, assaults or murder cases, the victim is grabbed or held, perhaps strangled by the perpetrator, often leaving "skin" prints. While it is readily possible to see fingerprints when a finger has been stained with ink, it is also possible to recover latent fingerprints from people's skin, living or dead. In fact it is even possible to recover prints for identification purposes from badly decomposed bodies; bodies charred in a fire; bodies that have been lying in water for long periods; and bodies that have been weather-damaged or interfered with by animals.

The system used sounds unpleasant but it is functional. Boiling water is used to enhance or recondition the fingerprint or palm area. The water rehydrates and reconditions the damaged skin, allowing for prints to be taken from the most distressed postmortem bodies. The prints can then be compared to databases or known prints of the person. With the ridge reappearing, the area is dusted with the usual powders and wrapped in tape. When the tape is removed a clear print should be visible. The system was developed as a result of disasters such as 9/11 and the tsunami in Thailand and has proved extremely successful. When used on skin surfaces, chemicals, reagents and powders such as dactyloscopic powder can also pick up prints, which are then shown up under forensic light surfaces.

Technology has allowed the use not only of fingerprints, but also palm and footprints, to short circuit identification of suspects. While it would have been possible to lift palm prints twenty years ago, it was somewhat pointless, as there was little to compare them to. Today, SOCO teams can lift anything from footprints to ear or even lip prints – the kiss of death – in serious cases. However, evidence relating to comparison of "prints" other than the standard finger, foot and palm, is not yet acceptable in all international jurisdictions, and there is currently little to compare ear or lips prints to, but undoubtedly these will feature more prominently in the future.

Footprints, particularly the toes, have similar ridges to fingerprints. The soles of the feet also carry marks and ridges similar to the hand. There are now "footprint databases" in both the US and UK, which investigators can access. Of course, as suspects would normally be wearing shoes, footprint identification is usually associated with a particular type of shoe or boot. The UK launched its FIT – Footwear Intelligence Tool – in 2007; it is updated daily as footprints are the second most common piece of evidence found at crime scenes. See "Footprints in the Sand" later in this chapter.

The Eyes Have It

With modern technology, fingerprints and DNA are not the only means of identification, as retina and iris scanning become the norm. In what was once only science fiction, machines can now recognise and identify an individual by scanning their eyes.

In retinal scanning, biometric technology "captures" the patterns of blood vessels in the nerves at the back of the eye. Like fingerprints, they are unique to each individual, including identical twins. While people can change the way they look, the colour of their hair or even, with contact lenses, their eye colour, they cannot change their individual retina pattern. Some people can change almost beyond recognition through age, illness or cosmetic surgery, but while their eyes may deteriorate or they may have laser eye surgery, their retina pattern remains for the most part the same, creating, together with their fingerprints and DNA, the ultimate identification tools. Undoubtedly there are certain medical conditions that can effect the eyes, such as glaucoma and diabetes, but taken in conjunction with fingerprints, problems of identification can be overcome.

Iris recognition is similarly unique in identifying a person and is used in many sensitive organisations to identify and allow staff access. More recently, the UK Information Commissioner's Office has approved its use in schools. Such technology is now widely used in security applications such as passport identification, and can be seen in many international airports, particularly in the US following 9/11. It is likely that it will eventually be used for everything from passports and driving licences to military applications, banking transactions, welfare payments, prisons, colleges, asylum seekers, computer access and routine security checks. Research and development organisations are constantly working to improve its capabilities and the speed with which a database can identify an iris/retina pattern.

The US Department of Homeland Security in conjunction with the Terrorist Screening Centre and the National Crime Information Centre currently use biometrics to identify Iraqi and other terror suspects. Covert retina and iris capturing is being developed in order to have advance information about possible terrorists, without alerting them to US government interest.

Hearing Voices

Voice recognition is yet another tool used by police forces worldwide. Of crucial importance in cases of kidnapping, blackmail, murder or terrorist threats, where a phone or other vocal message has been left, voice recognition techniques can help identify the perpetrator, even when they have disguised or distorted their voice electronically or otherwise. Voice identification can be used to identify the origins of the caller, pinpointing a particular country and even a specific region. Dialects, accents, voice pitch and style, taken with other clues, can narrow the field in identifying suspects.

Voice recognition is also used in political and commercial environments to check that the "spoken" instructions from a person are not those of an impostor. Imagine, for example, a recording of Barack Obama which appeared to confirm his plans to unleash a nuclear attack on Russia. Voice recognition and identification technology which identifies an impostor could be crucial in averting at least an international incident, if not outright war. Commercial environments are also susceptible to such attempts.

Footprints in the Sand

Fingerprints are not the only prints that can tell a tale. Footwear can leave prints on numerous surfaces, from the muddy shoe on the kitchen floor to the blood track left behind at the scene of a crime. These are known as "positive impressions". Most criminals don't wear special foot protection when they set out to commit a crime. A pair of runners or tough boots to protect their feet is probably more likely, depending on the task. Whether it is something sleek and light to make a fast getaway or just everyday trainers; whether they are made from leather, rubber or any other material, each has its own unique sole. Each shoe will make a different two- or three-dimensional impression.

Positive impressions are clearly visible to the naked eye but may disappear later when the mud or blood dries off. Footwear impressions form an important part of every SOCO's job. Photographs of the impression, alongside a measurement ruler or scale showing the shoe size, are taken as early as possible before the impression dries off, or under forensic lighting if it has already done so. If the impression is faint, it may be enhanced with the use of chemicals, such as a luminol reagent spray, which highlights the footprint under dark conditions, producing a glow-in-the-dark blue light allowing the footprints to be photographed. Certain fingerprinting powders can also be used in some cases. If it is possible to remove the print – say, for example, if found on a piece of timber or a removable kitchen tile – analysis may be done in the lab.

Other prints can be taken from sand, earth or even snow. After the initial photography, such prints are best preserved by taking a cast. They can be set in old-fashioned plaster or in new plastic-type castings, having been "sealed" beforehand by a polymer, such as common hairspray. The make and type of shoe can be identified and matched up from a manufacturer's database. The Garda Technical Bureau operate a computer comparison system known as SICAR using the SoleMate database, into which photographs or casts of footprints taken from a crime scene can be scanned. This can indicate when a shoe was made, what countries it was marketed in and what outlets sold it in a given area.

The size of the shoe can narrow it down to a particular suspect and even DNA, if later obtained from the shoe, can identify the owner. Areas of wear and tear can also point to a suspect – e.g. a particular gait may have worn the shoe down on one heel. In the case of the Dún Laoghaire Yacht Club killing (see Chapter 19), the marks made by the sole of the culprit's shoe on the bar wall were photographed, sized and preserved. Nike runners were later found in a suspect's house and still retained evidential material such as blood and sand from the crime scene.

The OJ Simpson Case
Most scanning machines today capture not only the fingerprints, but the biometrics of an individual's overall hand size and shape, and the thickness and length of the fingers, all of which have wide variations, not alone between men and women, but also between races, making it easy to isolate and identify individual hands in conjunction with fingerprints. This development in biometrics could have been crucial to the OJ Simpson murder trial, had it then been available.

On 12 June 1994 the bodies of Nicole Simpson and Ron Goldman were found on the path leading to her front door. The victims were awash with blood and both had multiple stab wounds, with Goldman stabbed more than thirty times. Nicole's head was virtually severed, her throat slashed from ear to ear, the wound so savage and so deep that it exposed her spinal cord. Nicole's ex-husband OJ Simpson was later arrested and charged with murder.

When the case came to trial, it was difficult to understand the litany of errors made by so many professionals investigating the case. There were many "mistakes" made at the crime scene, which wasn't initially cordoned off. Police took a blanket from the house and covered the bodies where they lay. The medical examiner – the equivalent of the state pathologist in Ireland – wasn't given access for several hours. At the trial, the forensic pathologist who carried out the postmortems admitted to making over forty errors in his PM examination. Photographs of the victims clearly showed blood spots on Nicole's back, which indicated that someone had cut themselves and bled onto her. When her body was moved to the morgue, Nicole had been turned on her back and put into a body bag, wiping away this evidence. A forensic blood expert hired by the defence in relation to this evidence was not called by them to give his interesting findings.

Simpson gave misleading information to police as to his whereabouts on the night of the murders, saying he was home between 9.36 p.m. and 10.56 p.m., when police had evidence that he made calls from elsewhere during those times. A limo driver waiting to take him to the airport saw him arrive home at 10.56 p.m. Simpson went into his house, coming out minutes later with his luggage and a small black bag, which had disappeared by the time they got to the airport.

Police noted an open cut on Simpson's hand, which he couldn't explain. Eventually he went on the run, leading to the famous TV and police chase of his white Bronco. When he was caught, police found a false beard and moustache, his passport, almost $9,000 in cash, traveller's cheques and a loaded gun. A note addressed to a friend was left at his home; it was never shown to the jury, but it gave a mixed message – he was either going to break for the border and head to Mexico or commit suicide.

Simpson pleaded not guilty; in fact, he pleaded "absolutely 100 per cent not guilty". The wealth of evidence included several instances of Simpson's DNA at the murder scene on a discarded glove soaked with both victims' blood; items of clothing found in the bedroom of his own house, stained with his estranged wife's blood; and blood belonging to the victims and Simpson himself, which was found in his car. Blood found in his driveway and in the hallway of his house matched Simpson's DNA; it possibly came from his cut hand, believed by the prosecution to have happened when he wielded the knife.

Simpson's defence team suggested that the evidence had been both contaminated and tampered with. Simpson denied ever owning a pair of Bruno Magli shoes. A size-twelve bloody shoe print, with its distinctive "waffle sole" design, was found at the crime scene, and an Associated Press Photographer had evidence of having photographed

Simpson wearing the same dark brown shoes at a New York stadium, nine months before the murders. Investigations showed that only 300 pairs of that make and size were sold throughout America at the time of the murders.

Simpson also denied owning the bloody "Aris" glove lined with cashmere, one of two pairs Nicole had specially made for him. Evidence showed that only 240 pairs were sold in the US. Simpson said the glove couldn't possibly have fitted him, showing his much "bigger" hand to the jury. The possibility that he was taking steroids as an anti-arthritis medicine, which would have swollen the size of his hands, was lost in the glare of the media lights.

After just three hours, the jury found Simpson not guilty. He got the best justice that money can buy.

The reaction of his defence team was strange; they were anxious to say that they hadn't defended Simpson because they believed he was innocent. They wanted to highlight certain points of law and how carelessness in handling samples could affect the outcome of a case. Had biometrics been around, Simpson's true hand size could have been shown, and if the glove fits . . .

Once Bitten . . .

When we think of bite marks, we generally think of animals, but some crimes involve incidences of human bites. Cases of assaults, vicious attacks, rapes and murder can sometimes feature evidence of sadistic bite marks on a victim. Some victims may also bite their attacker in an effort to defend themselves. These bites are different in site; a "defensive" bite is usually seen on the hands, arms or face, whereas an attacker in a sexual attack on a female will usually bite on the breasts or legs.

Simple crimes like burglaries have been solved, all because the burglars decided to have something to eat while they ransacked the premises. A piece of chocolate, an apple or a lump of cheese to keep them going has been the downfall of many a criminal. Obviously, most burglaries would not warrant such a detailed investigation, but where the criminal is suspected of serious crimes elsewhere – perhaps a rape or murder – there are a number of angles open to investigating police and forensic experts. Having sampled the food or perhaps had a drink from a glass, bottle or cup, the culprit most probably left behind a sample of their DNA.

The impression left in a discarded apple core or a bar of chocolate can be their undoing. Just as missing people can be identified from their dental records, so too can criminals. Each individual has a unique set of teeth, with a different history of extractions, dental problems or alignment of teeth. In a serious crime investigation, a forensic odontologist can photograph a bite mark, noting the size, shape and position of the teeth marks, both individually and collectively. If a suspect's dental records or an impression of their teeth is obtained, it can be enhanced with the use of computer technology and matched up to bites on the victim. This method has been successfully used in murder and rape cases, where the bite marks correspond with a suspect's dental records or where the DNA left behind after inflicting bite wounds on a victim also identified them.

Generally speaking people have thirty-two teeth, unless some have been removed. Each tooth has five different surfaces, known as the buccal (cheek), lingual (tongue), occlusal (forward from the midline), mesial (away from the midline) and distal (biting) surfaces. All dentists must record these details which are different to individuals due to treatment, damage, loss, etc. It is accepted as evidence of the identity of an individual, for example if there is no relative to compare DNA to for ID purposes. All of this allows for formal and legal identification of an individual, as it would be extremely rare for two individuals to have exactly the same work done, or the same wear and tear or absence of certain teeth. Given that there are eight trillion possible combinations, it is a good way to identify a victim, even if the rest of the body has been badly charred in a fire, as teeth can withstand temperatures of over 700 degrees centigrade.

Teeth are also a good indicator of the age of a victim, their diet and even their habitual behaviours. Stains can be an indicator of smoking, alcohol or substance abuse or even an eating disorder. Even their occupation may be identifiable – for example, if as part of their job, they constantly held nails, carpet tacks, hairpins or other items between their teeth as they worked, a pattern of wear occurs. Any dental or orthodontic treatment or lack of dental work can be an indicator of their background and wealth.

The famous case of Ted Bundy was groundbreaking in terms of bite mark evidence. Bundy was an American middle-class law student who was believed to have killed over one hundred women, having bludgeoned them, bitten them, and brutally sexually assaulted them before finally finishing them off by strangulation.

During their investigations, police had interviewed 3,500 people and had in excess of 200,000 items of information, which they fed into a computer to try to come up with a "profile" of the attacker. Some of the details, MOs and other facts related to more than one attacker, but the computer came up with a list of ten suspects. Top of the list was Ted Bundy. He had been added to the database following the murders of several college students. People came forward with information on a man wearing a leg or arm cast, who was seen talking to the missing girls. He usually carried a lot of books and asked for their help in putting them into his car – a tan VW. One person overheard him tell a student who was later found dead that his name was Ted.

Police issued a Photofit of the suspect; Bundy's girlfriend, realising it was Bundy, contacted Seattle police in August 1974, saying she believed her boyfriend "might be involved". She subsequently sent in photographs, but at that time the witnesses couldn't make a positive ID and he was removed from the list.

The murders continued. In one instance, Bundy approached an eighteen-year-old in a bookstore in Utah, showed a gold badge and said he was a police officer. Telling her that her car had been broken into, he lured her outside, put handcuffs on her and pulled a gun, threatening to kill her if she didn't stop screaming. Dragging her into his VW he drove off, stopped outside of town and pushed her out of the car. He was about to hit her with a crowbar when she kicked him in the groin and escaped. She managed to wave down a passing car, and the couple took her to the police, where she gave a detailed description of Bundy. In her struggle she had scratched Bundy, who bled on her coat – providing police with evidence of his blood type (O). Investigations showed that a series of stolen credit cards had been used by a man fitting Bundy's description in Colorado and other areas where the murders had taken place.

Bundy came to police attention for a traffic violation in August 1975, arousing suspicion when he tried to get away, speeding through stop signs with his lights off. He was eventually caught after a police chase. When police asked for his identification, he produced a driving licence in the name of Theodore Robert Bundy. Police found in his car a crowbar, rope, an ice pick, handcuffs and a pair of tights with eye holes cut out, together with other questionable items. He had also removed the front passenger seat from his car, enabling him to bundle a victim into the car with ease.

Initially arrested on suspicion of going equipped to commit a burglary, police recalled the earlier attack on the kidnap victim, who had described her attacker's car – a tan VW Beetle – and identified the brand of handcuffs he'd used on her. They matched Bundy's. She picked him out in an identification parade and he was put on trial for attempted kidnapping. Police felt sure he was also behind the series of rapes and murders over three states that had gone unsolved for over a year.

In February 1976, Bundy got fifteen years for the attempted kidnapping. In October, he was charged with a murder in Colorado and was extradited from Utah prison to stand trial. He chose to represent himself; his leg irons were removed and he was allowed access to the law library, where he escaped by jumping out of a window. He was caught a week later.

He escaped again in December and made his way to Tallahassee in Florida where he rented an apartment under a false name, using stolen credit cards to fund his lifestyle. He then broke into student accommodation and beat two women unconscious with a log, before raping and killing another. He then raped and killed Lisa Levy, biting her on the breast and buttock before being disturbed by someone. He left no other physical evidence, no fingerprints or any clues at the scene. However, a sharp scene of crime officer photographed and measured the bite mark, which was unusual to do then.

Bundy went on to kidnap and kill a twelve-year-old girl, mutilating her. He was finally arrested a week later, driving a stolen car. He pleaded not guilty to the charges.

When Bundy was captured, Dr Richard Souviron, a forensic dentist, took photographs of his uneven teeth and gums. He made moulds and blew up the photographs, showing the alignment, the tooth damage and size and the sharpness of Bundy's incisors. He pointed out the double-bite effect of Bundy's teeth and then superimposed it over a blown-up photograph of the bite marks on Lisa Levy. It was a complete match. The doctor showed how Bundy had bitten the dead girl, and then turned sideways to bite her again. The top teeth remained in the same position, whereas the lower teeth again left two rings – the double bite.

The Chief Medical Examiner of New York, himself a forensic odontologist, confirmed the findings and said that from the position and measurements of the bites, Lisa was no longer struggling. Bundy bit her after he'd killed her.

Bizarrely, during his trial Bundy called a girlfriend as a character reference and witness. She believed totally in his innocence. During the trial he married her and she was devastated when he was found guilty of multiple murders and sentenced to death. Bundy, after years on death row, was finally executed in 1989, caught by the bite mark.

19

Death at the Yacht Club: "Johnny" Shorthall

Dún Laoghaire is hardly the crime capital of Ireland. The mix of middle-class professionals and wealthy yacht owners at the renowned Royal Dún Laoghaire Yacht Club are the doyen of propriety, so what happened in 1992 was set to rock the close-knit community to its very core. On a cold January day, sixty-seven-year-old Richard Shorthall, known locally as Johnny, went about his business as usual, not realising it was to be his last day alive.

A single man, Johnny suffered from cerebral palsy, but nonetheless he had held down a regular job as a night watchman at the yacht club for over twelve years. He was a well-liked and affable character who had many friends. On the night of 23 January 1992, he met up with one or two of these friends to have a "few jars" before he went to work. Staff at the yacht club remembered that Johnny turned up as usual around 11.00 p.m. He had two cans of Budweiser and a packet of crisps with a few locals, before the bar closed at 11.15 p.m. Before leaving for the night, barman Kieran Melly paid Johnny Shorthall his wages of £60, the balance owed to him for that week, and he left the premises around 12.45 a.m., leaving a few club members to finish off their drinks.

When they all left for home, Johnny locked up and curled up on the couch to get a couple of hours' sleep, covering himself with a rug. It was a relatively short shift, as he usually left around 6.45 the next morning, with nothing much to report. It was a quiet area and little ever happened during his shift.

When the cleaner arrived around 9.00 the following morning, she realised something was wrong. The club had been broken into. Accompanied by the manageress, she went to the upstairs lounge where they found Johnny Shorthall lying in a pool of blood. A 999 call was put in and a garda squad car in the area responded immediately. A medical examiner pronounced Richard "Johnny" Shorthall dead at around 9.38 a.m.

Johnny appeared to have a fractured skull, but it wasn't immediately possible to judge the full extent of his injuries, as the upper part of his body and his face were covered in blood. He also had defensive injuries to his hands. His pockets had been turned out, and bits of bloody paper and matches lay close by the body. A broken, bloodied plank of timber lay close to the body. It now looked like a murder investigation.

Detective Sergeant Eamon Reilly and Detective Garda Dominick Herns from Dún Laoghaire garda station had the job of investigating the killing. Gardaí from the

Technical Bureau examined the scene and found blood spatter radiating from the body towards the bar. They found pieces of wood, including the 3-foot-wide, 1 3/4-inch-thick bloodstained length of timber, which had broken in two. The other part lay beside the body, apparently dropped by the attacker. From all appearances, they had found the weapon used to kill Johnny Shorthall.

To get an accurate picture, the crime scene investigators measured and photographed the scene, mapping out the area where the victim lay and itemising where everything was found. They measured the length and width of the blood splatter, dividing the width by the length, to arrive at what is known as the "arcsin number", a mathematical calculation that works out the radians of an arc, showing how far, and in what direction, the blood splatter travelled. Blood makes its own distinct pattern, depending on how it falls. If it falls perfectly vertically or at a 90-degree angle, the blood drop will be round, whereas when the angle of impact increases, the blood drop "stretches out" and looks like it has a tail, making the blood droplet narrower. The bigger the difference between the width and the length shows the angle of impact. From the direction of the spatter, it looked like the victim had most probably been killed where he slept, on the couch close to the bar. A blood-soaked raincoat lay beneath Johnny Shorthall's body and the rug was still wrapped around his legs.

The body was removed for postmortem examination by then State Pathologist Dr John Harbison. Mr Shorthall's body was fully clothed at the time of his death.

He had a fractured skull, having sustained five blows to the left side of his head. He'd suffered extensive injuries; his face and head were covered in blood. He had multiple lacerations on the left-hand side of his face, his cheekbone had been fractured, and part of the top of his ear had been cut off. His skull had multiple fractures and his eyes showed evidence of massive bleeding, due to subjunctive haemorrhaging. Had he lived, he would undoubtedly have been brain-damaged. The victim's lungs and trachea were full of blood, due to ingestion and inhalation. He also had indications of defence injuries to his hands, indicating he had tried to protect himself. He had irregular lacerations on the left hand, extensive bruising and abrasions as well as broken fingernails.

Meanwhile the Garda Technical Bureau continued to work the scene. The club had been ransacked, with telephone coin boxes pulled from the walls and cigarette machines broken; the locked bar had been broken into, its shutters forced open; a security camera was ripped out; and cans of Budweiser Light and other drink had been taken, together with around £600 in cash.

The Technical Bureau managed to lift fingerprints from the banister on the stairs leading to the upstairs lounge, around the bar counter and on the door handle in the gent's toilet, a cleaning closet and other areas of the crime scene. A clear print from the left sole of a runner was found on a wall inside the main bar, where the cigarette machine had been ripped from the wall. They had gained entry by smashing the glass on an upstairs balcony door overlooking the water.

Detective Sergeant Reilly and his fellow Garda Detective Herns discovered that a number of boats moored in and around the harbour had been broken into that night, with extensive damage done and numerous items stolen. Given the timing and proximity to the yacht club break-in and killing, it seemed more than a coincidence. A man on his way home from work had spotted two young men looking at a trimaran in the harbour close to the yacht club between 12.30 a.m. and 1.00 a.m. on the night in question. Earlier on the evening of the killing two members of the Old Conna Golf Club had challenged two youths acting suspiciously inside the club. They made an excuse of needing the toilet and left. The golf club members gave a clear description of the two men.

Gardaí interviewed the boat owners and discovered that the owner of the trimaran had left his overturned dinghy on the slipway, hiding the engine and oars, binoculars and other items. The dingy was later spotted adrift next to the west pier the following day. The engine had been left on the slipway, abandoned by the thieves, who had apparently used the oars to row out to the various boats. They worked their way systematically through the various craft, plundering and damaging them as they went. Gloves were found on the slipway, next to the engine. Manoeuvring the dinghy would have been difficult in the dark and it seemed that one of the men had removed his gloves to launch the craft, accidentally leaving the gloves behind.

More than ten boats, ranging from the trimaran to sailing boats, cabin cruisers and yachts had been plundered. Various items stolen from the boats were found dumped inside the yacht club and around the general vicinity. A distinctive baseball cap with the words "Emery School of Aviation" stolen from the *Welcome* was found close to the murder scene, as was another distinctive white hat, which had old brown paint stains two zip pockets, embroidered "Costa del Sol", stolen from the *Duke*. The hatch door was missing from the boat, along with other items which were recovered from the harbour waters. There was also a small bloodstain on the galley area in one boat and numerous fingerprints were lifted.

Meanwhile, garda subaqua divers were trawling the harbour around the damaged boats. They recovered a lot of items that were later forensically examined to establish a connection, if any, with Johnny Shorthall's death. Among the items recovered was a black bin-bag containing cans of Budweiser Light – the same beer stolen from the yacht cub. Forensics managed to lift clear fingerprints from the cans. It was a remarkable breakthrough and the first time in Ireland that fingerprints had been recovered from underwater. Divers continued to trawl the waters recovering possible evidence. Their haul included a Perspex window that had been ripped out from one of the boats and dumped into the water. It also had well-preserved fingerprints that could only belong to the culprits.

In addition to the footprint found on the club wall, which appeared to have been used as leverage to rip the cigarette machine off the wall, other footprints were found on the roof of the club. The concrete roof was black and dirty from atmospheric pollution over the years, and shoe prints were clearly visible on the surface, where the killers had walked across this area towards the balcony window, before breaking the glass and entering the building. The Technical Bureau photographed and preserved the evidence for comparison later if a suspect or suspects were identified.

Dr Maureen Smith, Mary Giblin and other forensic scientists from the State Laboratory at Garda HQ in Phoenix Park examined the evidence. The prints collected from the yacht club, the Perspex window recovered from the harbour and the beer cans all matched. There was no doubt that whoever had damaged and ransacked the boats had also been responsible for breaking into the yacht club and, more importantly, for the killing of Johnny Shorthall. The prints were subsequently matched to the fingerprints of two men known to gardaí. The men matched also the description of the youths seen at Old Conna Golf Club and, later, at the harbour checking out the trimaran.

Twenty-one-year-old Richard O'Brien and twenty-year-old John Doyle, both from Bray, were arrested and taken to different garda stations for questioning. They denied having killed Johnny Shorthall and claimed they didn't even know where Dún Laoghaire Yacht Club was. Investigating gardaí removed a number of items from the suspect's homes, including shoes and clothing belonging to the two men. When John Doyle's house was raided, gardaí found a pair of Nike runners. The sole of the left shoe matched the sole-print lifted from the bar wall.

The prints on the Perspex found by garda divers matched those of Richard O'Brien. Two packs of Giraffe and Whitman branded playing cards, missing from the *Myung*, had been found scattered on the floor of the club bar. Both Doyle's and O'Brien's fingerprints were found on the cards.

Forensic examination of the suspects' clothes taken in the house searches revealed trace evidence from the yacht club. Both men's hands were examined and showed signs of recent lacerations and abrasions, which had been caused by glass. One of the men also had puncture wounds on his hand and a cut to a finger. Blood samples matched his blood to the blood found in the galley kitchen on one of the boats. It later transpired that he had cut himself trying to cut a line which was tied too tightly. Finally, the prints found on the club roof were also matched to the second culprit. It seemed the game was up.

Doyle and O'Brien gave their version of the story. They had been drinking heavily all day and riding around on a motorbike. Having spent more time drinking in a friend's house, they left and drove to Bray, where they hid the bike in the sheds at Presentation Convent while Richard O'Brien went to sign on at Bray garda station under his conditions of bail. He had a pending charge for aggravated burglary and receiving stolen goods. With that over, they bought more drink and caught the Dart to Dún Laoghaire, returning to an ex-girlfriend's house after her parents went to work. John Doyle called another ex-girlfriend from a phone box on York Road in Dún Laoghaire at around 11.20 p.m. to ask her to tell his mother he wouldn't be home. They went back to the house and continued drinking until the girl's mother came home and told them to leave. It was then that they made for the yacht club. They climbed the railings and found the dinghy on the slipway. They didn't know how to start the engine, which wasn't attached to the dinghy, so they used the oars to row out under cover of darkness. They left the gloves behind, as it was too awkward to grip the oars properly with them.

Later, they used a stainless steel winch handle stolen from one of the boats to help them break into the yacht club. Crawling on their hands and knees into the lounge area, they spotted a man asleep on the couch. They argued as to who should hit him, to keep him quiet. O'Brien had a piece of timber he had taken from the toilets and he repeatedly battered the man on the head with the plank of wood. They heard him make a loud groaning noise, and saw that he was covered in blood. Having ransacked the place, they eventually left the premises via the route they'd entered. By then, the tide had gone out and, with it, the dinghy. They clambered over a wall and headed for the Dart station, where they hung around until the station opened. They caught the train just after 7.00 a.m.

Several staff members along the Dart route remembered them. The depot men at Bray station remembered them getting off the Dart and paying £2, in two £1 coins, as they had no ticket for the journey. They headed up the town where they got breakfast before collecting the motorbike in Presentation Convent. Doyle then dropped O'Brien home, as he was up in court at 2.30 that day in Bray. Investigating gardaí confirmed that the phone call had been made from the call box at York Road at 11.19 p.m. on the night of the killing, placing Doyle and O'Brien in the area.

With the mounting forensic evidence, including the shards of glass in their clothing, the fingerprints on the boats and in the yacht club, the stolen playing cards and money, the footprints matching the Nike runners, trace evidence found at the scene, matching the samples taken when they were arrested, and the groundbreaking prints on five cans of Budweiser Light which they'd stolen from the club bar and recovered by garda divers in the sea, it was an open and shut case. When the case came before the Central Criminal Court, Doyle and O'Brien pleaded guilty to manslaughter. They each got ten years. The dogged detective work of Eamon Reilly and Dominic Herns had brought two killers to justice.

20

Blood
(and Other Bodily Fluids)

Blood samples can give a wealth of information about an individual, particularly their DNA, which is extracted from the white cells in blood, known as leucocytes, as the red cells do not carry DNA. Blood samples can also identify blood type, known in forensics as the ABO system. Changes to the antigens in the body are measured to determine different blood types, which can be important in criminal investigation and can rule a suspect in or out. Where there are multiple victims, or even just one victim and one or more attackers, if different blood groups are identified at the scene, they must be matched to the victim and/or the attacker to identify who the blood belongs to. This is the job of a serologist, who will analyse and identify the various blood groups, although it is possible that two or more individuals have the same blood group.

In general terms the main blood groups are A, B, AB and O. These are subdivided into further groups of positive and negative; for example, A1+ or A1–; A2+ or A2–, and so on. This makes it easier to distinguish between even the common blood groups. That said, there are more than 200 minor subdivisions of blood groups that, being extremely rare, would readily identify a suspect if their blood was found at a crime scene. This applies more generally to international crimes, but with the diverging ethnic mix in Ireland, it may also be a consideration here. While O+ is the most common worldwide, some of the other groups can help to track down a suspect in a given scenario. For example, the AB blood group is the least common, found usually in Japan, China and Korea, which would narrow the possible suspects if found at a crime scene in Ireland, whereas type A is most frequently found in Northern and Central European countries, such as Norway, Denmark, Sweden and Poland. Almost fifty per cent of the Polish population belong to group A.

Bloodstain pattern analysis can help to reconstruct a crime. Blood spatter is the pattern and shape the blood forms when it hits a surface. Photographing or connecting a string line linking each blood spatter, and then using trigonometry, can reveal the sequence of events. If the blood spatter is teardrop-shaped, forensic investigators know that the impact of the blow was less than 90 degrees. The "tail" in the teardrop shows the direction from which the blow came. An angle of more than 90 degrees results in a circular-shaped bloodstain.

There are three main bloodstain categories: transfer, passive and active (also known as projectile). Transfer blood spatter happens when something or someone comes in contact with a wet, bloody surface. They may pick up blood on their shoes or hands, leaving bloody prints behind, as in the Grace Moore case (see Chapter 14). Passive spatter is caused by gravity, where blood drops or pools onto a surface, perhaps dripping from a bloody knife. Active spatter happens as a result of a blow to the head, or a stab wound to a main artery, which gushes. The type of spatter patterns differ in each case, depending on the surface they hit. If, for example, blood hits a pane of glass, there will be little distortion, whereas hitting lino will cause the blood drops to take on a scalloped shape, while blood spatter on wooden floors has a circular shape with "arms" or rays, much like a sunburst.

Blood spatter patterns can thus indicate the trajectory or the direction the blood came from; its spread over a surface area; and even the velocity or speed at which it hit the surface – i.e. if the blood flow was fast, such as from a gushing artery or from a gunshot wound, as opposed to a slow trickling bleed. Combining all this information can help to identify the type of weapon used, whether the person was moving towards or away from their attacker, or was motionless, perhaps lying in bed or standing still, and even whether it was a vicious attack or an accident.

If an injured assailant or victim was moving, or if the victim was hit with a weapon which itself became bloody as a result of the contact, the blood may have left a trail. Imagine, for example, that the attacker hit their victim with a poker or pistol-whipped them; the injury would leave traces of blood on the weapon, and as the attacker pulled back their arm, a trajectory of blood would be dispersed behind the attacker. This is often referred to as cast-off evidence, or cast-off blood, with a long, narrow, lighter weapon (such as a poker) creating a bigger cast-off area than, for example, a short weapon such as a handgun, if used as a bludgeon. As the blood is flung away from the victim, it lands on various nearby surfaces, such as a wall or floor, creating blood spatter. The pattern created by the cast-off blood can tell a lot about what happened, even down to whether the assailant was left- or right-handed.

The general population has a mix of "secretors" and "non-secretors". Secretors are people who have large concentrations of antigens A or B, which respond to an "invader" such as an illness in their body fluids – everything from sweat to saliva, semen, urine and other bodily fluids. Non-secretors make up a smaller proportion of the population, between eighteen and twenty per cent. Group O has no antigens. This can prove an important factor in establishing the person responsible for a bite mark, for example. If tests show that the perpetrator is a secretor and a suspect proves to be a non-secretor, the suspect, while not completely eliminated from the case, is ruled out as having inflicted the bite.

Equally, in a rape case, a semen sample from a non-secretor suspect should not rule them out. This was not always the case. Andrei Chikatilo sexually abused and murdered at least fifty-three women and young children in Russia between 1979 and November 1990. Russian investigators were unable to identify the killer, despite having arrested Chikatilo more than once. He was released when blood tests failed to match the semen found on victims. Police charged another young Russian with the murders and he was executed for the crimes, yet the killings continued. Police were aware of thirty-six murders, all with the same MO, but still had no new leads. Moscow police appointed a new investigation team, which included a specialist forensic scientist, Victor Burakov. Burakov believed that a non-secretor's blood group could show up differently in a semen sample, but other scientists refused to take his theory seriously. Eventually, when Chikatilo was re-arrested and confessed to fifty-six murders, Burakov's theory was proved right and it was then widely used until the development of DNA analysis, which made it superfluous.

21

Ballistics:
The Bullet Catchers

Ballistics is a catch-all word to describe the wider science that examines the identification, measurement and comparison of firearms, bullets or cartridge cases, often found at the scene of a crime. In truth, it's more about physics than pump-action shotguns and it covers the evaluation of information and data on the range and trajectory capabilities of certain weapons. The nature of wounds and trace evidence, such as chemical residues and powders left behind on the victim or gunman or woman, also form part of the overall investigation.

Any cartridge cases left behind have unique breech block or firing pin markings which can identify the type of firearm used. The lack of cartridges does not necessarily mean the gunman was clever enough to collect them as he made his escape. Certain types of weapons, such as a revolver, will leave no cartridges, so nothing should be ruled in or out at the early stages of the investigation.

If the crime scene investigation unit are lucky (and careful) enough to find spent cartridges, they can throw up a wealth of information. They may hold a print or partial print made by the gunman when loading the weapon. The bullets fired from a gun will have linear grooves or marks called striae. This happens when the bullet passes through the gun barrel and helps to identify the particular weapon. The lands (also known as ridges) and grooves in a barrel, known as rifling, are made during its manufacture. These make the bullet spin as it passes through the barrel, causing striations on the bullet, which laboratory analysis can link back to an individual weapon if it was used in other crimes.

As with most other aspects of an investigation, ballistics involves a wide range of other specialists who support the overall investigation, from a metallurgist, who gives details of the make-up of the bullet, to a firearms examiner who can, with the aid of chemical etching reagents, restore identifying serial numbers filed away by the criminal. As all guns have their own unique serial number, this can help trace the gun's movements, from the manufacturer and the point of sale, to those reported stolen or used in other crimes. Criminals are well aware that such identifying serial numbers can incriminate them and they make every effort to ensure that no serial numbers are found. The game – and that's often what they see it as – is to avoid getting caught.

Fortunately, modern forensic scientists have both the tools and the tenacity to catch them. Ballistic experts may link the weapon to other crimes, which will narrow the range of suspects. Of course, fingerprinting is also essential, and it is crucial that care is taken to ensure that any possible fingerprints are "lifted" from the weapon if found. DNA can also be identified on weapons, as hundreds of thousands of skin cells, invisible to the naked eye, are shed every day.

International police forces have their work cut out with the wide array of weapons available, both legally and on the black market. Forensic laboratories need the latest technology to identify every kind of firearm, from a small single-shot pistol, to semi-automatic pistols, where the force from the bullet fired loads a new round from the magazine into the chamber. These weapons come in many forms, with magazines holding anything up to 100 rounds. A semi-automatic rifle with a long barrel, which gives more accuracy, is extremely lethal. A .308-calibre copper-jacketed bullet can blow a hole in a quarter-inch thick steel plate – not something you want to mess with.

In recent years, gun crime in Ireland has included the use of revolvers, semi-automatics, rifles, sawn-off shotguns, submachine-guns, laser sights and silencers. Since 2005, gardaí have seized around 250 guns as well as ammunition from feuding Limerick gangs alone, proof that there is little difficulty in getting high-calibre weapons into Ireland undetected.

In early 2008, the gardaí, in co-operation with Dutch police and the PSNI, made major seizures of drugs, ammunition and guns, including machine pistols and other firearms. In September 2008, in another joint operation, police intercepted 165 firearms in a car and in offices in Holland, awaiting delivery to Ireland. The haul included seventy Glock pistols and Steyr submachine-guns fitted with silencers, along with 7,000 rounds of ammunition from a factory in Austria.

Handguns

Handguns are usually held and fired with one hand; they can be either revolvers or semi-automatics. Revolvers have a rotating cylinder that holds the cartridges, with various types holding different numbers of cartridges. Pulling the trigger rotates the cylinder, loading the next cartridge, ready for the gun's firing pin. When the gun is fired, the empty cartridge case remains in the cylinder.

Machine Pistols

Often seen on television and used by police forces as well as criminals, the machine pistol, also known as the submachine-gun, fires pistol ammunition. It can operate as either a fully automatic or semi-automatic. The Israeli Uzi or German Heckler and Koch are well-established manufacturers. Heckler and Koch is widely used by Special Forces and SWAT teams internationally. The MP5K 9mm fires 900 rounds per minute – definitely a deadly weapon. Croatia recently developed a mini ERO 9mm submachine-gun based on the Israeli mini and micro Uzis. It has a twenty-round magazine and is something for our law enforcement agencies to watch out for, as it is only a matter of time before it is brought into Ireland by criminals.

Shotguns

Shotguns also use cartridges, but with lead pellets or shots. They generally don't have the usual "rifling" associated with some gun barrels, which causes striations as the bullet leaves the barrel, though in recent times, new shotguns with rifling have emerged, alongside rifled ammunition for use with non-rifled shotguns.

Unlike other weapons, shotguns are measured by their gauge, so a twelve-gauge shotgun is really a measure of the diameter of the inside of the gun barrel. The bigger the gauge, the smaller the diameter of the barrel. A shotgun doesn't require a precise aim, as it is a wide-scattering weapon; the pellets spread out in a circular pattern, usually taking anything in their path.

Ammunition

People commonly think of bullets when they hear the word "ammunition". This is not strictly correct; the bullet is only part of the story. Bullets are usually enclosed in cartridges, which these days are often made of plastic. The primer can be found at the base (rim-fire ammunition) or in the middle of the base (centre-fire ammunition). The different elements are separated by wads, a mix of fibres made up of cotton, cardboard and other materials. When the trigger is pulled, the primer is struck by the firing pin and the primer ignites, setting off the gunpowder propellant and firing the shot. The metal covering on the bullet is referred to as jacketing, made famous by the film *Full Metal Jacket*.

A bullet recovered from a victim or a crime scene can tell its own story and will have marks and indentations or trace evidence such as blood, hair or fibres related to anything it struck, whether it was the victim, a piece of furniture or clothing. The spent cartridge can provide a great deal of evidence, from the company that made it to the identity of whoever handled it and even the make and model of the gun that discharged it.

Gunshot Residue and Nanotagging

After a gun is fired, there will also be gunshot residue. There are two types of residue: the bullet and the secondary "cloud" that emerges. This is a combination of the unburnt propellant and the primer, which explodes and causes the propellant to ignite and burn. As the propellant burns, it gives off gases which expand, forcing the bullet out into the barrel. When it leaves the barrel, the primer residue of gunpowder, usually a mixture of potassium nitrate, charcoal, sulphur and gases, with the remains of the primer explosion, follow it out. The emerging gases, laden with a mixture of lead styphnate (a toxic explosive often used in detonators and primers in guns), barium nitrate, sulphide and antimony, settle like disturbed dust, wafting down unseen onto the hands and clothes of the gunman, becoming gunshot residue, which can be used to identify the gunman.

New developments in the fight against gun crime could bring about more convictions, as a result of a DNA tagging technology developed at the University of Surrey, where "nanotechnology" is being used to coat gun cartridges with a special surface. Designed to capture a user's DNA, the nanotags are just 30 microns (0.03 of a millimetre) in diameter and are invisible to the naked eye. They are easily transferable to a user's hands and clothes and are extremely difficult to get rid of, making if hard for criminals to dispose of a gun and get away with the crime. It is expected they will also be used to trace the weapons used in knife crime in the near future.

Nanotagging leaves a trail of evidence, just waiting to be picked up by investigators. The technology is so sophisticated that the coating can be manufactured to make each batch of cartridges unique, thereby establishing a clear line between a user and a fired cartridge. A specialist UK database, NABIS, the National Ballistics Intelligence Services, is used alongside other information systems and databases and significantly improves information on gun crime and the use of firearms across Europol countries and further afield.

22

Lamb to the Slaughter:
Rhys Jones

It is every parent's nightmare – the inconceivable thought of a child shot dead on his way home from football. That's exactly what happened to eleven-year-old Rhys Jones, shot dead at 7.30 on a summer's evening, as he walked home from football training, a young child in the wrong place at the wrong time.

On 22 August 2007, Rhys was hit by a stray bullet, an innocent victim caught up in a feud between Liverpool gangs. The bullet was one of three destined for rival gang members; instead it hit Rhys in the neck, severing his carotid artery. Paramedics could do little to save him. He bled to death in his mother's arms. The gunman fled the scene on a mountain bike.

Detectives linked the shooting to two feuding gangs, locked in a bitter turf war in the Croxteth Park area of Liverpool. They believed that the hit was intended for a north Liverpool gang, the Norris Green Strand gang, better known as the Nogga Dogz. All three bullets missed their intended targets, but the fatal shot fired by the fleeing gunman took little Rhys Jones's life. Police knew that the Nogga Dogz gang's arch-rivals were the local Crocky Crew gang members, from the unlikely named Good Shepherd Close area of Croxteth and they quickly identified the likely lads in the gang.

Detectives recovered CCTV footage from the nearby pub, car park and street area, which showed the hooded gunman cycling along a path leading to the Fir Tree public house. He stopped briefly around the back of the pub before disappearing from the camera's view. The footage also showed Rhys walking diagonally across the car park. Two minutes later, the hooded man reappeared. Moving from the side of the pub to the car park, whilst still astride his bike, he took aim, steadying the handgun with both hands, and fired three shots. Rhys's attention was drawn by the first shot, which appeared to hit a blue container. Almost immediately, he was struck by the second bullet and fell to the ground, fatally wounded. A third shot hit a stone wall, giving off a puff of dust, captured on CCTV. Ballistic investigations confirmed that the trajectory of the bullets came from seventy yards away, across the car park.

Scene of crime officers searching the pub car park found a black BMW with a shattered window. Ballistic investigation showed the trajectory of the gunman's first shot had shattered the window of the BMW before being deflected, hitting the blue container.

A postmortem examination confirmed what was already known: Rhys died from a bullet wound. The bullet entered Rhys's back, slightly above his left shoulder blade, and exited through the front right side of his neck. It hit him either "partially or fully sideways on, producing a keyhole effect" on his body. Forensic ballistic experts said the bullet didn't make the neat round hole as expected from a cartridge fired from a rifled barrel. Instead, it tumbled "nose over base" rather that the more usual, nose-first, stabilised flight. This can happen when the cartridge used is too small or is discharged from a worn or smooth-bore barrel or is deflected by something *en route*.

The gunman made his escape on a black mountain bike, heading back the way he came. Police enhanced the CCTV images in an effort to identify the perpetrator.

A suspect can be identified from CCTV in a number of ways, even if their face is covered. Height, build, a particular gait or stance, jewellery such as signet rings or even the clothes worn can all be used to help identify a suspect.

It may seem strange in this era of mass production and international store chains that a single garment can be identified from CCTV. As a result of FBI forensic analysis developments, however, forensic photographic technology has been used successfully in an increasing number of cases. In 1998, for example, three brothers were convicted of numerous bank robberies in South Carolina, USA. They became so complacent they even robbed the same banks several times. All the robbers wore balaclavas and facial recognition was not possible. CCTV enhancement allowed FBI forensic photographic technologists to study the armed robbers' build and stance. They believed from the way they stood and held their guns that at least two of the three men had done military service and one was possibly even a cop. They studied CCTV from another robbery where a customer attempted to stop them; one of the robbers wrestled the man to the ground, just as police are trained to do.

Detectives were asked to look at the CCTV footage in an effort to identify any current or former colleagues by their stance. Several people picked out one individual who had been in the force for many years. The "feet apart, two hands on your weapon" training drill for an armed challenge of a suspect had superseded the previous "one foot forward" position, and some of the older cops had difficulty adapting, using a mixture of the two. Detectives reviewed footage of recent training sessions and noticed one cop in particular had an unusual "mixed" stance, combining both methods in one. He fitted the height and build of the suspect on the bank's CCTV. Checking his attendance records, they found that he had either been off duty or on sick leave at the time of the robberies.

Examining the bank footage more closely, they examined the thief's clothing, in particular a black-and-white check work-shirt, which had two breast pockets. Quality tailoring uses extra material especially cut to ensure the pockets on a garment are properly aligned, giving that seamless look, which is more expensive. Generally, on mass-produced cheap shirts, pockets are stitched on with waste material, with no effort to "match" the pattern. A random pattern analysis of the shirt in the CCTV highlighted the alignment of the two pockets and the areas of wear particular to an individual, due to weight, muscles, protruding bellies or individual traits, which can also cause fraying of a garment in specific areas.

Raiding the police officer's home, they found a black-and-white check shirt which appeared identical to the one on the CCTV, but given that they were mass-produced, anyone could have had one. The shirt was forensically examined by a photographic technologist, who cross-matched the random pattern with that of the one caught on the bank's CCTV. He superimposed the enhanced photographs of the material and the design of the pocket angles, the stitching, wear and tear areas and most importantly, the exact position of cloth threads with those on the policeman's shirt. They were identical in every detail. The persuasive evidence of CCTV and random pattern analysis convinced the jury they had the right man. The men were found guilty.

In the case of the Rhys Jones shooting, the digitally enhanced CCTV showed that the bike rider was wearing a black hoodie top, black tracksuit bottoms with a white stripe and white trainers. His hands and a small unidentifiable area of his face could be seen, indicating that he was white. Photographic technologists estimated that the gunman was in his later teens or early twenties, of slim build and approximately five feet eight inches in height.

Police appealed to the public for any information on the murder, which was widely covered by the media. Leslie Shimmen was at home watching the news when police released an enhanced CCTV photograph of the Specialized Hardrock mountain bike used by the gunman and appealed for anyone sighting the gunman or bike to come forward. Mr Shimmen realised that he had found the frame of a similar bike the day after the murder, while out cycling with his children. He immediately contacted the police and told them where he had found the frame, sticking out of overgrown bushes in an industrial estate close to his home. A forensic examination confirmed that the frame had come from a satin silver and black Specialized Hardrock mountain bike. The bike frame was nineteen inches, matching that seen on the video, and forensic scientists also found DNA on the frame.

As the investigation was ongoing, over sixty officers and four firearms recovery dogs conducted a painstaking "fingertip" search of the area looking for evidence. It was described as the most arduous search ever conducted by Liverpool police; 120 metres of hedgerow and undergrowth were cut down and everything was collected in tarpaulins to ensure there was no loss of "evidence" from the branches. Searches spread over eight areas involving thirty-two premises took over 800 man-hours, while forty pairs of forensic protective boots were worn out during the search. Police divers searched for evidence in lakes, ponds and larger areas of water.

Intelligence indicated that the hit was intended to take out key players in the Nogga Dogz gang, which comprised about forty members ranging in age from thirteen up to thirty years old. At least one twenty-five-year-old "general" was already behind bars at the time. There had been over seventy tit-for-tat shootings between the gangs since New Year's Day 2006, when twenty-year-old Danny McDonald, a Crocky Crew leader, was shot dead as he drank in a local pub. The gunman, who was wearing a ski mask, blasted him seven times, leaving him dead, as fifty stunned drinkers looked on. This first known murder within the gangs raised the stakes critically.

No one was charged with McDonald's murder, but the police believed the gunman was nineteen-year-old Liam "Smigger" Smith, a Nogga Dogz member, who was quickly promoted within the ranks. Smith was later shot dead outside Merseyside's Altcourse Prison in a revenge attack. He and his sisters were seen visiting a friend in prison by nineteen-year-old Ryan Lloyd, himself a prisoner and a sworn enemy of the Nogga Dogz. Lloyd borrowed a contraband mobile phone to arrange the hit. He was overheard saying, "Quick quick, give us the phone, I'll get the boys up here to pop them." As Smith left the prison he was surrounded by more than a dozen Crocky Crew members, who ranged in age from early teens to fifty-one. Smith was shot in the head with a shotgun from five yards and died in hospital a short time later. The postmortem, which confirmed he had died from the gunshot wounds, also found pellets still in his body from an earlier attack in 2005. The shooting was caught on prison security CCTV, which was enhanced to identify the already well-known gangsters. Ballistics identified the shotgun, while fingerprints and DNA were found on the murder weapon. As a result, eleven men were charged with Smith's murder. Three men aged between sixteen and nineteen were subsequently convicted of murder and one, a self-confessed close friend of Smith's, twenty-six-year-old Liam Duffy, was convicted of manslaughter.

With the Rhys Jones murder investigation still ongoing, police bought an identical Hardrock bike and asked a forensics specialist to examine and compare it to the one identified on the CCTV. Detectives also turned up an interesting piece of information. A sixteen-year-old member of the Crocky Crew gang had bought a new black and silver Hardrock bike four months before the murder, when his old cream and black bike was reported stolen. His mother had made a claim on their insurance policy and the bike had been replaced with a brand new £400 Specialized Hardrock satin silver and black mountain bike.

Local insurers who paid out on the claim gave police the serial number of the new bike; it matched the serial number on the abandoned bike frame found close to the lock-up. Police went in search of its owner, sixteen-year-old Sean Mercer, of Good Shepherd Close, who denied all knowledge of the shooting. He said he was at home watching DVDs with friends at the time. His friends, eighteen-year-old Nathan Quinn, James Yates (20), Gary Kays (25), and Melvin Coy (24) and two other teenagers aged sixteen and seventeen all agreed that they were watching DVDs when Rhys was shot. Forensic analysis of their mobile phone usage would prove otherwise.

The gang spent their days stupefied in a cannabis fog, playing video games or riding their bikes. They were into petty crime and liked to showboat their exploits on the internet or Facebook, which would later come back to haunt them. Computer investigators forensically examined computers found in the suspects' homes and uncovered emails, chat room conversations and photographs of "their" guns, showing their fascination with gang warfare and guns. Jurors in the trial were shown a video which the gang had put on YouTube glamorising their lifestyle, flaunting a range of weapons, including a Smith & Wesson similar to the one used to kill Rhys. Forensic expert Mark Robinson said the gun in the video was a match for the murder weapon. Both had a missing metal loop, designed for soldiers to hook onto their belts.

Gangs were becoming a serious problem in the UK, and Liverpool had its fair share of teenage "punks" trying to emulate US gangs. Police were tackling the problem with Operation Matrix, and Sean Mercer had already come to their attention. Two months before he killed Rhys Jones, Mercer rode a motorbike around rival gangland turf, waving a gun at members of the public, while just weeks after shooting Rhys, he was given a three-year ASBO (Anti-Social Behaviour Order) for terrorising security guards at a local sports centre. Mercer also had convictions for the possession of weapons.

Twenty-five-year-old Gary Kays, believed to be the gang leader and the instigator of the shooting, was the only one with any apparent trappings of success, and that was just a leased Audi Q7. At 6.40 p.m. on 22 August

2007, he received a thirty-second call from a named friend alerting him to the presence of a rival gang member in the area. Forensic evidence from the phone showed the call was relayed from a mast close to the Fir Tree pub. Thirty seconds later, Sean Mercer, who was at Dean Kelly's house, got a call from Melvin Coy. That call lasted twelve seconds. Gary Kays also made a call to Mercer, telling him that a rival, Wayne Brady, was outside the Fir Tree pub. Mercer and Kelly left Kelly's house at Swords Walk to collect a gun from James Yates. Mercer then rode his bike to the pub, intent on killing Brady and any other gang member with him. Twenty minutes later, as eleven-year-old Rhys Jones crossed the car park, he was shot dead.

Forensic mobile signal tracking identified two calls lasting twenty-eight seconds and thirty-seven seconds respectively, both made from Melvin Coy's mobile to Sean Mercer's mobile shortly after the shooting. Mercer denied getting the calls and claimed that he had lost his phone the weekend before the killing – yet Mercer made a call from his mobile to his mother's phone immediately after the murder.

Investigations also identified a flurry of mobile phone calls between gang members within half an hour of the murder. Mercer rang Kays and Yates and told them he was in Boy M's house. Kays immediately phoned "Boy M" (who could not be named, as he was under-age at the time) and told him to clean up the operation. They rounded up some of the other gang members and they all met up. Kays later told police he'd never heard of Boy M, despite the forensic evidence of his phone call and other covert surveillance evidence that put Kays, Kelly, Coy, Yates and Quinn, along with Mercer, at Boy M's house after the shooting. Boy M's job was get rid of a hat and gloves. He ordered two other teenagers to get rid of the bike, which Mercer had left with him. (CCTV of Mercer had shown him arriving at the Fir Tree car park with his hands clearly uncovered but he possibly put on the gloves before firing the gun.)

Numerous mobile calls made between gang members and others on the night of the murder were relayed from masts between Croxteth and Kirkby, a few miles away. Footage from every available CCTV camera from Croxteth to Kirkby on the night of the murder was recovered and enhanced. It picked up and tracked the progress of a Ford Galaxy car carrying gang members and known to be used by Melvin Coy, from Croxteth to the Acorn Business Centre, an industrial estate in Kirkby, approximately three miles away. The car stopped at a garage *en route* to fill up containers with petrol. It was established that Melvin Coy's father had a lock-up at the industrial estate. Police raided the lock-up and found several empty petrol cans. When questioned, Kays denied having left the Croxteth area on the night of Rhys's murder, despite being shown the CCTV evidence. Forensic evidence from his mobile phone calls also placed him in Kirkby.

Within days of the killing, covert bugging devices were secretly imbedded into the homes of Boy M and James Yates. These listening devices proved crucial in establishing the criminal conspiracy of the gang members. The covert surveillance picked up three of the youths – Mercer, Quinn and Yates – intimidating Boy M's elderly grandmother in an attempt to force her to help in covering their tracks. Sean Mercer's voice is identified telling her, "You have to say it was Tuesday."

The grandmother replied, "I'm not saying it was Tuesday."

Mercer then aggressively said, "You've got it completely f*** wrong, you'd better change it. F*** hell, why can't you? Say you've got a bad memory."

The grandmother said, "I'm not changing. I've signed the statement."

In a later recording, the grandmother is heard recounting to someone else what Mercer had tried to force her to do: "I said [to Mercer], 'If you haven't done it you've got nothing to worry about. I don't know what all this lying is about.' He said, 'I know I know,' but he went white."

After the murder, one of the gang, "Boy X", went on holiday to Florida with his sister, her husband, their baby and his nineteen-year-old brother, but while there, he received several mobile calls which were tracked by detectives. Sean Mercer made thirteen calls or texts to Florida in the space of fifteen minutes, to let him know his house had been raided and a cache of guns and ammunition had been found. When his family found out, they forced him to co-operate with the police. His sister phoned her younger brother's house while detectives were still searching it and arranged for the police to meet them when they touched down at Manchester. Boy X was arrested on the tarmac at Manchester airport on his return. Following this development, the under-age youth, who had never been in serious trouble before, also turned "Queen's evidence", and was granted immunity under the Serious Organised Crime and Police Act, 2005, only the second time it was ever used, and the first time on an under-age youth. Helen Morris the Crown Prosecution lawyer, said: "We used all the legal tools at our disposal to push at the boundaries of what the legislation allowed us to do." It allowed Boy X to give evidence as a witness from behind a curtain on a video screen.

The seventeen-year-old told police that twenty minutes after the shooting, he got a call from Mercer telling him to get over to Boy M's house immediately. He got a taxi and was taken straight upstairs to M's bedroom, where Sean Mercer handed him a Smith & Wesson .445 revolver and said, "Here you are, take that, you've got to put that in yours and don't say anything to anyone." The youth said he wrapped it in a carrier bag and then hid it under blankets in a dog kennel for five days. Boy X later moved the murder weapon from the kennel and hid it in the attic, along with three .45 Colt cartridges, a Walther PPK blank cartridge self-loading pistol and ammunition.

Forensic scientists test-fired the cartridges found with the gun and discovered that they made the same "keyhole" effect seen on Rhys's shirt. Swabs from the barrel and chamber of the Smith & Wesson were found to have type two FDR (firearms discharge residue), containing elements of tin. When the .45 Colt cartridges were test-fired, they gave off the same type two residue. A swab of the bullet hole entry point on Rhys's football shirt also identified type two gunshot residue, containing tin particles matching those found on the gun. Angela Shaw, a forensic science FDR expert, said tin in gunshot residue was "unusual" and was seen in less than five per cent of cases in the laboratory.

There was no doubt that this was the gun that killed Rhys. The unusual keyhole effect was due to two factors – the bullet was undersized by 0.08mm and the revolver's rifling was worn. In fact, the Smith & Wesson dated back to 1915 and had been used in the First World War.

Boy M confirmed to police that, after the shooting, Mercer had turned up at his house and then rounded up the others to help him. Gang members including James Yates, Nathan Quinn, Gary Kays and Dean Kelly also turned up, and later that night, they all went to Melvin Coy's lock-up garage in the Kirkby industrial estate. Boy M also told detectives that when his grandmother answered the door to Mercer shortly after the murder, Mercer rushed in, saying he had just shot someone and that a kid had "gone down".

The teenager (Boy M) admitted three counts of assisting Mercer but claimed duress, as he was afraid of Mercer. Forensic evidence from the CCTV, the gun recovered and the bike all proved Mercer had been the gunman. The dogs in the street seemed to agree as graffiti appeared in Croxteth naming Mercer. Gang members' Facebook and internet messages also claimed Mercer and the boys had gone after the rival gang, killing Rhys Jones instead.

Both M's mother and grandmother said Mercer had a bike with him at the time. They remembered Mercer was anxious to get away from the area and Coy drove them to the industrial estate in Kirkby, where they washed Mercer down in petrol, to try to remove any gunshot residue from the murder weapon, and then burned his clothes. M claimed he was afraid of what the gang would do to him if he didn't do what they told him.

Mercer, Yates, Kays, Coy, Quinn and Kelly were among eleven people arrested in dawn raids and questioned about the murder and DNA samples were taken from the suspects before they were released on bail. Sean Mercer's DNA matched the DNA found on the bike frame. Mercer, then just seventeen, was charged with murdering Rhys Jones.

When police questioned Sean Mercer's mother, forty-nine-year-old Janette Mercer, she confirmed her son's story – the boys were all watching DVDs at her house at the time of Rhys's killing. When asked if he owned a mountain bike, she told police he had a black and cream bike and had never owned a silver and black Hardrock mountain bike, claiming his bike was nothing like the one seen on CCTV. By then, police already knew she had put in the claim to the insurance company and had got the replacement Hardrock satin silver and black bike for her son Sean.

When re-arrested, Mercer declined to answer any questions, except to say he had been with a friend, "Boy K" (Dean Kelly). When Kelly was arrested he denied two counts of possessing a gun and ammunition. He also denied he had assisted Mercer. When the case came up before Liverpool Crown Court, twenty-year-old Wayne Brady, the intended victim and a member of the Nogga

Dogz Strand gang, gave evidence. There had been a long-standing feud between the pair and Mercer had said Brady was "gonna get it". Brady had been with two friends close to the Fir Tree pub car park, but had asked his friends to wait while he spoke to his ex-girlfriend to "apologise for some things". That apology saved his life. Brady said he heard three gunshots, and his two friends "dropped their heads and pedalled away as fast as they could. I got off straight away, away from where the shots were coming from."

Janette Mercer, who was also known to police, was working as a £50-a-time prostitute at the time of the murder. She was charged with perverting the course of justice by giving her son and his fellow gang members a false alibi, and lying to police about her son's bike. She was with her son when they gave police a false pre-prepared statement, which said: "I own a mountain bike, it's black, cream and orange. I do not own any others and have no access to mountain bikes." On 27 September 2007, Janette Mercer gave police another statement backing up her son's alibi and the statement about his bike.

Rhys Jones's parents were in Liverpool Crown Court to hear Judge Henry Globe tell Janette Mercer: "Your son was a key suspect in the murder and you knew he had told a pack of lies. You backed him up and you told more lies." Janette Mercer was jailed for three years.

Marie Yates, the fifty-one-year-old mother of James Yates, a member of the gang who provided Sean Mercer with the gun, was also charged with perverting the course of justice. She was jailed for eighteen months for burning a mobile phone SIM card, which she believed would incriminate her son. Covert surveillance bugs had monitored her speaking about the killer Mercer with admiration, saying, "He's got bottle." Together with her husband Frank (49), they discussed the damning potential of the SIM card from their son's mobile phone and decided to burn it; bugging devices recorded them saying that if they burnt it, it could never be used as evidence against him. Frank Yates admitted to destroying the SIM card and concocting an alibi for Sean Mercer. He was sentenced to four-and-a-half years in jail.

Their son, James Yates, who supplied the gun used in the killing, was sentenced to seven years in jail. He was also convicted of assisting Sean Mercer after the killing, dumping the gun and burning Mercer's clothes, for which he got two concurrent sentences of six years. Yates had been trapped by bugging devices secretly planted in their home by investigating detectives, who heard the family talking about their son's involvement with Sean Mercer and what they had to do to cover up for them to make sure they avoided detection. The Yates's were worried that Mercer would admit that James Yates gave him the gun. Yates was heard to say to his parents, "Do you really think he's going to sit there and say James Yates gave me the gun? No. End of story, what can they prove? Nothing."

Melvin Coy, Gary Kays, Nathan Quinn, Dean Kelly and a sixteen-year-old boy were all found guilty of perverting the course of justice by helping Mercer. They denied the charges. Kays, Coy and Yates were jailed for seven years. Quinn, Kelly and the sixteen-year-old, who was given a supervision order and a four-month curfew, got off lightly, cheering and yelling as they left the courtroom, as a sentence of just six years between them was handed down in January 2009. Taking into consideration their time served on remand, they will be out in less than three years. The unnamed sixteen-year-old had already been making a name for himself "inside". He was in constant trouble while behind bars on remand, having instigated no less than nine fights.

Sean Mercer's family had experienced the tragedy of murder before. His parents, Jannette Mercer and Joe McCormick, were second cousins and had shared the same great-great-grandfather, John Maguire. Almost eighty years before Rhys Jones's death, Maguire was convicted of murdering his wife Ellen, the mother of his ten children, having stabbed her in the back and then slashing her throat in a fit of temper. He was later hanged.

Rhys Jones's parents said that, in their eyes, the parents had been as guilty as their sons, covering up for them as they did, knowing a child had been killed. "As adults, they should have known right from wrong. To intentionally cover up Rhys's murder, to protect a murderer and his accomplices, and to prolong our agony is unforgivable. As parents themselves, they should have understood our pain, but instead they chose to ignore it. For us, no prison sentence for these people would be long enough."

Boy X, who is now living under an assumed name on a witness protection programme, will be looking over his shoulder for the rest of his life.

Sean Mercer, now eighteen, got twenty-two years in prison.

23

Brothers in Arms:
Joan Casey

Murder is everywhere. It can come to your door or mine, for no apparent reason. It can come from an unexpected source – the jealous husband next door kills his wife in a fit of rage; the innocent girl, like Donna Cleary, caught in a hail of gunfire when gatecrashers were refused entry to a party in her friend's house; or even a grandmother, minding her own business, asleep in her bed at night.

The Casey family never imagined that murder would knock on their door. Joan Casey was an ordinary working-class mother-of-five living in Tallaght. She had already lost one child to tragedy and now the family were to lose their mum, described by her family as "the most wonderful person on earth; we lost the most important person in our lives".

It wasn't ill-health or a tragic accident that took their mother away. The sixty-five-year-old grandmother was murdered by two young thugs who smashed their way into her house, armed with a shotgun, at 6.00 a.m. on 2 April 2004. Shot dead, alone in her bedroom, just because . . .

A few months earlier, Joan Casey had moved into the back bedroom of her house, thinking it would be safer, after her front bedroom window had been smashed. She was nervous and she made sure to lock her bedroom door and put on the burglar alarm, but it wasn't enough to save her.

Mrs Casey's neighbour was woken up by loud shouting and banging noises outside his house. He heard glass being smashed and then two loud bangs. He looked out of his bedroom window and saw two masked young men walking slowly away from Joan Casey's gate. One of them had a shotgun and they seemed in no particular hurry to get away. He watched as the men dumped two pairs of gloves in a nearby bin and then attempted to set fire to it. The men left before the fire fully took hold, and the brave neighbour rescued the evidence before the gloves were burnt.

The Technical Bureau arriving on the scene found that Joan Casey's front door had been smashed in; the shattered glass from the door was everywhere. Upstairs, the back bedroom door had been blown apart. Two shots had been discharged through the locked door. One hit the bedroom wall; the other went straight through Joan Casey. The grandmother lay dead inside her bedroom.

Investigating detectives believed that Joan Casey was a victim of mistaken identity. They believed the gunman may have been targeting her son Gerard, who stayed at the family home from time to time.

It was obvious to ballistic investigators that a shotgun had been used. A shotgun fires a shell which contains a plastic wad or "cup" of small round lead or steel balls called "shot". When the wad leaves the gun barrel, this shot scatters in a wide angle, which can leave extensive injuries or damage in its wake. A postmortem showed that Mrs Casey had died from a gunshot wound to the heart. The shotgun caused multiple injuries to a wide area of tissue, which resulted in massive haemorrhaging to her left lung. The gun was fired from very short range through the bedroom door. Trauma specialists say that gunshot injuries are usually immediately fatal if shot from less than nine feet. Mrs Casey was shot from a much shorter range than that. She stood little chance of surviving the attack. (If they do survive, a victim can face years of surgery to repair the extensive tissue damage, which is compounded by infections caused by imbedded wadding, fragments of their own clothing and necrotic or rotting tissue left behind by the buck shot.)

Forensic investigators took samples of the shattered glass from the hall door, as glass particles are often imbedded in an attacker's clothing or hair. Determining how the glass was broken – such as with a rock, a baseball bat or a shotgun – can help to build a case against a suspect. The technical unit knew the glass had been broken from the outside. Even where this is not obvious, it can be established from the conchoidal or stress factor lines that spread out from the area of first impact. When examined under laboratory conditions, the glass curves out and away from the impact area, in a convex seashell shape. On closer inspection, these stress lines will show tiny fracture lines, known as hackle marks, which radiate out at 90 degrees from the conchoidal lines, like the spokes on a bicycle wheel. If the glass had been smashed with a shotgun and the weapon was recovered, nicks or scratch marks on the gun could be forensically identified against the glass.

In a search of the area, Detective Garda Mark Collander found a blue bag hidden under a bush, close to a block of flats nearby. When he examined the bag he found a twelve-gauge double-barrelled shotgun, which had been disassembled into three pieces. He also found live and spent cartridges and a blank firing pistol. He checked the breach of the shotgun and saw two spent cartridges. Shotgun cartridges are usually made from a plastic case, the base of which is covered with a thin brass covering, although the old heavy brass shells are still being manufactured. The shell is tightly packed first with gunpowder, which burns, or the more efficient smokeless powder which may contain nitroglycerine for its explosive qualities; then wadding, which separates the powder from the shot and is usually comprised of bits of lead or steel depending on the type; and finally, overshot wadding which holds the shot together as it travels through the barrel to ensure that the gas doesn't escape, leaving it without a propellant. There was no question that the cartridges used by Joan Casey's killers were without a propellant. The shot blasted right through her bedroom door, killing her on impact.

Detectives discovered that the murder weapon had been stolen in a burglary on the north side of Dublin in

2003. Annette Forde from the Technical Bureau ballistics unit examined the shotgun in the Forensic Science Laboratory and found fresh scratches on it. The scratches contained powder which, when analysed, was found to have come from glass fragments. This in turn matched the glass found at the scene of the crime – the front door glass that had been smashed. This analysis is done by measuring the refractive index (how light is reflected through glass) of the particles found and comparing it to the glass in Joan Casey's door. By using stereomicroscopes with a zoom magnification system, the light from one part of the glass travels in different ways to the eye, making it easy to see and move around with a tweezers or a needle probe. This system is also used to identify glass fragments in clothes. So if a suspect was caught, their clothes could be examined by hanging them over a sterile metal collection unit, brushing the clothes down and examining any debris, including specks of glass that may be on them.

Annette Forde also found a fingerprint on the barrel of the shotgun. The fingerprint was made either when the gunman initially assembled the shotgun or while dismantling it later, as the main body of the gun had been wiped down after the killing. The fingerprint was identified as belonging to Tim Rattigan (26) of St Dominick's Terrace in Tallaght, a small-time criminal with a couple of previous convictions. As a result of this detectives arrested four men in their twenties and a thirty-one-year-old woman. During questioning, two of the men, Dylan Johnson and Stephen Johnson, made statements confirming they'd received a phone call from Rattigan in the early hours of the morning, and a second call, shortly after 6.00 a.m., saying he was "on his way back". Rattigan, along with Conor Grogan of Avonbeg Park, was subsequently charged with the murder of Joan Casey.

During the twelve-day trial, the court heard that Rattigan and Grogan had been drinking heavily and ended up in Rattigan's sister's flat in the early hours on the morning of the murder. The victim's son Gerard Casey was married to one of Rattigan's sisters and they had four children together. He was believed to have been the intended target of the gunmen. During the case, the Johnson brothers changed their evidence and withdrew the statements they'd made to gardaí about the early morning phone calls from the accused. They now said they'd only made the statements following coercion by gardaí.

Mr Justice Paul Carney told the court that these two witnesses Dylan and Stephen Johnson were hostile witnesses. He said, "I'm satisfied that they were each lying through their teeth." While saying that he would not pursue the matter, "that doesn't stop the prosecution from doing so". Justice Carney directed the jury to find Grogan not guilty, due to insufficient evidence against him.

After a trial lasting twelve days, in a majority verdict, the jury found Tim Rattigan guilty of the murder of Joan Casey. The forensic evidence against him had been damning. Mr Justice Carney handed down the mandatory life sentence. Rattigan was sent to the maximum security prison in Portlaoise.

Tim Rattigan's cousin, Brian Rattigan from Drimnagh, is also doing time in Portlaoise, keeping it all in the family.

Brian Rattigan had been a victim of a shooting in March 2002, while his brother was gunned down in July of that year. Brian Rattigan was sentenced to four years in 2004 for firing five times at a garda car with a shotgun and then pointing it directly at a plainclothes detective. With the gun cocked, he continued to hold his aim, until a garda drew his gun and fired a warning shot. Rattigan was then arrested. Defending Rattigan at his trial, Brendan Grehan SC said of Rattigan: "He didn't take the ultimate step of pulling the trigger." It was later shown that, by then, Rattigan's gun was empty. He had run out of ammunition. Rattigan was already doing six years, having been sentenced a year earlier, in May 2003, after being caught with €27,000 worth of heroin.

Brian Rattigan was also charged with the murder of another Drimnagh man, twenty-one-year-old Declan Gavin, who was stabbed to death outside Abrakebabra in Crumlin on 25 August 2001, in what gardaí described as "a targeted attack". Rattigan denied the murder and told gardaí he was with a married woman on the night in question, saying he hadn't been to that Abrakebabra in four months.

When asked to identify the woman to substantiate his alibi, Rattigan said: "No f***ing way, you can find her yourself." Gardaí questioning Rattigan put it to him that "a lot of people witnessed the stabbing that night". Rattigan replied, "They can say what they like but they'll all have to say it in court."

The matter finally came to trial in January 2009. Evidence was given of a silver Micra car screeching to a halt outside the fast food outlet at 3.00 a.m. on the morning in question. A girl walked to the car and had words with the occupants, before kicking the car and walking off. As the victim, Declan Gavin, walked out of Abrakebabra, he approached the car. Someone inside the car shouted at him, saying, "You rat". A man then jumped out of the car brandishing a knife, ran towards Gavin and stabbed him. Gavin stumbled down the steps of the food shop, followed by the attacker, who continued his frenzied stabbing attack on the man. The attacker then ran towards the Nissan and made his getaway. A local security guard called the gardaí and an ambulance arrived, but it was too late for Declan Gavin. Stabbed through the heart, he was already dead.

The jury was told that Rattigan's palm and fingerprints were found at the crime scene. Detective Garda Chris O'Connor, a fourteen-year veteran in the fingerprint section of the Technical Bureau, used developing agent of grey powder to highlight the mark, which was then photographed by Detective Garda Caroline Hughes. When the prints were compared to those taken from Brian Rattigan, there were twelve points of comparison in both. A twelve-point match is usually enough to identify a person.

Further prints on the door of the premises were also identified as belonging to Brian Rattigan. Either the fast food outlet hadn't cleaned their windows in four months or Rattigan was mistaken. He later said he couldn't remember saying he hadn't been there in four months. DNA extracted from blood found two inches away from Rattigan's palm print was identified as belonging to the murder victim Declan Gavin. Detective Garda Seamus Quinn from the ballistics section of the Garda Technical Bureau found a trail of blood starting at the bus stop outside Abrakebabra, leading all the way down the steps and into the fast food outlet.

Within hours of the killing, Rattigan's friend's car, a silver Nissan Micra, the same make and colour from which the killer emerged, was later found abandoned and burnt out. Mr Justice Barry White told the jury it could not be influenced by the fact that many witnesses in the trial suffered from loss of memory in the witness box. He said they were not to draw adverse inferences on the accused from this. He also told them not to anticipate what evidence the prosecution had expected these witnesses to give in the case. In the end, the jury failed to agree and the matter was put back for a new trial date.

The trial was beset with a series of delays resulting in Rattigan applying to have the case against him struck out. The Supreme Court awarded him € 500,000 in costs against the DPP, for his unsuccessful bid to halt his trial, in a reverse of the norm where costs are awarded to the winning side.

At the time of writing, Brian Rattigan is still awaiting a new trial date.

24

Hanging By a Thread: Fibre Evidence and Analysis

It may be hard to imagine that something so minute as a thread can play a crucial part in a criminal investigation, yet many a case has been solved by matching fibres found on a victim or at a crime scene to the perpetrator. Fibres are trace elements which can provide significant forensic evidence in a case, placing a suspect in close contact with a victim. The various methods of fibre analysis can yield different types of information and by using a combination of different tests, a full picture relating to the crime is more likely to emerge.

More than half of all fibres used in the production of textiles are man-made, with polyester and nylon being the most common. The shape of these fibres can be important in identification as, when examined under a scanning electron microscope, the cross sections of man-made fibres can be tracked to a specific manufacturer, particularly where they may have been part of a once-off production or in use for a limited timeframe, just as a "designer" garment can be tracked to a well-known designer.

How a fabric is constructed is an important factor in fibre transfer. Some fabrics, such as tightly knitted or woven items, shed less than more loosely woven fabrics. Fabrics made from spun yarn are rougher because when the twist is increased and tightened during the manufacturing process, the fabric becomes harder. A good example of this can be found in carpets. Carpets made with a spun yarn will shed excess fibre, especially when new, and they are more likely to leave "contact" fibres.

Cotton is the most common plant fibre. The type of cotton, the length of the fibres and the techniques used during its processing are all important clues to its identification. A procedure such as mercerisation can lead to a "unique" fabric ID: the cotton thread or yarn is treated in a solution of sodium hydroxide (caustic soda) giving the fabric a glossy sheen, causing an irreversible chemical change which can be picked up under microscopic laboratory conditions.

Sheep's wool is the most common animal fibre in use. The coarser grades are used in carpets, while the finer grades are reserved for clothing or furnishings. Other animal wools used, such as mohair, cashmere and even alpaca or camel, are more easily shed. The discovery of these less common fibres can more readily identify the source when transfer fibres are detected.

One of the greatest variations in fabrics and textiles is in the shade and colour. Pigments and synthetic dyes are categorised by twenty-nine chemical categories and by their application methods. Some products can take up to ten different processes before arriving at the finished colour. This may suggest that it is nearly impossible to break down and identify the myriad of colours, shades, hues, manufacturers and processes. Actually, this is not the case. While it is sometimes a painfully slow process of elimination, the worldwide annual production of most dye colours is only around ten tonnes and small batch processing has become the norm. Given that these dyes are used for a wide variety of products, it is now easier to pinpoint a dye to a specific fabric range.

Often a combination of more than one dye may have been used to get a specific colour or shade. When the dye was added is important, as some fibres can be coloured before being spun into yarns; the yarns themselves can be dyed or a manufacturer may add dye to the finished fabric. There are many methods of dyeing. Some fabrics have the dye or colour applied to the fabric surface, such as in "print" fabrics. How this colour has been applied and absorbed can be important in matching such a fabric to a specific victim or suspect.

In a typical crime scene, the Technical Bureau will check for trace evidence such as fibre transfer. Fibres can come from many sources apart from clothing, including car seats, sleeping bags, or even rope. Even within these groups, analysing what kind of material was involved forms part of the identification process; for example, if fibres from a rope were found, analysis can show whether it was braided, twisted or straight, the type of twist, the diameter of the cross-section, the colour, the nature of the cord, if it was natural or synthetic, the coatings if any, the number of twists per inch . . . and these are just some of the steps required in rope fibre analysis.

So, as you can imagine, narrowing the field down to possible matches is a vast task for forensic investigators. Fibre examination involves a comparison of samples found on a victim's clothing or body to fibres from a suspect's clothing or cross-transferred from the victim to the suspect. These are referred to as "known" and "questioned" sources. An example of this can be seen in Chapter 25, where John McDonagh's white jumper was found to have fibres from Siobhan Hynes's socks, jumper and fleece. She in turn had transfer fibres from his red fluffy car seats.

Fibres can be involuntarily exchanged between people or objects, such as from a woolly jumper or carpet fibres found on a shoe. To determine the source, the fibre type, the number and extent of such fibres, the colours and the possible or probable nature of contact, transfer and persistence must all be examined and evaluated. The nature and duration of the contact must also be established, as we can all pick up fibres from seats, for example in a cinema, a hairdresser's or even a car. Fibres can be transferred from one fabric to another by primary or secondary transfer.

The possibility of transfer can depend on the type of fabric as well as the nature and duration of the contact. For example, an angora jumper will readily shed fibres, while a plastic raincoat will not, although static electricity in the plastic coat may attract the angora fibres. Someone on a bus may brush off you, shedding a fibre from their clothing, but while it is possible to transfer a fibre or hair from that person to you, the transfer will be unlikely to persist following this fleeting contact, particularly when both parties are constantly moving.

Forensic evidence has shown that the clothing of a murder victim can retain transfer fibre evidence even years later, as they are no longer moving. Moving a body after the killing may dislodge some fibres but, nonetheless, the perpetrator may have transferred even more primary fibre evidence to himself, leaving a forensic clue of direct and violent contact with the victim. It is therefore advisable for scene of crime investigators to recover clothing, shoes and similar items from suspects as soon as possible, as the identification of cross-transfer of fibres between the victim and a suspect can be crucial to the investigation.

Despite the range of textiles produced annually, the relatively small amount produced from any one fibre type and colour dramatically reduces the odds in favour of investigators. The chance of any two manufacturers reproducing a fabric in an identical way, using the same type and number of fibres from the same original batch, the same cross-section, weave, colour batch and application, is highly unlikely.

The location of the fibres on a victim or at the scene can be an indication of their significance. The nature and duration of the contact, the transfer persistence, the characteristics or traits, and commonness or rarity of fibre types found can affect the evidential value. If several different fibre types are transferred between the suspect and a victim, the likelihood that close or even violent contact occurred between them is increased.

Over a period of just under two years, between 1979 and 1981, over twenty African-American youths and children were murdered around Atlanta, Georgia. Forensic scientists found greenish-yellow fibres on many of the victims' clothing. On examination, these proved to be fibres from a carpet. It was a real breakthrough but when the information was published in the press, the killer began stripping his victims, concealing them in the river. When yet another victim was recovered from a river, crime scene officers found a single strand of rayon on his underwear, which the killer had failed to spot. However, police still had no suspect in mind.

Random stakeouts were mounted and, in May 1981, while police were maintaining a watch on a bridge over the Chattahoochee River, they heard a loud splash. They came across a twenty-three-year-old man, Wayne Williams, who said he'd just thrown some rubbish into the water. After producing his ID, he was allowed to go. Two days later, a body was dragged from the river. Pathologists found a greenish-yellow fibre trapped in the victim's hair. FBI forensic scientists identified it as the same nylon fibre found on other victims made by a Boston company, which had sold it to carpet manufacturers between 1967 and 1974. A small company in Georgia used the dye on that specific nylon fibre between 1970 and 1971 but only sold the carpet in a limited area.

Detectives decided to search Williams's car. The fibres from his car mats matched the rayon found on one victim's underwear. They also found violet acetate fibres in the car and on a bedspread and blanket in his bedroom, which matched those found on other victims' clothing. Hairs from Williams's German Shepherd dog were also found on a victim. Williams was convicted of two of the killings in 1982 and given two consecutive life sentences.

With recent developments in forensic technologies, it is easier to locate and identify questioned fibres in a crime scene. In one typical crime scenario, where an attacker grabs a woman and there is a struggle, there may be cross-contamination between his clothes and that of his victim. It is important for the Technical Bureau to collect any hairs or fibres found and to ensure the continuity and non-contamination of the evidence. Different fibre or hair samples will be collected in separate evidence bags.

Hair can be a particularly important find at a crime scene as forensic scientists can identify not only DNA – provided they have a root, which is the main source of hair DNA, although mtDNA can often be found in the shaft or cut hair – but they can discover whether the person uses drugs or medication, whether they dye their hair, and they can even identify their natural colour. This is done by examining the hair structure, which is made up of three parts: the cuticle; the medulla, which is the middle or core which is not always present; and the cortex, which is the natural colour. Like all colours, hair reflects different wavelengths of light, giving us a range of natural hair colours from black to blond. There are two main pigments, pheomelanin, which produces red or blond hair, and eumelanin, which is responsible for brown and black hair, so dyeing your hair after a crime is not a solution – forensics can still find you.

Forensic investigators will examine a victim's clothing as soon as possible after a crime in order to recover any trace evidence fibres, which may be later examined against a suspect's clothing. The methods of recovery can vary. Some examiners extract the individual fibres with a tweezers, or tape, making sure not to contaminate them, while some laboratories use a specialised vacuuming system for the recovered clothing. This blows the fibres onto a special sterile filter system. The most common method of recovery is to lift the fibre sample with a specialist tape designed for this purpose.

The examination is sometimes initially done using a stereomicroscope, which can examine two fibre samples side-by-side to determine if they are from the same source. Using a stereomicroscope, the forensic scientist will note the physical properties such as the colour, diameter, length, damage, the sheen or the cross-section of the fibres. Digital stereomicroscopes can also take magnified pictures of the specimens, which can be shown on a computer or television screen in court.

By using a polarised light microscope forensic scientists can identify the different types of synthetic fibres, measuring the refractive index (how fast light passes through them) and their birefringence (when the fibre "splits" the polarised light into two rays). The "sample" fibres are placed on a clear acetate film or a glass slide before being visually examined by a forensic scientist specialising in fibre analysis, using a low-powered stereomicroscope. This is a slow and tedious job and if the "sample" and the suspect or target fibre are similar in colour, the eyes become tired and it is easy to miss a possible target fibre. As a result, a number of fibre finder systems were developed to allow for the quick identification of a large quantise of fibres.

Where a number of different fibres were lifted, identification can be made using a "fibre finder". An automated system such as MaxCam can isolate and identify a large number of different fibres and colours over a short timespan. As a result of a 2002 project between the University of Rhode Island and the FBI in Quantico, Virginia, the FBI now have a Datacolour Dyeing machine – a database of every dye known to have been manufactured worldwide. Combined with a Fibre Database developed by the textile chemists at Rhode Island, they are a source of valuable fibre-related information to international police forces and forensic scientists. By direct comparison of fibres from a known source – for example, clothes worn by an assailant – to transfer fibres found on a victim, the characteristics, type, colour and manufacturing process can be identified. When compared and evaluated, the scientists must consider the frequency of such fibre types in the relative area, the persistence and transfer rate of the questioned fibres and whether they were most likely transferred by primary or secondary contact. These are all factors in interpreting the evidence, either confirming or refuting the theory that a suspect had close and possibly violent contact with the victim. This evidence will ultimately have to be explained and demonstrated by the forensic specialist in court, leaving no room for a margin of error either way.

Fibre analysis proved crucial in identifying and convicting the killer of Sarah Payne, an eight-year-old girl who went missing in West Sussex in the UK in July 2000. Shortly after her disappearance, her brother remembered seeing a white transit van in a lane near their house. A local man, Roy Whiting, who was on the sex offenders register, became a suspect. Police raided the man's house and took items from his white transit van, including a check shirt, socks and a curtain with a clown pattern for forensic examination. A red sweatshirt found in the van was examined and a full DNA profile of the suspect was produced. They also found a petrol receipt for a garage close to the missing girl's home. An examination of the van showed that that the driver and passenger seats were made from different fabrics.

On 17 July, over two weeks after she went missing, Sarah's decomposing body was found buried and a forensic examination recovered fibres from her hair and from her black shoe, which had a Velcro strap. Two balls of Sarah's hair were retrieved from the burial site and in the body bag which had been used. Forensics identified fibres from a red sweatshirt, the suspect's white socks and from the passenger seat of his van.

Fibres believed to have come from Sarah's dress were also found, although the dress itself – being the control sample – was never found. Sarah's friend owned a similar dress in green. When forensics examined the fibres against this dress, the structure and fibre patterns were the same;

only the colour was different. Twenty-five blue polyester fibres were found on Sarah's silver jacket, which she was wearing the day she went missing. These fibres matched the nine blue polyester fibres found on the red sweatshirt, as well as others found in the suspect's jeans pockets.

The shoes were positively identified as being Sarah's and importantly, the Velcro had over 350 fibres, including blue polyester and cotton fibres from the girl's school uniform, as well as four dark red fibres which were trapped in the strap. Forensic scientists individually picked each fibre off with a forceps and isolated and retained them under Sellotape.

An examination of the suspect's clothes revealed that the red sweatshirt fibres shed easily and were unusually dark. A hair identified as belonging to Sarah was also found on the red sweatshirt. Using a comparison microscope, scientists matched the red fibres on Sarah's shoes to the sweatshirt. It was the first real breakthrough in the case. The sweatshirt and clown-patterned curtain contained fine hairs, which were sent for DNA analysis and produced a full DNA profile of the child. Sarah's DNA had been identified from a milk tooth her mother had kept as a souvenir when she lost her first tooth.

The unusual clown curtain had been made in four colours, only 1,500 metres of which were in yellow. Narrowing the field, police discovered that this yellow clown curtain had been made for Boots Chemists, to be used in their baby-changing rooms. A single multi-coloured fibre from the curtain had also been found on Sarah's Velcro shoe strap. It was a match to the curtain found in the suspect's van.

Following months of investigation costing over £2 million, analysis of over 500 items of forensic evidence by over twenty forensic scientists, including entomologists, geologists, environmental profiling experts, DNA and crucial evidence from fibre specialists, in December 2001, Roy Whiting was convicted and sentenced to life imprisonment – hanged by a thread.

Fibre comparison analysis was also used to convict child killer Ian Huntley, who killed ten-year-old friends Jessica Chapman and Holly Wells in the UK in 2002. Police found the bodies two weeks later at two different locations in Soham and Mildenhall, but were able to link both murders back to Huntley by forensics.

Scientists from the Forensic Science Service in the UK linked hairs and fibres from his house and clothing to the two girls. Recovering a bin from Soham College, where Huntley worked as a caretaker, crime scene officers found two partly burnt Manchester United shirts, tracksuit bottoms, underwear and shoes, believed to have been worn by the girls when they went missing.

Under forensic examination at the laboratory, scientists found surface debris such as leaves, pollen and insects, as well as hair and fibres, both inside and outside the bin. Some of the items had melted in the fire, including part of the Man U shirts, but everything was tested for the presence of blood, semen or saliva. No semen was found, but saliva was found on Jessica's shirt, and fourteen blood spots were found in the caretaker's lodge. Holly's trainers were also bloodstained. Forensic tests of the clothing and the burial site identified the presence of accelerants, which proved to be petrol. The girls' clothes had been cut off with very sharp scissors.

In a search of Huntley's home, over 40,000 fibre samples were taken from curtains, rugs, bedding, sofas and his car for forensic examination. Each fibre was loaded onto an acetate sheet and examined under a microscope. Manchester United provided sample shirts which, unusually in sportswear, were made up of a mix of wool and four types of synthetic materials. Man U shirts bought from market stalls and other outlets were also examined. Their make-up was different to the genuine article. Scientists found evidence of fibre transfer from Huntley's blue cord carpet, which was made up from five different colours, and the girls' genuine Man U shirts. Fibres from all five colours in his carpet were found on the girls' clothing, and over 154 fibres were found as a result of a direct two-way transfer between Huntley and the girls, both from his clothes to their Man U shirts and track bottoms and from the Man U shirts to his clothing and house. This was conclusive evidence that Huntley had direct contact with both of the girls, despite the fact that their bodies were found at different locations.

The forensics extended over other areas such as environmental profiling and entomology, based on the insects found both in the bin and at the burial place of the girls, and involved five different forensic science laboratories and more than fifty scientists. It was enough to convict, as Huntley was sentenced to life imprisonment for the murders of the little girls.

25

"Ní Dhearna Mé É": Siobhan Hynes

Siobhan Hynes died a week after her seventeenth birthday, brutally murdered in the harsh Connemara hinterland of County Galway. It was December 1998 and as she left home with her sister and a friend on that fateful Saturday night, heading for a disco in Carraroe, no one knew the fate that awaited her.

Had she not been turned away from Óstán an Dóilín, the only disco in town, due to her tender years, things might have been different. Her sister and friend were old enough to pass the scrutiny of the ever-cautious security men on the door. They were only doing their job, after all; the place could lose its licence if the gardaí arrived and found the underage teenager on the licensed premises.

By the end of the night the gardaí had far more important things to worry about. The young girl was missing, in the bleak terrain of a Connemara winter. Siobhan was last seen just after midnight by a school

friend and her mother as they drove through the Gaeltacht
village of Carraroe. The only other sighting put her close to
An Réalt, a village pub close to the disco. With few places to
hang out late on a freezing Saturday night, she spent the time
sitting in a car with two male friends, listening to music
tapes. One of them, John Paul Connolly, later told gardaí that
he remembered seeing a "big blondie fella in his twenties"
sitting on a wall near their car. Siobhan left the car to go to
the toilet in the disco but came back minutes later, saying the
doorman wouldn't let her in. Siobhan said she'd spoken to
the man sitting on the wall. She said he wasn't a nice guy and
that he had been "in trouble". As the other teenager left the
car, John McDonagh, whom he knew to see, continued to sit
on the wall, just watching Siobhan and Connolly. He walked
back and forth past the car a few times, before returning to
the wall, where he sat staring at them. Connolly remembered
Siobhan saying the guy "was a weirdo".

After a while Siobhan, still needing the toilet, left the
car to try the local chipper, An Feadóg. That was the last
time Connolly saw her. When his friend returned to the
car, they went to An Feadóg to look for her, but was told
she hadn't been in. They drove around Carraroe trying to
find her but finally gave up and went home at 1.40 a.m.
The next morning Siobhan's mother rang Connolly's
house looking for her daughter. On hearing that she was
still missing, he and his friends went in search of her but
they still couldn't find her. By then, she was already dead.

Although Siobhan lived almost eleven miles away,
Carraroe was her nearest village and she was well known
there. It was hardly a busy village, with a total population

of just 629 people. Not much got past the locals, yet they had no idea where Siobhan could be.

It wasn't until the following afternoon that news of Siobhan came through. It was the worst possible news, something no parent ever wants to hear. The teenager's body had been found by a man walking his dogs on the beach. The dogs seemed very interested in something on the beach, and as he got closer, the man saw the young girl's body hidden by boulders that sprawl the sandy, isolated stretch of beach. She was lying face down. Thinking she was asleep, he asked if she was okay, before realising that she was dead. But for that small blessing, Siobhan's parents, Aindi and Bríd, might never have known what had happened. By then the tide was already in. Siobhan's body was soaked through and she was only visible as the waves washed back out to the receding sea. The tide would have simply washed her away, which is probably what her killer hoped would have happened.

When gardaí were alerted it was initially thought to have been a drowning accident, an exuberant teenager messing about on a Saturday night, caught short by the tide. When they examined the scene more closely, they realised there was a killer in their midst. The quiet Connemara coastline showed signs of a struggle and, even to the uninitiated, it appeared to have been a sexually motivated assault. But that was the job of the pathologist and forensic scientists to determine. Meanwhile they had the harrowing task of informing Siobhan's family.

Gardaí sealed off the area as the crime scene unit began the slow trawl for any clues that could help them find Siobhan's killer. A painstaking task at any time, it was made all the more difficult by the changing tides, liable to wash away crucial evidence in the hunt for the murderer – for murder it undoubtedly was.

The main routes from Carraroe village to the beach were closely examined. The easy route leading to the beach is well trawled by courting couples all year round, but in the stormy winter nights they usually found warmer places to go. There was little evidence that the killer had taken the easy route to the remote beach. Siobhan's body had been found in rocky ground, three or four hundred yards away from that route. It was rough and remote and gave no easy access to cars or on foot, especially in the dark.

During the following weeks, crime scene investigation officers found bits and pieces of Siobhan's property scattered around the beach at Tismeáin. They discovered a chain, later identified as Siobhan's, which appeared to have been ripped from her neck, the crushed heart-shaped locket bearing witness to the struggle she'd put up. Clothing, including Siobhan's blue fleece jacket, was found buried close by, hidden in the sand. Garda divers also searched the shallow waters, looking for any other evidence discarded by the killer.

A postmortem showed that the young girl had been savagely raped with a foreign object, leaving her body mutilated. The killer had tried to finish her off by choking her, before leaving her for dead beside the incoming tide, in the belief or hope that, by morning, all his problems and the evidence would be washed away. But Siobhan wasn't dead when he left her, just unconscious. The postmortem showed that she had finally succumbed to death by drowning; her lungs were full of sea water, her battered and unconscious body overcome by the incoming tide. The State Pathologist Dr Marie Cassidy could offer little comfort. While saying that there was a "strong possibility" that Siobhan was unconscious when she came in contact with the water, she couldn't be sure. It was possible that she had come around, revived by the water, but was unable to save herself due to her injuries.

Superintendent Jim Sugrue, who had been involved in twelve murder investigations, said, "This was the most brutal, horrendous case that I have ever dealt with. A young girl, barely out of her childhood, was sexually abused with an instrument, her larynx fractured and her body dumped on rocks for the tide to take her out." Siobhan had severe bruising to her breasts and scalp and her attacker had also tried to rape her anally.

The people of Connemara were horrified that such a vicious murderer could live amongst them. They feared for their families and no one could rest until the killer was caught. Investigating gardaí had their suspicions. Whoever the killer was, he knew the lie of the land. An outsider could not have found his way through such difficult terrain in pitch darkness to the isolated spot on Tismeáin beach and then manage to get back again unseen, having murdered the young girl. They believed the killer was probably close to home and knew the ground well. They had one man in mind.

John "Demesne" McDonagh was well known in the area. On the night Siobhan disappeared, he had been in trouble twice, having instigated two fights in the village. McDonagh started a row in the town with a former girlfriend, the mother of his child. Seeing her with her new boyfriend as they queued to get into the club, he hit her over the head and beat up her boyfriend. Gardaí were called to the scene and cautioned McDonagh, telling him he would be watched. It obviously didn't worry him, given that within hours, he would brutally sexually assault and murder a young teenager.

Later that night McDonagh started a second fight in An Feadóg fish-and-chip shop. It later emerged that this was done to create an alibi for himself after he'd murdered Siobhan. He was unaware that several people had spotted him driving back from the direction of the beach, just before he started the fight in the chip shop.

During the investigation into Siobhan's death, gardaí took over 650 witness statements, including two over a two-day period from the then twenty-three-year-old McDonagh, who denied any knowledge of the murder. Detectives asked him to produce the clothes he had been wearing on the night. McDonagh didn't hesitate, handing over a bundle of clothes for forensic examination, confident that the forensic scientists would find nothing incriminating. He had given them a different set of clothes to the ones he had been wearing on the night, unaware that he had been caught on CCTV wearing jeans and a white jumper. The CCTV footage was recovered and digitally enhanced. Though he denied it, several local people also said that McDonagh was wearing a distinctive white V-necked ribbed jumper on the night in question.

241

Video enhancing technology has also been extensively used in the area of textile enhancement since 1996, when the FBI analysed unique wear patterns on denim jeans from a bombing and robbery crime scene caught on CCTV. As denim is washed and worn the dye wears off, exposing the white cotton underneath in varying degrees. The wear and tear from a washing machine, a packet of cigarettes or a wallet constantly rubbing a pocket can all cause "bumping" against a seam. This is unique to individual wearers, depending on the body size, height and general build, as different areas wear in different way, making an individual "fingerprint" in a pair of jeans. The accused's defence attorney put up strenuous opposition to the FBI's evidence. He produced 400 pairs of jeans from a second-hand jeans exporter as "proof" that forensic scientists could not identify the defendant's jeans from thirty-four pairs which he'd picked at random. He was proved wrong, as twenty-four separate wear "fingerprints" were identified on one pair of jeans, which the defence admitted belonged to his client. The defendant was found guilty.

Six days after Siobhan's death, on 12 January, investigating gardaí brought McDonagh in for further questioning. They removed several items from his house for forensic examination, including a white V-necked ribbed jumper, which had been freshly washed in an effort to remove any evidence, but it was not enough, as forensic scientists can use specialist techniques and equipment to identify persistent fibre transfer and their colours down to the exact composition of the dyes used, though invisible to the naked eye.

Within days detectives had a report from forensic scientist Dr Louise Kennedy, who said that forensic tests of this trace evidence had found "very strong support" to connect McDonagh to Siobhan's murder. Forensics had found "numerous" fibres on McDonagh's white V-necked jumper. They identified the structure, composition and colour of the fabrics of both Siobhan's clothing and those of McDonagh, having analysed the dyes used. When examined against a "questioned" piece of fabric, in this case McDonagh's white V-necked jumper or a piece of Siobhan's clothing, they were a match. Fibres identified on the suspect's white jumper came from Siobhan's black socks and her wine-coloured acrylic jumper, indicating that there was "primary" fibre transfers, directly from person to person. Equally, fibres from Siobhan's blue polyester fleece jacket, which gardaí found buried on the beach at Tismeáin, were also found on McDonagh's clothes.

Dr Kennedy had also found "strong" forensic evidence to show that Siobhan had been in John McDonagh's car the night she was murdered. Fibres from his fluffy red car seats were found on Siobhan's clothing, while fibres from her clothes were found in his car, again showing a primary transfer of fibres. Given her dislike of McDonagh, as expressed to her friend Connolly on the night she was murdered, it is unlikely she was in his car willingly.

On 15 January 1999, John "Demesne" McDonagh was again arrested in connection with the rape and murder of the schoolgirl. His mother Maggie was arrested on suspicion of withholding information. Supporting her son to the last, Maggie looked straight at him and said: "Ná h'abair tada leo agus seasfaidh mise leat" ("Don't tell them anything and I'll stand by you"). Maggie McDonagh was very protective of her son and refused to tell gardaí anything, except to agree that she had recently washed her son's V-necked jumper.

John McDonagh was charged with the murder of Siobhan Hynes. His family – his two brothers, three sisters and mother – immediately rallied around him, although his father John urged him to tell the truth if he knew anything. John Jr had nothing to say. He denied all knowledge of the killing. His mother Maggie was steadfast in his defence. During her detention she whiled away the time by singing to herself in Irish.

With the garda investigation ongoing, rumour abounded in the area that John "Demesne" McDonagh had an alibi. When gardaí investigated this "alibi", it transpired that there was no basis to it. Not much passed the locals in the valley of the squinting windows, and five weeks before the trial, a journalist from the *Sunday Independent* followed up on the rumours and spoke to a local man, Cólin Ó Conghaile, a neighbour of the McDonagh's. Mr Ó Conghaile confirmed that it had been suggested to him that he tell gardaí he had seen John McDonagh in Carraroe around 1.15 a.m. on the night that Siobhan disappeared. If true, this would put McDonagh in the clear for Siobhan's murder.

This "new information" was investigated by Detective Garda Pat Ferriter, but Ó Conghaile, whose land adjoins the McDonagh's, refused to confirm the alleged sighting to Detective Garda Ferriter, saying he wasn't even in the village that night. He later confirmed this to the *Sunday Independent*.

The damning forensic and circumstantial evidence was stacking up against John "Demesne" McDonagh. His house was less than half a mile from where Siobhan's body was found. He was familiar with the beach area where the body was found and forensics had identified the cross-trace evidence of the fibres from Siobhan's clothes both in his car and on the clothes he was wearing on the night she disappeared.

At 5.45 a.m. on the morning of 18 June 1999, six months after Siobhan's death, John "Demesne" McDonagh was arrested for her rape and murder. In accordance with court rules the identity of a defendant charged with rape is not disclosed unless and until they are convicted, in order to protect innocent people from malicious claims. Superintendent Jim Sugrue would later tell the court that when they came to arrest McDonagh, he was asleep in a lorry at a compound in Kildare. When he saw the gardaí, McDonagh extended his wrists to be handcuffed, saying: "Put them on, I was expecting ye."

By July, the vicious killer was out on bail and would remain so until he came to trial two years later. There were conditions: he had to stay away from Galway, Clare, Mayo and Westmeath, which meant he still had twenty-eight counties to wreak havoc on, and he took full advantage of it. While on bail, he was convicted of soliciting a prostitute and was alleged to have raped and attempted to kill another.

At his request, members of Siobhan's family were also excluded from the courtroom when he gave his evidence, as he claimed they were not directly connected with the case. In the end, to cries of relief from the Hynes family, the jury of nine women and three men unanimously found John "Demesne" McDonagh guilty of murdering Siobhan Hynes. The Irish-speaking McDonagh threw out his arms and said: "Oh for fuck's sake, ní dhearna mé é" ("I didn't do it"). Banging his fist on the bench, McDonagh repeatedly shouted "Jesus Christ" as he sat crying in the courtroom. Mr Justice Smith adjourned the court until order was restored.

Siobhan Hynes's extended family, together with her best friend Jayne Lee and locals from Connemara, all hugged Siobhan's parents, Aindi and Bríd Hynes, as they thanked the investigating gardaí for bringing McDonagh to justice. Over 146 witnesses had given evidence during the trial.

Back in the courtroom, McDonagh's defence counsel requested that sentencing for the rape conviction be adjourned to another date. Mr Justice Smith said, "In relation to the murder I am obliged under statute to impose a sentence of life imprisonment and I do that now." McDonagh was subsequently sentenced to a further ten years for raping Siobhan. Mr Justice Smith detailed the evidence and described it as "the most cruel rape". He said both sentences should run concurrently, with the rape sentence to be backdated to June, when McDonagh was found guilty. He refused leave to appeal. This is common practice but refusing leave to appeal does not necessarily preclude an appeal and that's exactly what McDonough did.

In February 2007 the Court of Criminal Appeal dismissed McDonagh's appeal on all grounds. Undeterred, in November 2007, nine years after he'd murdered Siobhan Hynes, McDonagh made another attempt to have his conviction overturned and again he tried to bring his case before the Supreme Court on points of law, which included a challenge relating to how the evidence given in Irish at the trial was recorded.

In a three-man court, the presiding Judge, Mr Justice Hugh Geoghegan, sitting with Mr Justice Roderick Murphy and Mr Justice Dan Herbert, said they were "quite satisfied" that McDonagh had no grounds for appeal, either on a point of law or on the other issues raised. They added that they were satisfied that "no injustice" had been done to McDonagh.

All "lifers" are entitled to have their sentence reviewed. Originally done by the Sentence Review Board, this was replaced in 2001 by the Parole Board of Ireland. The board, which is usually made up of ten people drawn from the Probation and Welfare Service, the Prison Service, officials from the Department of Justice, Equality and Law Reform, the Medical Director of the Central Mental Hospital and community representatives, make recommendations to the Minister for Justice for the parole or early release of prisoners. Prisoners serving fourteen years or more, including life sentence prisoners, can have their application for parole reviewed after seven years, with a few exceptions, which include the murder of a garda or prison officer, or for certain offences against the State. "Lifers" who are not granted parole after seven years will have their case reviewed again at the ten-year point. While no information is given with regard to review applications by individual prisoners, McDonagh has now served eight years. Under these rules, he won't have long to wait for a sentence review.

26

Playing with Fire
The Forensics of Arson

Fire: the word evokes both comfort and fear. When that fire has been started maliciously and lives are lost, it is either manslaughter or murder.

Investigators face an unenviable task working in burnt-out buildings, among charred debris. The devastation, destruction and possibly the danger of an unstable building, combined with the acrid smell, wet ashes and pools of fetid water make tough working conditions all the harder, especially if it is a crime scene involving someone's death.

From the investigator's point of view, it is important to establish a number of things: firstly, where the fire started, how it started and what was the cause. The discovery of more than one "seat" of a fire, or trails, are indicators of arson, for example. Most fires tend to burn upwards in a V-shaped pattern along walls, and are aided by combustible materials such as plastic. The varying colours of the flame are a good indicator of the temperature of the fire at its height.

A number of people are involved in the investigation of a fire, from the initial call-out of the fire brigade to the fire investigator. If the indications are suspicious, the gardaí and forensic scientists will also become involved, and perhaps an insurance investigator. Debris from the fire is collected and sealed in airtight conditions for forensic analysis back in the Forensic Science Laboratory.

Without some intervention, fire follows a predictable route from start to finish. The fire starts or ignites, then develops, radiates and reaches its maximum point, before finally decaying. In between, several variations can occur, depending on the nature and location of the fire. For example, a fire in a chemical factory, forest or house fire may have different additional contributory factors.

Fire is described by Redvers Skelton, a forensic fire investigator, as a "rapid exothermic oxidation reaction". That may sound complicated, but all it really means is that fire is something that generates heat quickly, but it needs oxygen to stay alight. Oxygen alone won't keep a fire burning, as there are three other components needed to sustain it. Commonly known as the "fire tetrahedron", as well as oxygen, a fire needs heat, fuel and a chemical reaction. If any one of these components is removed, the fire goes out. It sounds simple, and it may make you wonder how or why forest fires or house blazes seem to take forever to put out, but the science is not quite that straightforward. It doesn't take much to start a fire, but it can take quite a lot to put it out. The same principles apply. Remove one of the four essentials and the fire will go out. When the fire brigade hose down a fire with water, it will eventually go out (unless that is, the fire is oil-based, e.g. in a chip pan). It is essential therefore to know what caused the fire, to ensure that it is not accelerated, which is why fires are put out by different methods such as a fire-retardant foam fire extinguisher, or one that sprays carbon dioxide, which deprives the fire of oxygen. Throwing sand on some fires will also starve it of oxygen, while water can cool it down. By removing one of the four elements, such as the heat or oxygen, or perhaps isolating the chemical reaction or fuel source, the fire will go out.

Chemical fires are usually dealt with by reversing or balancing out the chemical reaction. The trick is to know which is the most immediately effective in a given fire; that knowledge comes with training and experience, so the fire brigade are the experts.

Where there are suspicious circumstances, the investigation takes on a number of objectives. Was it accidental or arson? Arson was not an uncommon cause of fires in Ireland in the 1980s and many were believed to have been the work of criminal gangs, who either bought run-down properties themselves or provided a "disposal" service to "clients", who recouped their investment with dividends following an insurance payout. There were several cases where sitting tenants were evacuated from a property for "renovation purposes", only to find that an unfortunate fire occurred within days, completely destroying the building.

Some cases involve clear-cut evidence of arson, with the interior of the buildings lined with plastic bags full of petrol, and trails leading from one room to another, to accelerate the spread of the fire, which "spontaneously combusted" with a little help from the arsonist. Such fires are sometimes started by incendiary devices with a delayed action or by using a retardant to slow down the process, giving the arsonist time to make his getaway.

In recessionary times, there is often an increase in such "unfortunate" fires, where a property has become more of a liability than an asset. It was not unknown for an individual to have more than one insurance policy on such properties, paying off the lender and still walking away with a tidy sum in compensation, though that has largely changed since computerisation of records and sharing of information became commonplace. The premises would usually have burnt to the ground by the time the fire brigade were alerted. In some instances, despite garda investigation, the insurers were forced to pay out, as no one was caught for the crime. The "unfortunate" owner of the property only learned of his or her loss on their return from holiday abroad or after a bank holiday weekend.

If a fire is believed to have been set deliberately, samples of what remains of the furniture, carpets, curtains or other items are taken for analysis. The samples are usually isolated in a sterile container, which may contain activated charcoal to trap any volatile gases or liquids. The samples will be analysed by forensic scientists in the laboratory using a gas chromatograph mass spectrometer (GC-MS), which separates the different elements, not only identifying any accelerants, but pinpointing them to a certain type and brand name. From this, detectives can identify the outlets selling the brand

and work back from there, to find out who purchased such a product in the area, within a specific time frame. It can be a time-consuming business. The forensic investigations can take weeks or even longer, as the evidence is extracted, analysed, crosschecked and interpreted to the extremely high standard of proof required for criminal prosecutions.

Other reasons for arson can include revenge. This is usually when the perpetrator knows the victim – for example, an embittered former employee or business partner, or an unfaithful spouse or their lover. In some instances, it has been just one final act in a series of domestic violence incidents. One case I was personally involved with as a private investigator came about following a series of vicious and violent attacks against a young pregnant mother and her young children, which included scalding, rape and other horrendous crimes by her bodybuilder husband. Despite eventually getting a barring order, he returned under cover of darkness and poured petrol around the house. He then sealed up all the windows and doors, right down to the letterbox, before igniting the fire, knowing his wife and young children, including a newborn baby, were inside. The timely arrival by the fire brigade saved the family – the loss of the house a cheap price to pay in return for their lives.

Following an investigation, the husband was arrested and charged with the crime. A forensic investigation proved his fingerprints were on the tape used to seal up the windows and doors. CCTV evidence identified him filling a can with petrol at a local garage shortly before the fire and the empty container was found in the boot of his car. He was sentenced to ten years' imprisonment. Arson is also quite common after a murder or robbery when the getaway car is torched in an attempt to destroy evidence.

Arson is also associated with pyromaniacs – people fascinated by fire who, time and time again, set fires for the thrill of seeing things burn. Pyromaniacs can often be identified by their MO (how they go about it) – the type of fire, which can often be very basic small fires; the accelerants used; the locations and timings – sometimes re-creating their "best" fires in order to relive the scene. Usually such people have some form of psychiatric illness. The fire gives them a sense of empowerment and control. When they are caught, it often emerges that they were the one to call the fire brigade, report the fire or give interviews to news media. Internationally, some pyromaniacs have even joined the fire services, helping to fight fires that they themselves set.

Fires in California and Australia are often linked to arsonists. The most recent fires in Australia, which claimed the lives of over 180 people and destroyed 2,000 homes and other buildings, were the worst in Australian history. A thirty-nine-year-old man, Brendan Sokaluk, was arrested in "Operation Phoenix", which investigated the fires. He was charged with setting fire to a timber plant in Southern Victoria, where the fires first started. Accelerants were found at the seat of the fire in the Gippland timberyard. The hot and windy weather conditions fanned the flames into raging infernos and reduced entire communities to ashes. Sokaluk initially faces twenty-five years imprisonment on the main charge, with a further twenty on additional arson and child pornography charges, and he may yet face additional manslaughter charges. Police also arrested a part-time firefighter from the County Fire Authority. The volunteer was suspected of starting the blaze in Marysville, which killed thirty-nine people in Victoria. Forensic evidence again located accelerants at the seat of the fire.

An arsonist may be trying to destroy evidence of other crimes, including murder, in the misguided belief that the fire will destroy all the evidence of the killing. While it will certainly do some damage, it will not cover up the fact that the fire was deliberate or that the victim was already dead before the fire started.

For example, many arsonists use accelerants to start a fire, or retardants, to slow its onset, giving them time to get away and have an alibi. As the fire rises, these substances will settle into a carpet, flooring or furniture or soak into the walls. Modern fire investigators have elaborate technological tools to establish the cause of a fire, from instruments known as "sniffers" – portable detectors which show changes in the oxygen levels on a semi-conductor – to specially trained dogs that can locate the presence of fire accelerants or retardants at a crime scene. The portable "sniffers" are an indicator of areas likely to produce good samples for laboratory analysis.

In murder cases, bodies are often found near the seat of the fire, the killer attempting to destroy evidence of blood, stab wounds, strangulation or gunshot wounds, unaware that postmortem examination and forensic analysis can establish that the victim was *already* dead before the fire started.

A recent example of this in Ireland was the horrific case of thirty-year-old Sharon Whelan and her two daughters, seven-year-old Zarah and two-year-old Nadia, who were found dead in their isolated burned-out house at Roscon, County Kilkenny, on Christmas Day 2008. At first it looked like a dreadful accident, made all the more tragic given that two little girls died on Christmas morning in such terrible circumstances. However, it became even more grotesque when it was established that the fire had been caused maliciously, to cover up a murder.

Local people spotted the fire in the rented house, two miles from the town, shortly after 8.30 on Christmas morning and called the fire brigade. As firefighters fought the blaze, they recovered the body of Sharon Whelan and her two little girls. Initially they thought the girls were unconscious and efforts were made to resuscitate them. But it was too late; they were already dead. They never woke up to see if Santa had come.

Forensic investigation showed that the cause of the fire was not accidental, as it is believed that an accelerant was found near the seat of the fire. Postmortem results on the bodies of the young mother and her two little girls showed that, while the children died of smoke inhalation, their mother Sharon was already dead before the fire took hold. She had no smoke in her lungs, and ligature marks on her neck indicated that she'd been strangled. It appeared that the fire was started to cover up the killing and the case was upgraded to a murder hunt.

Forensic scientists from the State Laboratory sent the DNA and toxicology reports to the investigating detectives. Following extensive investigation by the gardaí, a twenty-three-year-old postal worker, Brian Hennessy of Windgap, County Kilkenny, was arrested and charged with the murder of Sharon Whelan and her two children, Nadia and Zarah. He also faces criminal damage and other related charges. Detective Sergeant Jim Lyng gave evidence of his arrest, charge and caution to Judge Gerard Furlong. When taken to Kilkenny garda station, Hennessy said, "I'm guilty" to each of the three charges.

27

The Techno-Experts: Computer and Mobile Phone Forensics

In the high-tech world of crime, the use of computer forensics in identifying fraud, uncovering conspiracies or tracking emails and internet surfing or searches is a crucial part of an investigator's job.

Crimes involving computers have increased dramatically and cross-border crimes are no longer the preserve of the well-travelled international criminal, as many criminals don't even have to leave home. Computer crime is not just about fraud, banking scams or boiler room scams; today it encompasses everything from pornography, intellectual property theft, child sex abuse, financial scams, extortion and murder, amongst many other crimes.

Forensic computer investigations and cyber-crime units are now part and parcel of every police force and have been crucial in cracking major crimes which otherwise might have escaped detection or conviction due to a lack of substantial evidence. To this end, Ireland has been to the forefront in establishing a groundbreaking Master's degree course run by UCD in conjunction with the Garda Bureau of Fraud Investigation (GBFI), covering such areas as cyber-forensic recovery, examination and analysis of computer information, password-breaking, encrypted data, and steganography, which extracts hidden messages or data embedded in "cover" files. The course was founded in 2006 and has already seen its first police force graduates from a range of countries including Britain, Italy, Norway and Austria as well as students from Interpol itself.

Forensic computer evidence can fill in possible gaps in circumstantial evidence and produce enough hard evidence to allow a jury to convict. In recent years, this has been proved time and time again in the Irish courts, where the Garda Computer Investigation Unit has been responsible for getting convictions in key serious crimes. Often working in conjunction with other international computer investigation agencies, from the FBI to Interpol, the "link" between co-conspirators can be identified, allowing a case to be built. Computer forensics are part of the overall puzzle, putting the pieces of the jigsaw together until the full picture emerges.

Recent successful cases in Ireland include the Sharon Collins case. Under the pseudonym "lyingeyes98@ yahoo.com", Collins searched the internet for a hit man to kill her lover so she could inherit his fortune. To her delight she found "hitmanforhire", a US site run by Las Vegas-based poker dealer Essam Eid, an Egyptian Walter

Mitty, who also called himself "Tony Luciano". The rest, as they say, is history, as the cyber-crime unit stopped Sharon and her "hitmanforhire" in their tracks. Collins is currently serving six years for her part in attempting to have her lover and his two sons murdered, while her accomplice, Essam Eid, is also spending time in an Irish jail, no doubt contemplating his next great business idea. (See Chapter 29.)

Other cases involving computer forensics include the case of "Doctor Death", Harold Shipman (Chapter 9), and Colin Whelan's murder of his new bride Mary (Chapter 28). Despite a qualification in computing, Whelan was unable to hide evidence of his means and motive for her murder on his work computer.

But how does it all work? How were they caught? Well, one of the most common misconceptions is that when you press the "DELETE" key, everything is erased. It may seem as easy as that, particularly if you can't find something you've just deleted by mistake; it would be easy to assume that it has disappeared forever. This is not the case. What happened is that it has just been removed from a specific area, freeing up space and allowing you to overwrite it. It still remains on the hard drive. With the right expertise and technology, computer forensic experts can recover everything you have ever done on your computer, so if you have been checking out crime sites or looking at something you shouldn't have, be warned: there is no hiding place from the forensic computer scientists.

It's all about how computers manage memory and disks. Active data is there for the user or anyone else to access at will; it may be password-protected, but that is readily accessible by a computer analyst. When a computer operating system writes a file to disk, it allocates a number of sectors, details of which are recorded in a "directory" for later access. When a file is deleted, that space or sector is then listed as "free" or unallocated, but the information remains on the disk. Files or information that have been deleted can be "recovered" via the hard drive. It is either in an easy-to-recognise format – for example, entire files – or it can be recovered from fragmented bits and pieces made up of unused parts of the hard disk.

Files are also created when a system goes into hibernation. For example, a laptop running Windows XP will write the entire contents of the RAM to a file when going into hibernation. These files can contain large amounts of "hidden" information – embedded messages or encrypted data not found elsewhere on the system. It is all a matter of knowing where to look and how to extract the data, sensitive information that forensic computer investigators prefer to keep to themselves.

Computers leave a trail of information which is as almost as good as having full-time surveillance on the owner. They can identify everything from our areas of interest, likes and dislikes, friends, finances, medical conditions and just about everything we do as a matter of course in our everyday life. It may be harmless shopping on the internet or dodgy dealing, falsifying accounts, taxes, sales or purchases for illegal purposes. Specialised "doctored" software accounting packages are known to have been used to pay salaries to "dead men" or non-existent people on some large organisations' payroll. Forensic computer accounting can recover and reconstitute the original true files on the hard drive.

The great mystery of computer science is often played out in the courtroom, when an expert gives evidence for the prosecution on the trail of planning, sourcing equipment, contacts and the execution of the crime. Computer forensics is sometimes the most crucial element of a prosecution and it needs to be explained in detail, in a manner that members of the jury, with no prior knowledge of the workings of a computer, can clearly understand. This technological witness can be the most damning of them all.

Mobile phones have played a significant part in criminal cases in recent years, appearing in a number of well-known trials, including the Sharon Collins case, the Northern Bank robbery and, most famously, the trial of Joe O'Reilly for the murder of his wife Rachel.

O'Reilly's alibi – that he was at a bus depot in Broadstone – was shot to pieces when mobile phone tracking evidence clearly placed him in Balbriggan at the time of the murder. O'Reilly's appeal against his conviction for murder was turned down by the Court of Criminal Appeal. The judgment said that O'Reilly's statement regarding his movements on the day of the murder were "found to conflict directly with the evidence . . . of the prosecution": "The data derived from his use of his mobile phone showed that his movements that morning were markedly different from those set out in (his) statement." Clutching at straws in a desperate attend to overturn the conviction, O'Reilly even suggested that the gardaí has accessed these records illegally under the 1999 Act, as no "proof" had been shown that O2 Ireland was a licensed operator under that Act.

The system used to track mobile phones, identifying the location of the user, is based on GPS technology. Global positioning identification makes use of satellites to "lock on" to a signal from various technological devices, including phone SIM cards. It can track the movement of a signal as it bounces from a phone to a mast. It measures the time it takes for a signal to leave the mobile phone and hit the mast, much like establishing where thunder is by counting the time between thunderclaps. More precise identification can be done by a system known as triangulation – measuring the time it takes to bounce a signal between three masts, which can pinpoint an exact location. This service is commercially available in the UK and Northern Ireland to keep track of employees, sales personal and even family members. Subscribers can follow their movements on the internet and, combined with Google Earth, they can even "home in" on a mobile, a particular street or house.

28

Insured to Kill:
Mary Whelan

"The most calculated and callous killing I've ever encountered" was how Judge Paul Carney described the murder of Mary Whelan.

Twenty-seven-year-old Mary Gough worked as a solicitor's clerk and, like any young woman in love, was excited about her forthcoming wedding. She had been with the man of her dreams, Colin Whelan, for almost seven years and she was finally planning her wedding.

Thirty-year-old Colin was a freelance computer analyst working for Irish Permanent – which would later turn out to be somewhat ironic. They couple were well set up as they already had their own home, having bought a house at Clonard Street, Balbriggan, from a relation of Colin's.

Mary and Colin married in March 2001. They were still newly-weds when, six months later, tragedy apparently befell Mary. As she made her way up to bed, she fell down the stairs, tripping on her dressing gown cord. Her distraught husband rang the emergency services, who arrived within minutes, but too late for Mary, who was already dead.

The ambulance crew were less than convinced about the manner in which Mary Whelan had met her death. When the investigating gardaí arrived on the scene, they too had concerns. They were not so sure that the grieving husband's tears were genuine. Following an investigation and an examination by the then Assistant State Pathologist, Dr Marie Cassidy, the "accidental death" was upgraded to murder. Mary Whelan had indeed died as a result of a cord, but not from her dressing gown. The cord came from her husband's pyjamas and her death was no accident – it was strangulation.

After choking the very life out of his young wife, Colin Whelan then dragged her body from the bedroom and threw her down the stairs, making it look as if she'd fallen. He had made sure there were no ligature marks on her neck, shielding it with a towel before he choked her – a trick he'd learned on his murderous trawl through the internet. Only then, when he was satisfied she was dead and beyond help, did he phone the emergency services.

Investigations into Colin Whelan's background unearthed a murky past, one that his young wife had known nothing about; for if she had, she'd never have married him. While still a teenager, Whelan had been involved in a lengthy relationship with an older woman. He had a history of sexual and physical abuse towards her and she became terrified of him. To escape from his constant threats and violence, she had fled to England, leaving no trace of her whereabouts. Whelan didn't seem too worried, as he coolly moved on to his next victim, the innocent Mary Gough.

A full-scale investigation launched by gardaí revealed some interesting information. It seemed that Whelan had been planning to murder his wife since long before the wedding. He had played the long game, knowing his ultimate plan was to kill his new wife Mary, to reap the financial rewards. His prowess with a computer was, he believed, the key to realising his dream. A forensic investigation by the Garda Computer Investigation Unit examined Colin Whelan's work computer at the Irish Permanent Building Society. Forensic analysis of the computer's hard drive revealed he was doing more than his job, as the EnCase and FRED analytical programmes operated by forensic computer detectives discovered. At least six months before the wedding, Colin Whelan had been trawling through internet sites to find out the best way to asphyxiate someone, without leaving the telltale ligature marks usually found on a strangulation victim's neck. He had accessed sites advising the use a thick towel to prevent ligature marks, and recommendations as to make a murder look like an accident.

Whelan had also scoured the internet for stories about serial killers and their methods, what mistakes they'd made, how they evaded detection for long periods, and how they disposed of their victim. He was obsessed with the prospect of quick, easy money, and had the stomach to do whatever it took to achieve his dream, even if it meant killing his young wife.

Six months after the wedding, he put his grizzly plan into action, putting his new-found knowledge to use: killing his young wife and making it look like an accident.

They also discovered that Whelan was involved in yet another relationship with an older Welsh divorcee. Perhaps he was lining up yet another victim for when he disposed of his wife? Whelan's wasn't an unhappy marriage, but for him it was a marriage of convenience, a sure way to make easy money.

Mary Whelan was no heiress, but if his plan had worked Colin Whelan would have been a wealthy young man. He had taken out an insurance policy for £400,000 payable to the surviving spouse, should either of them die within ten years. They were both young, healthy and a good risk. Colin wasn't expecting his wife ever to collect on the policy, but he was already making plans for the money. The only obstacle to his fortune was the now inconvenient matter of Mary, his bride of just six months, and that, he believed, had been sorted out.

But for the investigating detectives, it might well have been. Following the pathology report and the forensic computer evidence, together with the significant insurance policy on Mary's life, not to mention his previous history, detectives were in no doubt they had a killer on their hands.

Whelan was arrested and charged with his wife's murder and was due to stand trial at the Central Criminal Court, but he fled the jurisdiction while on bail in 2003. His car, together with his clothes, were found abandoned at the cliffs in Howth in Dublin, suggesting he had committed suicide. He disappeared from sight. No contact was made with any family members or friends and it looked like he just hadn't been able to face the impending trial.

Dogged detectives were more sceptical. They were proved right when, almost eighteen months later, he was spotted working in a bar in Majorca by an Irish tourist, who immediately reported the sighting to the gardaí. Spanish police confirmed he was well known in the area, spending his money on the local prostitutes and flirting with the female tourists. It later transpired that the day he disappeared, he had caught a flight to Spain, travelling on false documentation "stolen" from a friend.

Whelan's party was over as an extradition warrant was issued. Murder squad detectives brought him back from his island paradise to face charges for the murder of his wife. Whelan again sought bail but, not surprisingly, was refused by Mr Justice Paul Carney. Unexpectedly, when the case was called, Colin Whelan pleaded guilty, to the relief of Mary's family. He is currently serving a life sentence, convicted by his own stupidity and a trail of his intent on the internet.

29

Lying Eyes Meets Hitman for Hire:
Sharon Collins and Essam Eid

If ever a story was stranger than fiction, this one surely was. It is a tale of the bizarre world inhabited by a middle-aged blonde lover and erstwhile gold-digger, who would stop at nothing to get her hands on her boyfriend's cash.

Sharon Collins was the epitome of the average woman. From Ennis, County Clare, the separated working mother of two sons, she took home just £850 a month, which only allowed her to live a modest lifestyle. In November 1998, following the death of his previous partner Bernie Lyons that February, Collins had met PJ Howard, a wealthy businessman from Kilrush, County Clare, and quickly moved in with him. The ever-generous PJ "topped up" her wages, giving her another £1,000 a month for herself.

She enjoyed the good life, splitting time between his luxury home at Ballybeg House overlooking a lake in Ennis, his boat *Heartbeat* and his luxury penthouse apartment in Fuengirola. Howard too was separated, having married at twenty-five, long before he met either Bernie Lyons or Sharon Collins. After his wife's death in 2003, Collins saw no obstacle to their marriage, but Howard had other ideas. Concerned that it would complicate his sons' inheritance, he was reluctant to marry her. His two sons worked in the family business, Downes and Howard Ltd, a low-key property company in the nearby Westgate Business Park, and PJ wanted to make sure that they got everything when he died. Sharon wasn't having it. She worked in the business too, albeit part-time, and she wanted it all for herself.

Collins constantly put pressure on PJ to change his mind and even went as far as arranging a wedding in Italy, but Howard refused to budge. His only concession was to have a "blessing" in a tiny church in Sorrento, where they pledged themselves to each other. They were not married and no legal ceremony had taken place. Returning to Ireland after their holiday, Collins told friends that they had married, and she threw a party at the Admiralty Lodge in late 2005 to celebrate. To ensure there was no misunderstanding, PJ Howard gave a letter to his sons, confirming that no wedding had taken place in Italy, and he had documents drawn up and lodged with their respective solicitors, to clarify any "misunderstanding" as to their status.

Having repeatedly tried unsuccessfully to persuade him to change his mind, Sharon Collins hatched a plan to make sure that she and not his adult children inherited his €60 million fortune. In fact, the party to celebrate their "wedding" in Italy was just Sharon's way of laying the ground for her murderous intent. Although Howard knew they hadn't married, Sharon Collins told anyone who'd listen that they were now man and wife and PJ indulged her; after all, it meant nothing, it had never happened. By 2006, she was ready to have him bumped off, but first, she had to "marry" him to make sure she was his next of kin and the legal heir to his fortune.

Sharon searched the internet and eventually found a site that offered proxy marriages, which was legal under Mexican law. All she had to do was sign forms giving some stranger at the other end of the internet special power of attorney. That and a few thousand dollars and she and PJ would be legally married under Mexican law. Normally, marriages legal in another jurisdiction are recognised by other countries, and the US in particular recognises such proxy Mexican marriages, despite the fact that neither party has ever stepped foot in Mexico.

Sharon filled in the "Bride's Information Sheet", which notably had the most important details at the top – "Total US $" – the deposit and the "Balance due". Other than that, it was basic: name, address, nationality, occupation and parents' name. The groom's form was exactly the same. All that remained was an internet signature and, of course, the money. The price varied according to the "urgency" of the wedding. An "Emergency Marriage" cost $1,495, and guaranteed you'd be legally married within twenty-four to forty eight hours – handy if you wanted to wed someone on the way out in order to inherit their fortune – and you could have the marriage certificate FedExed to you within three days. If time was on your side, you could get the "cheap" version and in three weeks you could be legally married for a mere $1,095. Sharon paid $1,295. She was in a hurry, but could afford to wait a few days extra and save $200.

There were no "difficult" formalities, such as the need to have an affidavit certified by a Notary Public or even a Commissioner for Oaths. It was almost too easy; Sharon couldn't believe her luck. Clutching her new (and legal) internet marriage certificate, she produced it at the passport office and was issued with a new passport in her "married" name. She was now officially Sharon Howard.

But that wasn't bringing her any closer to PJ's fortune. As things stood, even if he died, the boys would still inherit his money, leaving Sharon without a cent. Having succeeded in her intricate plan to "prove" they had married, her next move was to ensure that, as PJ's widow, not only would she collect the insurance, but she would inherit the business, his properties and his €60 million fortune. Collins decided on a plan of action; she would do whatever it took, even if it meant murdering her lover and his two sons, twenty-three-year-old Niall and twenty-seven-year-old Robert. The idea of letting them come between her and a life of luxury was incomprehensible. She decided to get rid of all three, removing any possible obstacle between her and the money. Despite being the mother of two sons herself, David (23) and Gary (25), Sharon lost no sleep over her decision to have her lover's sons killed.

In April 2006, the then forty-three-year-old Collins wrote an email to *The Gerry Ryan Show* on RTÉ radio, telling of her "unbearable" situation with her unnamed lover, building a picture of a man who frequented prostitutes and transvestites, claiming he was urging her to join swingers' clubs with him. Collins initially denied ever having written the email, although when it was subsequently located during the forensic investigation of Collins's computer, she agreed that she had written it, but said she hadn't realised she'd sent it by email. Surprisingly, she chose to call Gerry Ryan and the show's producer, Siobhan Hough, to give evidence in the case. It was probably the most incredible and bizarre outcome to a listener's email ever, but it certainly boosted his already large audience.

On 2 August 2006, using an Advent computer at work, she accessed her personal emails on her "sharoncollins@eircom.net" account and trawled the internet in search of everything from travel to Tesco diets and Reductil – a dieting product she had previously bought – before moving on to search for information on her rights to inherit her "husband's" fortune, whether cohabiting as "partners" or if they were actually married. Incredibly, she also searched sites for a hit man. She came across exactly what she was looking for: a site called "hitmanforhire". The website claimed: "hit man is the perfect solution for your killing needs. We offer a variety of professional assassination services available worldwide . . . We are a privately owned independent enterprise that specialises in reliable contract killings."

At 1.54 p.m. that day, Collins set up a new email address from the computer at work, with the user name of "lyingeyes98@yahoo.com". Ironically, or perhaps not, she picked the name from the Eagles song about a woman cheating on her older lover, although she later denied ever having heard of it. From there on, her plan was put into rapid action.

She immediately made contact with "hitmanforhire" – Las Vegas-based Essam Eid – using her new email address and told them what she wanted – three men dead. The following note was later found in Eid's file, his notes of request: "*2 male marks in Ireland. Asap. Usually together. Mu like accident. Then possibly a third within 24hours.Prefera like suicide. Would appreciate a call by return.*" Sharon did not realise that, with this email, she had started to leave a long forensic trail that gardaí would later follow.

Using the name S Cronin on the "application form" on the "hitmanforhire" website, Sharon gave her contact details. Later, when asked by detectives if the name S Cronin meant anything to her, she replied, "Not a thing". In fact, her mother's maiden name was Cronin.

"Hitman" emailed Sharon and said: "*I got your email. We will call you within 30 minutes. Can you email us back with more info before we call.*" Collins, still calling herself Sharon Cronin, phoned "hitman" – "Tony Luciano", aka Essam Eid – and then followed up with an email from her new "lying eyes" email address, which she again signed "S Cronin". Giving her Irish mobile number, she asked "hitman" to contact her within fifteen hours. Sharon had her own ideas about how she wanted the Howard men killed. She wanted them to die in a car or boat "accident".

Sharon subsequently emailed "hitman" from an Iridium laptop computer at Ballybeg House: "*Hi, we were just talking* [on the phone, which was later tracked]. *As you can imagine, I'm extremely nervous about sending this message and even talking on the phone. There are actually three but two of them would probably be together and the third would not be in Ireland, he would be in Spain. I don't want to give you the names of the people involved just yet but I will give you the location and tell you what I want, ideally."* The lengthy email went on to describe the Howard boys, giving their ages, saying that they worked and socialised together, adding that they shared a house with two other people in Ennis.

After exchanging many emails, it was decided that the brothers would be poisoned when they were in Kilkee, County Clare, where they kept a boat close to their holiday home. Her lover would be dealt with later, after he'd learned of the tragic death of his sons. Collins wanted this to happen in Spain, at his Fuengirola apartment, where his murder could be explained away as suicide. She suggested that it should look as if he had thrown himself over the balcony of his fourteenth-floor apartment, on hearing of the death of his beloved sons.

Collins then said she needed to know how soon it could be done – would it take days, weeks or months? She added: *"if the first job is done in Ireland, is it possible for the second job to be done with 12 – 24 hours in Spain, that's where he is? How much would it cost and how much of a deposit would be needed up front?"*

Following a series of these emails between Collins and the Las Vegas hit man, Collins was told it would cost $50,000 a "hit". Ever the businesswoman, she negotiated a discounted $90,000 to kill all three.

The "hitman" replied to "lyingeyes98@yahoo.com" on 8 August: *"Hello, well we discuss about your situation and we assume that these people is your 2 stepson and your husband. . . . if that so we can do 2 males first and after cool off we will do the third one."*

On 8 August, Collins logged on to the internet to check her "sharoncollins" email account. She also checked out bank sites looking for a personal loan of around €20,000, to pay the deposit on the contract killing. At the same time, she accessed her new "lyingeyes98" account and emailed the hit man from Ballybeg House using the Iridium computer. In a long and detailed message she said: *"I would prefer it if it was just my husband, but because of the way he has arranged his affairs, it would be way too complicated if his sons were still around and I'd still be in the same situation as I am now."*

According to emails sent by Sharon to Luciano, which were later forensically recovered following analysis of the computer hard drives by the Garda Computer Investigation Unit, Collins changed her mind about taking out a bank loan. PJ was well connected and she was worried that word about a loan, which she couldn't explain, would get back to him. Telling Tony that her husband was friendly with the bank manager, she said a record of larger bank drafts were kept but added: *"I could send a few drafts. I'd be worried that if the cops got suspicious though, and looked into it I wouldn't have answers. Do you know if cash can be parcelled up and Fed Ex safely?"*

She kept in touch with "hitman" and was now on friendly terms with him, saying *"Hi Tony"*, while he replied

"Hi Babe". She asked him for more details about his plans to "top" her "husband" and the "cooling off" period between killings.

On 11 August an email from Tony advised Collins not to worry about the Howards finding out she'd taken money, *"cause they will be gone we are planning 18 or 19 and your husband aug 20 we can arrange to meet you and get the key or we have our ways in without keys and we have a pic of the two guys and your husband too."*

Sharon was reassured. She wrote: *"I suppose your right I should just leave to you and not worry but I do worry. I could send the keys of the apartment to you or leave them somewhere in Spain near the apartment for you to collect."* Explaining the *"further complications about Spain"* she said PJ could be away on his boat – she wouldn't know until nearer the time but *"we could stay in touch by text if he and I are on the boat but if I'm on the boat I wouldn't want anything to happen to him there. I guess if he were to get news about his sons he would immediately return to the apartment to pack anyway."*

She said she didn't want the Howards to *"get suspicious of me in any way I'm already walking a very fine line here"*. She even offered to pay "hitman" over the odds after the job was done, saying there was a considerable amount of cash in Spain, *"once my husband is taken care of I'd be 'bringing him home' and any balance can be sent immediately once I'm back here."*

The kind-hearted and flexible "hitman" agreed, saying the balance of $45,000 would have to be paid *"no later than 72 hours after the job is done, this is our contract or you will be the target."* Collins replied from Ballybeg House: *"You most definitely will be paid within 72 hours. In addition, there may possibly one more person I might add to the list a little later but Ill get this job done first."*

Time was getting tight and Collins still had not sent on the deposit. On 14 August "hitman" emailed her: *"If you cant send the Money today forget about it it will be too late. My people not wait."* Collins replied immediately saying: *"I will be sending the money later today. It is 11a.m. here now so once I get the envelope to Fed Ex by 5p.m. today we're ok. Will you email the address for delivery. Im at work right now have to behave as normal and when i'm sent to the bank later I will sort out the money. Don't worry im going to do it. Ive decided. I also need to spend some time here with one of the sons to find out what he will be doing next weekend. Will let you know as soon as I do. Talk later Sharon."*

In the end, Collins decided to raid her own bank account at the AIB, withdrawing €13,000 and a further €2000 from the credit union, believing it was a good investment, given what she stood to gain. Within hours the agreed deposit was on its way to Las Vegas. Would-be killer Collins personally called to the FedEx office and sent the €15,000 deposit concealed in a "gift" box, to the address Luciano had given her, in the name of T Engle – later described as Tony Luciano's "wife", Teresa Engle.

Later that week, Collins checked her personal email from home on the Iridium computer at midnight and again at 8.10 a.m. Immediately afterwards she checked the "lyingeyes" email looking for her FedEx tracking number she received when she sent off the hit man's deposit. She contacted "hire_hitman@yahoo.com" from Ballybeg House and said: *"Thanks for getting back to me so fast. Wow. Im a bit scared to be honest. The two guys usually go to a place called Kilkee on the West coast of clare each weekend. . . . They drink in a bar called the Greyhound Bar on the main street in Kilkee. Its easy to find. What do you plan, putting poison in their drinks? I have to ask you what poison it would be, autopsies would be done and I need to know what they would conclude from the autopsies. I think it might be easier for your people to stay in a hotel in Kilkee and get talking to them in the bar but then you know your business I don't. I would be in Spain with my husband when the job would be done if its arranged for next weekend or even after that. What would you do about him? Especially with me around. You say you will take care of him yourself. You'd be coming a long way from the US to Spain. I could get the keys of the apartment to you and arrange a time to be out. I would be a suspect if anything looks suspicious, especially when I would be the one to inherit."*

The lengthy and detailed email rambled on: *"I have no conscience about my husband, he's a real asshole and makes my life hell, but I feel bad about the others, however I thought about it long and hard and I realise that it is necessary or there is no advantage to getting rid of my husband other than not having to look at his miserable face again. But I must be sure that I will be ok financially etc S."* In further emails from Collins to Tony recovered from Eid's Gateway computer by the FBI, she said *"I can't stand him now and have been wishing him dead for a long long time."*

Making sure "hitman" had the full picture, she sent him a photograph of herself and PJ, taken at a Christmas party in Dromoland Castle. She identified herself in the picture as *"the devil in the red dress"*. Tony replied: *"You look so great I cant wait to see you."* In other emails they referred to each other as Tony and Sharon. On 15 August he wrote: *"I just wondering if all info in the package what's there beside the Money? Is everything we need inside? Don't get mad when I see you in Malaga if I like you I will kiss you. If I don't do it I just joke Thank Tony."*

More emails flowed over the following two days as the deadline approached. Collins booked a flight to Malaga on the internet; she and PJ were heading to the holiday apartment in Fuengirola on 16 August. She continued to stay in touch with "hitman", as they phoned, texted and emailed each other on a regular basis. She passed on details of their plans while they were in Spain, telling him they would be on their boat heading to Porto Banus for a few days but *"In any case he will surely have to return to his apartment after he gets the 'sad' news of his sons!"*

Many of the emails were more personal. Tony said: *"I guess from your voice no one can touch you and I guess you are beautiful too."* Collins flattered him, telling him: *"you're very handsome yourself, Italian of course! I had to smile when I saw your photos. For as long as I can remember ive been saying that would love a sexy yellow sports car and as Ive always wanted to visit Las Vegas maybe you'll take me for a ride in yours if I ever get there. Now that's cheeky isn't it?"*

Emails continued between "lying eyes" and "hitman" after 15 August. She gave him the alarm code for the business premises and she told him where she'd leave the office keys. The email went on to give very specific directions to different locations, including the Downes and Howard office, as well as details of the location of the door locks and light switches at the office, giving him the alarm code and instructions of what to do there. The plan was for Eid to steal the computer there to get rid of the email evidence.

Everything was in place and it seemed that Sharon's plans were finally about to be realised. She kept in regular contact with Luciano, exchanging over seventy phone calls and texts with him, on landlines and their respective mobiles – Sharon had both Irish and Spanish ones, while Tony had American and Spanish mobiles. These transmissions were tracked and the constant traffic between "hitman" and Sharon was later identified. It also placed them in the US, Ireland and Spain at times consistent with their email correspondence.

Eid decided to contact a friend, Ashram Gharbeiah, to do the job for him, but he couldn't get hold of him, so the hit was put back a few days. Eventually, on 30 August, Eid's partner Teresa Engle flew to Ireland and met Gharbeiah, known as Ash, and the pair discussed how to dispose of the Howard boys. She said Gharbeiah had planned to poison them with prescription drugs, to bring on heart attacks while they were drinking in the Greyhound pub in Kilkee – not a very plausible plan and one which, had it succeeded, would have undoubtedly resulted in exposing their murders when postmortems were done. To paraphrase Oscar Wilde, for one to die this way might be regarded as misfortune; "to lose both looks like carelessness". However, before the plan was put into operation, Gharbeiah decided it wouldn't work. He went back to America, as did Engle, leaving Sharon with a problem.

Collins was getting extremely anxious; she had handed over her deposit and now wanted the job done. The pressure was on. In September 2006 Tony Luciano flew to Ireland, using his own passport in the name of Essam Eid, accompanied by Engle. The pair stayed in room 208 in the Two Mile Inn in Limerick. The original plan was to retrieve the computer from the business premises to prevent the police finding the incriminating emails. Sharon had already given them the keys and the alarm code to the offices.

When the Howard brothers turned up for work on 26 September they found that their office at Downes and Howard at Westgate Business Park seemed to have been "broken into" and two computers – a Toshiba laptop and the hard drive from an Advent PC – as well as computer cables were taken, together with other items, including a digital clock and, strangely, a poster of an old Irish £1 banknote.

Detective Garda Fahy from Ennis was sent to investigate. Seeing that no damage had been done in gaining entry, and no windows or doors broken, he checked the alarm and found it had been turned off just before 9.30 p.m. the previous night. Crime scene gardaí found nothing to suggest that it had been an ordinary break-in, despite the missing computers. Any fingerprints found were those of legitimate staff and even if Luciano's prints or DNA showed up, they had nothing to match them to at that time. As it transpired, he wore gloves while he was there.

They checked the CCTV coverage from the business park and found that the camera nearest to the offices was either already broken or had been interfered with. Other CCTV cameras in the business park proved more fruitful, and they recovered footage which picked up a car entering the "closed" business park at virtually the same time the Howards' alarm was deactivated. To all concerned, it looked like an inside job. The thieves had the alarm code and apparently had keys to the offices of Downes and Howard. At the time, Sharon and PJ were sunning themselves in Spain.

In a bizarre twist of fate, the one thing Sharon hadn't considered was that she was not alone in her greed. Frustrated at being unable to contact her in Spain, Eid saw a way of making even more money, without the messy job of three "hits" thousands of miles from home.

Before police could properly investigate the thefts, they got another call from Robert Howard. He reported a strange and startling call to his mobile at around 10.30

that night. The call was followed up almost immediately by a visit from a stranger. The caller said, "I heard you lost a couple of computers. I'll be at your house in five minutes." Worried and intrigued, Robert Howard wasn't sure if it was a joke, someone who'd heard about the robbery messing with him. Within five minutes he found out. Answering a knock to the door, he saw a foreign-looking middle-aged man who introduced himself as "Tony". To Robert's disbelief, the man handed him the Toshiba laptop missing from his office. Incredibly, he also told him that there was a contract for $130,000 on the lives of the Howard family. Saying he didn't really want to do the hits, he offered him a deal. For $100,000 Robert could buy out all three contracts.

To prove he meant business, Tony showed him photographs of the Howard family – PJ on his boat, the Howard brothers, and one of Sharon and PJ together. He also had detailed directions to their homes. There was no mention of a contract on Sharon or her boys, just the Howard men. Robert Howard was really worried; whatever this was, it was serious and was more than just the theft of a few computers. He grabbed the photographs – printouts from computer scans, and told his brother to call the cops. Tony didn't hang around and, despite efforts to follow him, he escaped. Thinking they had frightened him off, they were amazed when a couple of hours later – well after midnight – they got another call. A casual Tony asked if they had started to get the money together. Robert Howard was no fool; he played along, reassuring Tony that they were working on it.

Stringing Eid along to give them time, the Howard boys called the cops and told them the bizarre story. A full-scale covert investigation was launched. Following a forensic investigation of call traffic, the seven-minute extortion call was identified. It had come from a mobile phone registered to an "Essam Eid" at a Las Vegas address. The call, made from County Clare, had been routed through the US back to County Clare to an Irish landline number, the same day as the Howard boys had reported the extortion call.

The next day Tony rang again, chasing up his "ransom". He wanted Robert to meet him at the Ennis bus station with the cash. Detectives working on the case advised against this and told Robert to arrange to meet somewhere less remote, where a surveillance operation could be mounted. The "payoff" was arranged for the Queens Hotel in Ennis. Robert was told to sit at the bar and wait for Tony. In the best "shake-down" style, Tony phoned and told him to go to the hotel toilets, where he would be met by a woman who would check that he had the money. Letting the surveillance unit know about the new development, Robert went to the toilet area and met a dark-haired middle-aged woman wearing a leather jacket, who was later identified as Teresa Engle. When another woman (a plain clothes garda) walked by, Engle got jittery and left in a hurry. Afraid their cover was blown, gardaí moved in and arrested Engle and Eid at two different locations where they had been kept under surveillance. Later that evening, both Robert and Niall Howard picked out Tony from an ID parade, confirming he was the man who had called to their house with an "offer they couldn't refuse".

When gardaí raided their hotel room at the Two Mile Inn Hotel, they found black leather gloves, a mask, wigs, a black balaclava, and items missing from the Howards' business premises including the digital clock, the poster of Irish money, computer cables and two keys. They keys fitted the lock of the Downes and Howards' offices.

Detective Sergeant Mick Gubbins and Detective Peter Keenan of the Computer Investigation Unit of the Garda Síochána were assigned to the case. Working closely with the FBI, they conducted a year-long forensic investigation, which focused on an analysis of eight Irish hard drives, including the Iridium laptop seized from Ballybeg House and computers from the Howard's business premises at Westgate Business Park, including the Advent computer which was found hidden in bushes behind the Two Mile Inn Hotel, as well as three US hard drives. It was essential that any data recovered was maintained in an unaltered fashion, as any "contamination" or alteration would make it inadmissible in court.

Computer forensics detects otherwise "invisible" evidence and can deal with everything from hard drives, DVDs, CDs, flash memory sticks or cards, floppy discs and even tapes. Using a system called EnCase, they can locate and identify when a file was created, accessed, written up or modified, whether innocently or to conceal evidence. It can undertake complex searches and filter out unrelated matters, while locating any hidden, unallocated or deleted files and it can even handle encrypted data.

Two other tools, known as FRED (Forensic Recovery of Evidence Device) and FREDDIE (Forensic Recovery of Evidence Device Diminutive Integrated Equipment), are also used for "on-site" mobile computer forensic investigations. They can acquire the hard drive data, without losing any data or damaging the evidence. By removing the suspect hard drive and plugging it into FRED or FREDDIE, forensic investigators can interrogate a computer and access hidden or deleted files, whether encrypted or fragmented. Between these systems, they can overcome write-blocking techniques, can locate "key" words or recover passwords to enable investigators to locate and examine emails, free space, where files or part files may have been transferred to free or empty space, or recover deleted files. The Garda Computer Investigation Unit used a combination of EnCase and FRED to recover deleted emails from Collins's computers, as did the FBI in Las Vegas.

The emails found revealed Sharon's detailed instructions to kill the Howards and her preferred methods of getting rid of them. The investigating detectives were even more shocked than they could have imagined, as the level of Sharon's greed and deceit unfolded. Working in conjunction with Interpol and the FBI, Essam Eid's home was raided. FBI agents forensically examined the hard drives of three computers found there. They deconstructed and retrieved information from them that directly linked "Luciano", aka Eid, with Sharon Collins. The FBI found damning unencrypted emails between "lyingeyes98@yahoo.com" and "hire_hitman@yahoo.com" from the house in Las Vegas, which told of their grand plan to murder for money.

Working closely with the Yahoo organisation, the FBI established that the "hitmanforhire" site had been set up on 3 June 2006, almost coinciding with Sharon's search for a hit man. The website "owner" was identified as someone using the name Tony Luciano. At that time, it was still unknown if this was a genuine name, but it subsequently emerged that Luciano was in fact Egyptian Essam Eid. The "pidgin" English used in his emails would also help the FBI to identify that the emails had either come from someone whose first language was not English, or who was trying to disguise their natural writing style.

The investigation initiated in Ireland involved tracing all calls and emails made between Eid and Collins from Spain and the US, and detectives travelled to Spain in search of additional evidence of Collins emails sent while she was in Spain to Tony, following up her quest to kill the Howards. They discovered that various email addresses used by Collins and Eid were used to plot the "hits".

The FBI also identified other emails to Ireland connected to the case. Brian Buckley, a twenty-three-year-old Irish soldier, inadvertently got caught up in the web of murder and deceit as he trawled the internet looking for computer games. At the end of July 2006, Private Buckley, who had been in the army for just two years, was searching for "cheat codes" for a game called *Hitman* when he came across the "hitmanforhire" website. He thought it was a joke, as the front page had a cartoon character of a man holding a gun, wearing sunglasses and a hat. He filled out a form on the website, using the pseudonym "Will Buckimer" and gave background information that was a mixture of truth and fantasy. He claimed to be experienced in handguns, rifles, submachine guns, shotguns, sniper, heavy weapons, grenades and limited poisons.

At the beginning of August he got an email from "Tony Luciano" to his email address. It simply said: *"I have a job for you if your interested. Two males in Ireland. One in Spain. Asap. Let me know. We will try and call you."* Eid also contacted Buckley by phone and email, saying, *"We have intended targets, one in Spain and two in the west of Ireland."* Buckley ignored the messages, still thinking it was a joke.

Just over two weeks later he got another message from Luciano: *"Please help us out for this. I need some strong poison. One of us will be in Shannon. We cannot shift this stuff for security reasons, you know that, so please help us out. Will pay and will owe you favourite. Thanks brother. Tony."* Buckley was worried. He got a number of phonecalls someone who said he was Tony Luciano. He cut him off, telling him he had the wrong number. He eventually forgot about it, until he was contacted by detectives investigating the Sharon Collins case. Buckley was happy to co-operate and agreed to give evidence in court, telling of the strange messages he'd received from "hitman".

In the meantime, following her arrest, Teresa Engle quickly opted to turn "States evidence", becoming a prosecution witness for the state in return for immunity. Detectives established that Eid and Engle had flown into Shannon from the US, having booked the flights and hotel accommodation with PJ Howard's American Express card. Sharon Collins had given them the details of the card in one of her emails, expecting the Howards to be dead long before the bill came in, with no one left to question it. When the scam later emerged, she claimed that she had lost the card in Spain, but she had never reported the "loss" to American Express.

Teresa Engle had a lot to say for herself. She told detectives that the computers had been stolen to order, as Sharon Collins wanted to get rid of them, worried that the incriminating emails could put her in the frame when the Howard family were wiped out, particularly when she claimed the money. Engle said that Eid got very angry after the break-in when he couldn't contact Sharon. It was then that he had decided to contact the Howards directly, phoning them and then turning up at their door minutes later.

When first arrested, Eid claimed he had been having an affair with Collins for two or three years. He said they spoke on the phone often – that part was true, as the pair plotted murder for money. He said he'd visited her a month earlier in Malaga, when she was on PJ's boat, but said he had stayed in a hotel.

When Collins was arrested for questioning she denied all knowledge of the assassination plan. She denied writing any of the damning emails, saying she wasn't that stupid, as most people knew emails could be traced. She certainly knew it by then, as she had already been found out by forensic internet traffic analysis. Collins said she knew that emails could be tracked, as she had done a computer studies course when she was seventeen – of course, this was twenty-six years earlier, long before email became globally available.

But Teresa Engle provided good information, telling detectives about the money Sharon had FedExed to the US, and the stream of calls and emails between Sharon Collins and Essam Eid. When confronted with the evidence that she had withdrawn money from her accounts, and of her personal visit to the FedEx office in Shannon and her subsequent tracking of the "hit money" delivery to Las Vegas, Collins claimed that her laptop had been stolen but, like her credit card, the alleged theft was never reported to the police or an insurance company. The forensic investigation unit cross-tracked the time the FedEx account was accessed. It matched exactly the internet dial-up times from Sharon Collins computer operated from her home.

Collins came up with another excuse. She claimed she was being blackmailed – not by Luciano, but by a mysterious woman called Maria Marconi, who was supposedly helping her to write a book. Collins said she'd been forced to give this woman the tracking number of the money she'd dispatched to the US, claiming that the elusive Marconi was blackmailing her about a derogatory email she'd sent her, in which she told Marconi private and intimate details, alleging that PJ indulged in unorthodox sexual practices. She said she had called him vile names, saying that he used transvestites and swingers' clubs, claiming he wanted her to work as a prostitute and have sex with other men while he watched. She claimed she was terrified that PJ would ever find out about the email.

When confronted with the extracted emails, she eventually admitted sending a similar letter to *The Gerry Ryan Show*, which she said she didn't realise she had sent by email. The language in this email was consistent with the language of her emails to others, including "hitman", using similar phrases and talking about her "unbearable situation". Consistencies in style, format, spelling and terminology can be traced, even when a writer tries to disguise their style. There was no denying that Sharon had written the damning emails.

Collins could produce no evidence of the existence of Marconi, despite her detailed description of a tall attractive American in her late forties, and despite her supposed visit to Ireland, when Collins claimed she took her sightseeing. No photographs were taken, nor was there any record of her having entered the country. Sharon could not produce a single person who recalled meeting Marconi, nor could she give details of where she had stayed. Despite their "close friendship", she had not invited Marconi to stay with her, nor had the exotic creature even been glimpsed in the area or introduced to Collins's family. Sharon claimed she was unable to contact Marconi, the only person who could corroborate her tale. Her excuse was that her computer address book with details of Marconi's email address had been wiped from her computer, making it impossible for her to provide any information to help locate her star "witness".

Indeed, this was probably the only time Collins told the truth. She couldn't provide any information to help locate Marconi, because she'd never existed. The combined forces of the Garda Computer Investigation Unit and the cyber-crime teams of the FBI fared no better. They could find no forensic evidence of any Maria Marconi, nor were there any emails that would match her profile in any of the computers' hard drives, either in Ireland or elsewhere. Marconi had vanished in a puff of Sharon Collins's fertile imagination.

It escaped Sharon's notice that the detectives' talents and forensic investigative skills had already uncovered material she had "wiped" from her computer, as well as accessing her text and telephone records. The detectives in Harcourt Square could break passwords, timepass and encrypted codes, so a little thing like an erased address book was small change to them. Collins felt comfortable in her naivety, unaware that the computer forensic investigation unit could and would have found any contact with Marconi, had it ever existed.

Teresa Engle kept her promise to turn State's evidence. She admitted her complicity in the plot and described how she had helped Eid to make the toxic poison ricin, from acetone and castor beans, following instructions they had found on the internet. She admitted travelling to Ireland and Spain to recce the killing sites. Married three times (to the same man) before she "married" Eid, Teresa Engle had already pleaded guilty to similar extortion charges in a separate case in the US. She was awaiting sentencing when she made the deadly trip to Ireland with Eid, whom she "shared" with his legal wife Lisa. (Eid claimed that as a Muslin, he was entitled to have several wives, despite the US laws prohibiting polygamy.)

Following Eid's arrest, he was detained in Limerick Prison awaiting trial. It was here that the toxin described by Teresa was found. Eid kept it in his cell, sleeping with the deadly poison concealed in a contact lens case. An Army bomb disposal team headed by Commandant Joe Butler, dressed in full "fall-out gear", removed the lethal poison from the prison and using a RAMP (Rapid Analyte Measurement Platform) check, they made an initial analysis, which indicated that it was ricin, the deadly biological toxin, one of the most dangerous poisons known to man which, even in small doses, brings about a lingering and painful death.

For the purposes of a court case, however, the sample must be tested by forensic scientists qualified to deal with biological warfare products. As the Garda Forensic Laboratory were not equipped to deal with such biological warfare toxins, the sample was sent to the Home Office Laboratory of the Government Chemist in Middlesex in the UK. Joanna Peet from the LGC confirmed the initial findings. It was definitely ricin.

Eid denied any knowledge of the deadly poison but FBI forensic net analysis of Eid's computer in Las Vegas found documents on how to make ricin from castor beans. Also, Special Agent Ingrid Sotelo found evidence of ricin manufacturing at Eid's house. She found a drum of acetone in the garage, one of the ingredients required in its manufacture. She also found a food mixer which still had white power residues and other items which indicated that ricin was being concocted there.

The court case gripped the nation like no movie plot could, falling between farce and outrageous tragedy. After weeks of hearings, the plot unravelling to an incredulous courtroom, the jury found Sharon Collins guilty on all counts. They found she had solicited a hit man, Essam Eid, to murder the man she lived with, PJ Howard, and his sons, Niall and Robert, young men in the prime of their life.

She was sentenced to six years in jail. Despite the damning forensic evidence from police forces from two continents, Collins continued to protest her innocence to the very end. She denied having any part in the plot to kill the Howards, claiming it was a set-up by her mystery blackmailer. The jury didn't buy it and both Collins and her "hitmanforhire", Essam Eid, are languishing in jail contemplating their failure as criminal masterminds.

Essam Eid was found guilty of handling stolen goods, and of attempting to extort €100,000 from Robert Howard, and he is currently serving six years, the jury having failed to agree on the conspiracy to murder charges. Fifty-three-year-old Eid appeared philosophical about his conviction, having already spent almost two years in custody and facing further similar charges in the United States. In a copycat case, the FBI said they were investigating Eid in connection with an extortion racket in which, it was claimed, Eid had been hired by a former boyfriend of Anne Royston to assassinate her, but in September 2006, he gave her the option of "buying out" the contract for $54,000. Royston contacted the FBI, who raided Essam's house and seized weapons including a 9mm Browning, two semi-automatics, magazines, 9mm Luger ammunition, tazer guns and silencers. If he is found guilty of these charges in the US, he could face a far heavier sentence. For now, it seems he is quite happy to remain in the custody of the Irish State.

As for Sharon, amazingly the self-described "devil in the red dress" had the full support of her family throughout the ordeal. Throughout the trial Collins's own two sons, David and Gary, sat steadfastly beside her, holding her hand and comforting her, never believing for a single minute that their mother could be capable of being a cold, calculated murderer, had her plan succeeded. Even her ex-husband Noel, who'd split from Sharon eighteen years earlier, and his wife Fiona supported her and were in court to the end. They all must have been deeply shocked to hear one of her email messages to Eid: "*I was sitting with my son last night and thinking if only he knew what his mother was planning. He would definitely wonder if he ever knew me at all. My boys would be devastated if they thought I would do such a thing.*"

Whatever Svengali-like powers Sharon Collins had over PJ Howard, he refused to believe what the prosecution described as the "overwhelming evidence" that his beloved Sharon tried to have him murdered for his money. After concluding his evidence in defence of Sharon, saying he still loved her, PJ told a shocked court that he would wait for her. The packed courtroom watched in disbelief as he left the witness box and kissed the woman who had paid a "hitman" to have him and his sons killed. Her greed was so great that she was prepared to have him thrown to his death from a fourteen-storey balcony, so she could get her hands on his money and yet, he said he still loved her.

30

The Drug Busters

The little island of Ireland is famed for the beauty of its rugged coasts and countryside, which attract tourists from all over the world – but who would have thought it would also prove such an attractive stopping-off point for some of the biggest drug deals in the world?

There is no shortage of demand for illicit drugs worldwide as international cartels of dealers ply their evil trade, selling to the highest bidder. The CIA drugs intelligence unit identified Ireland as being "a transhipment point for, and consumption of, drugs to the UK and Europe" with "an increasing consumption of South American cocaine". Delivery is the only problem, but the beautiful and rough terrain that stretches around Ireland's rocky coastline, from the Atlantic seaboard to the east coast capital, wrapping itself around the Cork shoreline, with its myriad of bays, inlets and coves, gives ideal cover for international drug smugglers to make clandestine drops.

It seems like Ireland is a soft touch, an easy target, with a tiny navy and few resources to fight drug crime, as day after day we see crime lords killing each other for an extra piece of the action. It wasn't so many years ago that this was the stuff of television, *Miami Vice* and other American cop shows, so removed from life in Ireland or even Europe. Now we live with it on a daily basis, as the media report murders, stabbings and shootings as a matter of routine. We have become almost inured to the crime surrounding us – just so long as it doesn't stop at our door. Crime pays, and pays handsomely, and the drug dealers are willing to take the risk.

Even when caught, they continue to run their empires from prison. Many are their own best customers, which leaves them exposed to the new kids on the block, ready and willing to do whatever it takes to become the new crime boss. While we have had some very dramatic drug seizures in recent years, it is easy to become complacent and believe we are on top of the situation. That is not the case, as the huge hauls are only the tip of the iceberg.

Major hauls in Ireland in recent years have been the stuff of movie-makers. In the summer of 2007 the perfect script landed right in their laps – though it would be something of a farce. Even the name of the smugglers' vessel would come back to haunt them.

It all started when a UK gang which included three Englishmen – Perry Wharrie, Martin Wanden and Joe Daly Jr – set out to make their fortune smuggling drugs, but things didn't work out quite as well as they'd planned. Through a combination of bad weather and their own bungling, they were caught attempting to smuggle over €440 million worth of cocaine into Ireland, when their RIB (an inflatable boat) sank at Dunlough Bay in West Cork, after they'd filled the petrol-driven outboard motors with diesel in error. The stranded, overloaded boat capsized in the rough seas, tossing its cargo of cocaine adrift.

At 8.00 a.m. on 2 July 2007, a very wet and agitated young man banged on a local farmhouse door just outside Goleen in West Cork, looking for help. Saying his name was Gerry O'Leary, he claimed he'd been fishing with friends when their boat capsized in stormy waters, north of Mizen Head. He refused to let the farmer, Michael O'Donovan, call the coastguard, despite the fact that his friends were still at sea. Although it was mid-summer, the weather conditions were poor, with a force five gale blowing. Trying not to alert the stranger, the farmer quietly called his sister and asked her to scramble the coastguard to the rescue.

Soon, the tiny road leading to the bay was packed with cars and personnel, with little room left to park. A coastguard member unthinkingly blocked in a green UK-registered jeep in an effort to get on with the job. It was a small place and locals knew everyone in the area, but the man remembered noticing an unknown woman standing close by the jeep. She quickly disappeared from the scene, leaving the jeep behind. Later identified as Sonja Wanden, she left Ireland in a hurry.

With the rescue in full swing, two men appeared at the scene; one of the men (later identified as Perry Wharrie) approached the rescue team and told them there were two more men in the water. As gardaí arrived, the men (Wharrie and Joe Daly junior) didn't hang around to watch the rescue, but disappeared across nearby fields, making no attempt to get to the jeep.

At around 9.15 a.m. the lifeboat pulled a man from the sea. Lucky to be alive, he was wearing a lifejacket which had kept him afloat until the rescue. A rescue helicopter was also sent to the scene and the man was taken to Bantry hospital where he was treated for hypothermia. He claimed to be a South African national and gave his name as Tony Linden, one of several aliases he used. Unaware that "O'Leary" had already made it to the shore, he urged the rescue crew to keep looking for his friends, saying they were still in the sea, which was now awash with bales of what was suspected, even then, to be drugs.

Sixty-two bales of what was believed to be cocaine, weighing 1,554kg, were recovered from the area surrounding the sunken boat. Whoever was behind the major cocaine deal had invested big money into the venture, but they stood to make a vast profit. With the realisation that this was a major drug-smuggling operation gone wrong, customs and drug squad detectives from West Cork were summoned to the area, while the drug enforcement unit's boat, *An Suirbheir* and the *LE Orla*, were also sent to the scene. The operation was headed up by Chief Superintendent Tony Quilter, who assigned 150 gardaí from the drug squad, the Technical Bureau, the national criminal investigation unit, along with the air support and intelligence units, to the major investigation, liaising with the Maritime Analysis and Operations Centre–Narcotics (MAOC-N), the international unit set up the previous year, with its HQ in Lisbon, which, in conjunction with the Irish investigation, was also trying to track the location and progress of a suspect boat, believed to be out at sea.

The consignment was formally examined by garda forensic scientists who confirmed the haul was cocaine, using gas-chromatography. (Other methods, such as infrared spectrophotometry (IR), or nuclear magnetic resonance spectroscopy can also be used.) This analysis can identify the purity, dilution or even the adulteration of the drugs with potentially lethal ingredients, but this time it was strictly high-quality stuff. The street value was estimated and re-estimated as forensic results came in.

Geraldine O'Neill of the garda forensic science unit examined the hallmarked cocaine from Dunlough Bay and found that it was seventy-five per cent pure. Street cocaine usually varies in purity from around twelve to fifteen per cent. The valuation, based on a purity of seventy-five per cent, was put at €440 million, more than four times the original estimate. When compared to her calculations for adulterated street value cocaine with a purity of 6.7 per cent, the final adulterated value of the haul could have been worth €1.28 billion, despite the drop in prices in recent years.

Forensic science can also provide intelligence as to the source of drugs by identifying the packaging material. It was clear that the cocaine had originally come from South America, probably from Colombia, which shares a border with Venezuela, where FARC guerrillas, who control the drug trade in the area, also have a base, supported by President Hugo Chavez. Thirty per cent of the 600 tonnes of cocaine smuggled out of Colombia each year is smuggled through Venezuela. Most of it ends up in Europe.

A short time later, a car was reported stolen in the Dunlough bay area and later an unoccupied holiday house in Ahakista near the Sheep's Head peninsula was broken into – both unusual occurrences in such a rural setting. A forensic examination was made of the house, which identified that two beds had recently been slept in. The crime scene unit found human hair and fibres from clothes on the beds and on other surfaces in the house, where it appeared that someone had taken shelter for the night. It is virtually impossible not to leave trace evidence and DNA, as each day we shed millions of skin cells and hairs. Unseen fibres are picked up and shed from our clothes and virtually everything we touch can provide evidence, as every contact leaves a trace. At least two separate sets of DNA were found at the scene, together with a number of fingerprints, which were later matched to known UK criminals via NAFIS, which has more than seven million fingerprints on its database.

Two days later, on 4 July, the men were spotted hiding in a hedgerow by a local man, in Gubbeen, outside Schull in West Cork. Dirty and dishevelled, they had trekked over fifteen miles across the rugged terrain in force five gales. Forced to abandon the jeep and all their personal belongings at Dunlough Bay, they were at the mercy of the West Cork weather. They'd had no food for days and seemed almost relieved to have been caught. The men were identified as Joe Daly Jr from Bexley in Kent and Perry Wharrie, also known as Andrew Woodcraft, from Essex.

Daly had strong links with his father's home in West Cork and in recent years, his father, also Joe Daly, had returned from England to live in the area. Joe Jr often visited with his wife Jennifer and their two children. At the time, Joe Jr was on holiday there, as was his brother Michael. Joe Jr had borrowed a fishing rod to go fishing that day and, on hearing the news of the "accident" Joe Sr had contacted gardaí, concerned that his son was involved. Gardaí took Joe Sr to the hospital but his son was not there. However, he recognised one of the rescued men, a man called Martin, who was a friend of Joe's. The man had told gardaí that his name was Tony Linden. Detectives using international co-operation resources such as NAFIS, the UK's National Automated Fingerprint Identification System, quickly identified Tony Linden as a well-known UK criminal, Martin Wanden, who used a number of aliases, including Stephen Witsey. Wanden was originally from the UK but he had moved to South Africa, where he had substantial assets. Detectives established that Wanden held passports in the various names of Linden, Witsey and Wanden.

Joe Daly's other son, forty-eight-year-old Michael, had joined the London Metropolitan Police as a young seventeen-year-old cadet and was quickly promoted through the ranks, becoming a detective sergeant in the drug squad before leaving the force in 1994. He drove a taxi for nearly ten years but he lost that job when his licence was suspended. Daly was now a dirty ex-cop. He had the convictions to prove it.

The flurry of police activity was all over the news, leading to the early and hasty departure of a number of men who had been staying at the Glengarriff Hotel. It was believed that up to eight accomplices were now fugitives on the run. Some of the men had been in the area for a while, under the pretext of being tourists. They drank in the local pubs, played golf and generally splashed the cash while gathering local intelligence. Detectives were able to get good descriptions of the strangers from the locals. CCTV footage from shops and clubs in the area was collected and digitally enhanced before being painstakingly scrutinised by gardaí. Ports and airports were checked and again CCTV footage was examined to locate and identify any fleeing suspects.

Detectives were also liaising with international police organisations to establish if any of the captured men or hotel guests had connections to the drug haul. They learned that Perry Wharrie, one of the two fugitives arrested outside Schull, was a convicted cop killer. In 2005, he had been let out of a UK prison on early release, on licence, having served seventeen years for murdering PC Frank Mason. Wharrie shot him in the back during a bank robbery. Having broken the terms of his licence, there was a warrant out for his arrest even before the Dunlough Bay job.

Gardaí found two more UK-registered jeeps abandoned in the area, which were forensically examined. DNA and clothes fibres, together with various documents, were found. As a result, detectives raided a holiday house in the Kilcrohane area, which had been rented by Alan Wells, one of two properties the gang rented near the Sheep's Head peninsula.

The crime scene unit found an Aladdin's cave of forensic evidence. It appeared that some of the drug gang had been based at the holiday home, co-ordinating the mission for at least three weeks prior to the drugs being landed.

They found satellite phones, which when forensically analysed provided information on the date and location of all calls made, as the signals were bounced between international satellites to specific satellite phones, identifying the phone users. In fact, it was established that Joe Daly Jr had flown into Cork Airport on 8 June with another man, Allan Wells, also known as Charles Goldie, a "friend" of his brother Michael's. Wells paid for the flights. They picked up a jeep at the airport and drove to Bantry where they bought supplies at Murphy-O'Connor's hardware shop. They spent two days making up mooring weights to anchor the RIBs, before flying home two days later on 10 June.

The same day Joe Daly Jr got a call from Michael asking him to drive a jeep to tow a boat to Ireland later that week. Michael Daly backed out of going himself, sending his brother and Martin Wanden instead. Wanden paid for the ferry at Pembroke and travelled as far as Rosslare. The pair split up and Wanden made his own way to West Cork, while Daly Jr continued to tow the RIB. When Daly Jr arrived in West Cork, he drove to his father's house, where two men, Alan Wells and a man called Alex, collected the jeep from him.

During the following two weeks Joe Daly Jr spent time at his father's home and in Durris (where the second RIB was later found), as well as visiting the house in Kilcrohane, the command headquarters, where Alan Wells was staying, surrounded by an array of state-of-the-art technology, which included encrypted communications systems.

GPS – global positioning systems – were also found in the house at Kilcrohane. GPS can identify the precise position of a user and has continuous course acquisition data capabilities; it can map a journey between Dublin and Cork or Bantry and Barbados, either on land, by air or sea. It has been in use by the military for many years, more recently by commercial airlines and maritime organisations and is now commonly used by drivers. The more sophisticated GPS systems, known as "standard systems" can provide a predictable position of a yacht, car, aircraft or individual and is accurate to 100 metres horizontally and 156 vertically within 340 nanoseconds (a nanosecond is one-billionth of a second), whereas precise positioning systems (PPS as opposed to GPS), used in military applications, give a minimum accuracy of 22 metres horizontally and 27.7 metres vertically. This information is delivered to the PPS even faster, quicker than the blink of an eye, within 200 nanoseconds, all accurately tracked via satellite data point measurements.

It is likely that their GPS helped the gang track the incoming drugs shipment. Detectives identified that the vessel that had offloaded the drugs was called the *Lucky Day*. The final message sent via the satnav phone gave away the gang's plans for *Lucky Day*. On 6 July 2007, the *Lucky Day* was intercepted at sea and escorted to the port of La Coruna, the largest port in northern Spain. Two Lithuanian men on board were arrested by Spanish police and refused to co-operate with them.

The men captured in West Cork were charged with possession of cocaine for sale or supply and were remanded in custody. But for a stupid mistake and the inept way they dealt with the situation afterwards, the dumb drug smugglers might well have gotten away with the scheme. It had been a long time in the planning and, up to that point, that planning had been meticulous.

The gang come across an advert on the internet for a yacht. Called the *Lucky Day*, the luxury catamaran was offered for sale by a marine trading company in Fort Lauderdale in Florida. The 1997 Fountaine Pajot built Tobago 35 had been privately owned by wealthy Austrians. The catamaran, which travelled between Grenada and Martinique, had a stateroom in each hull, each with a queen-sized bed. It also had another eight berths, a luxury kitchen and living-room area, along with additional accommodation. Stripped of its luxurious accommodation, the 35-foot catamaran was ideal for transporting large quantities of drugs. They bought the catamaran and set about their audacious venture.

The precious cargo travelled from Venezuela to Barbados, where it was picked up by the inaptly named

Lucky Day catamaran, crewed by two Lithuanians, Aras Sturnbrys and Rolandas Karnatake, who were joined by an Englishman named Gerard Hagan, or Gerry O'Leary as he called himself when he later knocked on the farmer's door for help.

At the end of May 2007, some of the gang travelled to West Cork, having already rented two holiday homes on Sheep's Head peninsula, under the guise of being on a fishing holiday. One of the gang members, Perry Wharrie, had already been to West Cork some time earlier to recce the place. During a later trip he left clues that were to come back to haunt him. Suffering from a toothache, he got the receptionist at the Ramada Hotel in Blarney, where he was staying, to make a dental appointment for him. He visited dentist Liam O'Sullivan in Tower, Blarney, County Cork, at 2.00 p.m. on the afternoon of 20 June 2007. Saying he was in Blarney to play golf, he filled in a medical questionnaire giving his correct name, his date of birth as 2 August 1959 and an address in Essex. He was given a prescription for an antibiotic, Amoxicillin, which he had filled in a local chemist. Later, while investigating the cocaine haul, detectives found scraps of paper in a field at Dunlough Bay. When forensically analysed they were found to contain the words "Perry Wharrie", "pharmacy" and "Tower". Perry Wharrie, who had been to school with the Daly brothers, was later picked up in Schull, along with Joe Daly Jr.

Martin Wanden had been in County Cork the previous January to check out the area. He bought a mobile phone in Bantry, which he registered in the name of Steven Witsey, one of his many aliases. The mobile phone was to become crucial to the State's case, as forensic evidence would later prove.

The logistics and financial outlay involved in planning the drugs landing was enormous. As well as purchasing the luxury catamaran for $132,000, the group bought three Land Rover Jeeps, a diesel 275-horsepower single engine, rigid inflatable boats (RIBs), as well as a number of mobile phones, GPS and satellite phones. They had booked into hotels and B&Bs, had flight and ferry costs and rented houses and at least one car and had a number of false passports in their possession – and these were only the "foot soldiers".

The GPS would be of use in rendezvousing with the catamaran the *Lucky Day*, which was dropping off the cocaine in the remote location thirty miles south-west of Mizen Head off the West Cork coastline. The rendezvous point was marked by a weather buoy and the gang had already entered the coordinates into their GPS, which would later prove to be another nail in their collective coffin. One of the RIBs would rendezvous with the catamaran and later transfer the cocaine to the second RIB, at Dunmanus Bay, where they had jeeps on standby to shift the cargo.

Somewhere along the line it was decided to change the 275-horsepower single diesel engine on the RIB and replace it with two 200-horsepower Yamaha petrol engines. The plan ran adrift when the men forgot about the change and inadvertently put diesel into the petrol tanks. In a force five gale, the engines cut out and the RIB got into difficulty, eventually capsizing, losing both its crew and its precious cargo.

With hindsight, it was an easy mistake but after all their planning, that simple mistake led to their downfall. Perhaps the gang became complacent as they neared the end of a long journey, or perhaps it was the Irish weather conspiring against them; either way, their luck ran out.

As navy divers recovered the bales of cocaine from the sea, they also found something else crucial to the forensic investigation – a waterproof container known as a "Pele box" close to the sunken RIB. It held a treasure trove of evidence, including a mobile phone, which was later traced back to Martin Wanden, aka Steven Witsey, who had bought the phone in Bantry months earlier. The stash also included a two-way radio and a satellite phone, which would all play a role in the hapless crew's downfall. Forensic examination of the mobile phone tracked a series of calls bounced through various phone masts to a number of contacts and specific phone numbers in the UK, a system known as triangulation. It put a date and timeframe on the operation and linked the captured foot soldiers back to the armchair generals who were financing the crime. Detectives now had a solid line of enquiry as to who was pulling the strings on the operation. Subsequent records on these phones confirmed that the Wanden-owned phone had both received and made calls to these people. Around the same time, news came through that Spanish police had arrested the two Lithuanian crewmen aboard the *Lucky Day*.

Forensic tracking on the satellite phone showed calls to a number in Spain and regular check-in calls were made to another satellite phone as the *Lucky Day* sailed the Atlantic. Wharrie's and Wanden's fingerprints were all over the phones and on a notebook containing the same telephone numbers they found on Martin Wanden's phone, the one he'd bought in Bandon in the name of Steven Witsey. Not expecting to be caught, it had never occurred to these seasoned criminals to "wipe" the evidence, especially as their very lives were at stake when the RIB sank.

When the recovered RIB was examined, Joe Daly Jr and Martin Wanden's fingerprints were found on the seating and in other areas. The same prints were discovered on seating from the boat found at the rented house at Faramanagh, near Kilcrohane in West Cork. The evidence was building up, when police had yet another find. They discovered a Volkswagen Passat car rented by Perry Wharrie's wife, with mobile phones and two more passports in a bag in the boot.

The mobile phones found in the VW Passat were forensically examined and provided further evidence of the conspiracy to transport, import, sell and distribute the cocaine. Telephone records indicated that the men and at least one woman had been in close and regular contact during the pre-planning, setting up and execution of the crime. Two weeks before the incident in Dunlough Bay, a text message was sent to Martin Wanden on the Nokia phone he'd bought in Bantry. The text came from "Big Al" (Alan Wells aka Charles Goldie) which said: "any sign of the gruesome twosome?" Other messages sent in June said "where are the keys 4 boat", "Can you drop off

Joe's bag? it is in the front of the car?" and "Mooring sorted". The day the RIB capsized on 2 July, there were thirty-four frantic calls from the gang members to Wanden's phone.

One of the passports found in the car had a photograph of the man who'd escaped the sinking boat and turned up at the farmhouse, but the name said Gerard Hagan and not Gerry O'Leary as he'd claimed. When gardaí investigated the passport, they found it was genuine; the man actually was Gerard Hagan, the Englishman who had travelled in April with the two Lithuanians on the Catamaran from Barbados.

Twenty-two-year-old Hagan had been living in Fuengirola in Spain with his girlfriend when he was offered £5,000 to take part in the drug-smuggling. He flew to London in February 2007 and applied for a passport at the Irish Embassy, using the birth certificate of a long-dead Irish child, Gerard O'Leary. "Confirmation" of his identity was supplied via fax from the office of a firm of non-existent solicitors in the UK. Hagan flew to Trinidad and Tobago using the illegally obtained passport. He met up with the two Lithuanian sailors on the *Lucky Day* and set sail. When they were 250 miles out to sea they picked up their illicit cargo from the "mother ship"' and headed for Ireland.

Linking this information with the satellite and telephone data, it was matched to maritime backtracking intelligence, which identified the *Lucky Day*'s long journey from Florida to La Isla Margarita off Venezuela's north shore, through the Caribbean, until it eventually arrived off the Irish coast. En route, Hagan produced the O'Leary passport to Barbadian officials on 6 May 2007, as they checked out the arrival of *Lucky Day*. According to their records, there were three men on board, the two Lithuanians and "O'Leary".

Satellite phones also pinpointed the location of the *Lucky Day*, as international calls ricocheted between Hagan and his bosses. The under-resourced Irish navy proved their mettle when the gardaí asked Commander Eugene Ryan to chart the progress of the *Lucky Day*. By plotting maritime charts, evaluating tides and predicting wind values and meteorology, based on his calculations, Commander Ryan said that from the West Indies, where it picked up the drugs, to the Irish coast close to West Cork, it would have taken the *Lucky Day* twenty-six days, travelling at a speed of 5.1 knots, to cover the 3,300 nautical-mile journey (over 6,000 kilometres) The satnav communications, supported by the coordinates found on the GPS, indicated that the handover from the *Lucky Day* to the RIB had taken place thirty miles off the coast. Based on the information from Barbados, Trinidad and Tobago, combined with satellite phone-tracking information, which pinpointed the location of the catamaran as it crossed the ocean and the subsequent capsize of the RIB, Commander Ryan's calculations were spot on. Between the calculations of the Irish naval service, the gardaí, the MAOC-N (which had been set up just over a year before), and the forensic scientists, the forensic evidence against the men was stacking up.

Just when the drug smugglers thought their luck couldn't get any worse, in a complete coincidence, local salvage expert Colum Harrington was asked by customs and excise to recover the submerged RIB from the sea and take it to Castletownbere. When he raised the craft, Harrington immediately recognised it. While returning from a Sea Works exhibition in England in June 2007, just over two weeks before the drugs haul at Dunlough Bay, he noticed the RIB queuing for the ferry in Pembroke. He remembered thinking it unusual to see such big engines on a RIB and thought whoever owned it must be in a big hurry to get somewhere. Being in the business, he had had a good look at it and was surprised when the owner made no attempt to speak to him, as is the norm with boat owners when someone shows an interest in their boat.

With the information already uncovered, the net now widened and, in co-operation with the UK police, CCTV was recovered from the ferry port. Digitally enhanced, it showed Joe Daly Jr and Martin Wanden, travelling under the name of Tony Linden, driving a blue 4x4 jeep onto the Pembroke ferry on 15 June 2007. They were towing the RIB that ended up at the bottom of Dunlough Bay.

Gardaí also seized a number of vehicles in the area, including two UK-registered jeeps. They found insurance and registration documents linking the three 4x4 blue, green and red jeeps to the gang. In an elaborate plan, all the vehicles were registered to their previous owners between 3 and 16 November 2006 and then changed again four months later, over a four-day period in March 2007. Evidence produced by the UK driver and licensing authority in Swansea showed the red and blue jeeps were both registered to a Paul Young, at a Bexley, Kent address in south London. Insurance for the blue 4x4 was provided by Mastercover Insurance in the UK. The initial deposit of £113 was paid by Joe Daly Jr using his own credit card, with the subsequent direct debits coming from his Halifax bank account.

Forensic examination of the 4x4s linked them to the cocaine gang. DNA was found in the cars, while Perry Wharrie's DNA was found on a toothpick discarded by him in one of the jeeps.

When the case finally came to court, twenty-four-year-old Hagan from Liverpool pleaded guilty at Cork Circuit Criminal Court and was sentenced to ten years in prison. Despite his reluctance to call the coastguard, the judge said the sentence reflected the fact that Hagan had left himself open to capture by getting help to save a human life. Wanden's other co-conspirators had left him to drown in a force-five gale. He was suffering from hypothermia when he was picked up. Hagan had also co-operated fully with detectives, admitting his part in the scheme within thirty-six hours of capture and he had stood to gain only £5,000 for his efforts on behalf of the British-Spanish gang behind the €440 million Colombian cocaine drugs deal. Detective Sergeant Fergal Foley spoke up for Hagan – but for Hagan raising the alarm, he said, gardaí and customs would never have known about the cocaine.

Gardaí believed that up to ten people had travelled to West Cork from the UK to set up logistical support for the operation. Others linked to the drug smuggling included Joe Daly's brother Michael and Alan "Big Al" Wells who was also know as Charles Goldie, along with two women.

The men all claimed they were being accused in the wrong, just because they had gone to the aid of a friend and relative of Joe Daly Jr, who'd said he'd been told his brother Michael was in trouble in the rough seas. Daly claimed that he and Perry Wharrie rushed to the scene to help, unaware there was anything criminal involved.

After a ten-week trial, in which evidence from over 300 witnesses was heard, the men were unanimously found guilty at Cork Circuit Criminal Court. Martin Wanden and Perry Wharrie, who had denied the charges, were sentenced to thirty years in prison, while Daly got twenty-five years. A fifth man who had been on the RIB, believed to be Michael Daly, had fled. The cost of the garda operation was said to be in the region of 1 million, while free legal aid for the defendants cost over €300,000, at taxpayers' expense, despite the substantial assets of the convicted men.

Wanden, who had moved from the UK to South Africa eight years before his capture in Cork, was known to have substantial assets there. Johann Joubert, Senior Special Investigator of the South African Forfeiture Unit, said Wanden had used various aliases to buy up South African property since 2001, spending millions on the "Pink Palace", a large house in Hout Bay, as well as numerous other expensive properties, boats and flashy cars. Just months after buying his first property in South Africa, Interpol had issued an arrest warrant for Wanden, who had escaped from a French prison after being caught red-handed in possession of a drugs cache destined for the UK. The drugs had already been loaded onto a RIB but once again, the weather spoiled his day and he was caught.

Wanden and his wife's bank accounts were monitored and were constantly growing with "foreign" payments coming through. After Wanden's arrest in Ireland, the Financial Intelligence Centre froze their accounts.

His "business" ventures had taken him around Europe, South and Central America and ultimately to Ireland. Immediately after his arrest in West Cork in July 2007, his wife Sonja attempted to sell off these assets, including a mansion outside Cape Town, but was prevented from doing so under a South African magistrate's order. The assets were later sold at auction and the proceeds went to the South African criminal assets agency.

Sonja Wanden, who was bipolar, also known as manic depression, committed suicide in a mental hospital in the UK, leaving the couple's nine-year-old daughter Jade without either parent.

In a postscript to the West Cork seizures, UK police kept an even closer eye on ex-drug squad Detective Sergeant Michael Daly, who was believed to have escaped from the capsized RIB.

In May 2008, forty-eight-year-old Michael Daly was arrested in England and charged with the attempted importation of cocaine from France into the UK. Michael Daly was out on bail, awaiting trial, when the gang came unstuck in West Cork. In March 2009 Kingston Crown Court heard how Daly and four others planned the collection, delivery and transportation of cocaine, smuggling £4 million worth of the drugs in from France, landing a small boat on a remote beach at Capel-le Ferne in Kent. A former member of the Met's Drug Squad, Daly, from Beech Way in Bexley, was the brains behind the plan. Together with another man, Paul Young, of Bexley, Kent – the man listed as the registered owner of the blue and red jeeps involved in the Dunlough Bay cocaine haul – they set sail for France on 19 April, unknowingly being tracked by the MAOC-N and surveillance GPS, but the boat ran into trouble. Three weeks later, they tried again with a different RIB – not having learnt from their experience in Dunlough Bay. When the RIB arrived back in England, Daly and Young were arrested. Daly was found in possession of two padlock keys which fitted a storm drain thirty yards away. A search of the drain turned up eight holdalls with 200 kilos of cocaine, skunk cannabis and amphetamines. Both men's DNA were all over the holdalls and their mobile phone records showed a conspiracy to supply Class A and B drugs. They pleaded guilty to the charges and each were sentenced to eight and five years, to run concurrently.

In July 2009, ex-Detective Sergeant Michael Daly, who was already serving time on drugs offences, was charged with conspiracy to import 1.5 tonnes of cocaine into Ireland, part of the Dunlough Bay seizure. He was remanded in custody to appear before the Old Bailey on 7 August 2009. Alan Roger Wells from south east London, who rented the holiday home in west Cork and John Edney from Kent were also charged with the same offence and remanded in custody to appear before the Old Bailey.

31

The Write Stuff:
Questioned Document Analysis

Although often overlooked as a specialist area of
forensics, handwriting analysis, often wrongly referred to
as graphology (which is more about identifying personality
types) is crucial to identifying forged documents in both
criminal and civil matters. Everything from Aunt Maggie's
will leaving her fortune to a stranger, to contracts, dodgy
bank drafts, priceless autographs, confession statements,
suicide or ransom notes or malicious letters are all part of
the daily work of the forensic handwriting analyst. It is a
highly skilled and technical area of forensic science, and
questioned document experts are now employed in many
areas of the criminal justice system, in banking and in the
private sector, providing expert evidence in court for both
the prosecution and defence in criminal matters, as well as
acting for various parties in commercial disputes or
private matters.

The importance of document examination could well be illustrated by the fate of Irishman Roger Casement, who was said to have been hanged by a comma. A hero at home, he was deemed a traitor by the British. Charged with treason following a court case, he was convicted of conspiring to bring about an insurrection in Ireland in 1916 during the Easter Rising. The case was marked by controversy. The offence came under the Treason Act of 1351; that's not a misprint – the archaic law was scrutinised as to its interpretation, which all hung on the existence and placing of a comma. It seemed that the infamous comma appeared in some versions of the law and not in others and, small as it was, it was the difference between life and death for Roger Casement. Before coming to a decision, two of the five judges (there was no jury) went to the Public Records Office where the original 1351 document was examined with a magnifying glass. The document was written in Norman French, which made its interpretation all the more difficult. The point of law rested on the comma and where it was placed, which allowed the judges to decide that the definition of a traitor included someone who acted outside the realm. (The charges related to events that happened in Germany.) The judges decided that the comma was indeed there, and hence they found Roger Casement guilty of treason. He was hanged three weeks later in Pentonville prison, in August 1916. Had a forensic scientist been involved, they may have examined the document and found otherwise.

The FBI maintains a database of paper and ink samples supplied by manufacturers worldwide. They also hold thousands of case files relating to handwriting cases, watermarks, logos, counterfeit documents, cheques, ransom and robbery demands, and automated machinery used by government and large commercial operators to print staff or government cheques. This short-circuits the investigation by not having to go over old ground. An initial database check may well be sufficient to identify a document.

The mass use of computers and printers has not eliminated this specialist area, as even printed documents usually need signatures. Beyond the handwritten word, document analysis is almost an everyday requirement of an investigator's work. With modern technology, comparison analysis equipment can identify everything from forged bank notes to anonymous or threatening letters. The problem is that a sample of the genuine article is needed in order to compare the disputed document.

One generally unknown advantage discovered in recent years is that some printers have a built-in identikit that can secretly track documents back to a specific user. The system, known as the CDS, was set up by the US Federal Reserve Board to "deter the use of computers, digital imaging equipment and software" in order to protect against counterfeiting but it has proved invaluable for police in investigating timelines in kidnap demands and other crimes.

The technology was designed by a consortium of banks in the US, England, Japan, Canada and Europe. In co-operation with manufacturers, they encrypted a series of dots on ink jet and laser printers, designed to show up microscopically on all printed pages. The individual printer can be identified, together with other identifying information. This speeds up the investigation process by eliminating the immediate need to identify the source of the paper, ink and printer.

Before the development of computers, forensic investigators had to identify the make of typewriter a note was written on, and from there, it was possible to identify the source. Though many models were produced, individual keys would be damaged over time and some letters would be distorted, making them unique to a particular individual or workplace. Harold Shipman was found out this way, by using his own typewriter to forge a patient's will – despite having a computer. He also used his computer to alter patients' records after their death. (See Chapter 9.)

In commercial disputes, computer forensic analysts may measure the indentation, angles, pressure, speed and style of writing used in an electronic business transaction, where it is accepted as authentication of a document or contract. This is an increasingly common scenario in the fight to eliminate fraudulent transactions in business and commerce.

To get back to handwriting: while it should be relatively simple to compare the handwriting in a questioned will against samples known to be the genuine signature, it's not quite so easy when it comes to a ransom note or malicious letter. This takes further investigation to identify possible suspects before any accurate analysis can be done. Most initial examinations will be done by the naked eye, then with low-power stereoscopic microscopes, and if necessary by equipment such as a video spectral comparator (VSC), which can bring up writing or text not visible to the naked eye, which has been erased by correction fluid or other means, bombarding it with variable light-wave sources, gas chromatograph mass spectrometer (GC-MS), infrared or UV, which can pick up the various types of ink, making the missing text "reappear". Other marks hidden to the naked eye can be picked up under ultraviolet light using electrostatic detection apparatus known as ESDA.

It's all too common to find that the writer tries to disguise their handwriting. For example, where samples are requested from staff in an internal investigation, they will sometimes "alter" their writing, consciously or otherwise. In general cases, such as written demands in a bank robbery or anonymous letters, the writer uses only capitals, or writes with the left hand if they are right-handed, or slant the writing in a different direction, in order to conceal their identity. However, their distinctive handwriting characteristics can still be identified in a number of ways. An experienced handwriting expert can even pick out indentation – where the person emphasises a word or letter without even being aware they are doing so. This indentation is readily picked up by comparison analysis equipment, which can even pick up words written on a discarded page from the indentation on page layers below. Each individual letter, for example a "G", is compared to every other "G" that appears in the script. This is carried through for each letter and eventually emerges as a pattern, much like a picture appears from the pieces of a jigsaw.

Another "indicator" is the fact that handwriting varies with age and illness, just as our outward body visibly ages. An old or ill person's handwriting shows up as shaky, as often does that of a person under severe stress or agitation – for example, during a robbery, or while drunk or on drugs. Other variations occur when something is written hurriedly, and we can all identify that rushed note, indecipherable even to ourselves, as opposed to the carefully composed handwritten card or letter. Nonetheless, there remains an identifiable "pattern" that makes each individual's writing unique. The slope, style and use of language, spelling, letter features, such as flowery swirls or how the "t" is crossed, unusual personalised punctuation marks, and so on, all form a picture of the characteristics of the writer.

Other indicators can be spelling mistakes – some deliberate, others natural – and the linguistics of a document, which can point an investigation in a certain direction. The use of words, syntax, inflexion, diction and how a note or letter is composed can indicate the person's origin and background, and identify their country or region of origin. Their use and grasp of English or other languages involved is a pointer to where they were brought up, educated or have been living and whether they are writing in their first language.

Even regions within a country have their own dialects and peculiarities, which will come through in the written word. For example, most Europeans write the number seven with a line through the centre, 7 as opposed to 7. It is easy to identify the writings of a person from Texas, as opposed to a Londoner, by the language and style of writing. Through the combination of all these factors, a profile emerges.

Sargur N Srihari, a professor of computer science at the State University of New York, undertook a comprehensive study which confirmed beliefs that everyone's handwriting is unique. Studying a four-paragraph handwritten letter written out on three different occasions in black ink by some 1,500 people, representing all ages, sex, race, country of origin and educational levels, he was able electronically to identify the individual authors from samples of their handwriting taken beforehand, in ninety-eight per cent of cases.

Just as important as the handwriting is the paper it's written on. If Aunt Maggie's will is written on paper that wasn't manufactured twenty years beforehand, at the time she supposedly made the will, it is probably safe to say it is questionable. Paper investigation can be important to forensic analysis, as it can narrow the field by identifying watermarks, quality of paper, whether it is specialised or mass-produced, sold throughout the country or limited to a particular area or industry, all help the investigators to identify the suspect.

Even if the document or will *is* the original, it may have been altered or a codicil added; it may be something as small as a date changed, which could change the legitimacy of the document or alter its value. It is part of the questioned document analyst's job to detect any erasures or changes made to the document, no matter how inconsequential they appear; as always, the devil is in the detail. Analysis of the type of ink used, even today, with mass-produced pens, can be a vital clue. The presence of chemicals which may have been used to erase certain clauses, substituting others more favourable to one party, can also be identified.

Banknotes are often secretly marked before the handover in blackmail, theft or ransom cases, and can later be identified not alone through their serial numbers, but through unseen marks or writing such as the initials of the investigator made for identification purposes. These will show up under ESDA or ultraviolet light along with other incriminating evidence.

Credit card fraud poses major problems for banks, customers and the outlets accepting them. For every security measure, there is inevitably a way around it. Despite use of chip-and-pin, encryption data and built-in security measures, many cards still have a strip designed for the owner's signature. Theoretically, the signature cannot be wiped off, but by applying a specific chemical solvent, the signature can be erased, and when dry, a fraudster can replace it with their own signature. In a counter-move, infrared light can readily identify if a card has been manipulated, as the chemical solvent used to remove the genuine signature leaves a mark that shows up, and with it, the shadow of the original, genuine signature, can also show up.

Going with the rule that every contact leaves a trace, documents can of course also be fingerprinted as, unless gloves were worn, the natural oils and moisture present in our hands and fingers will be absorbed by the paper, leaving clues invisible to the naked eye. This does not of itself prove they wrote the ransom note or other document, unless the handwriting or computer generated note is traced directly to them, but at least it indicates that they had some involvement in the activity. Such cases demand swift results, as lives may depend on the outcome.

On occasion, handwriting analysis is used to check the validity of suicide notes, as it has been known for the victim to have been murdered and a note left to mislead any investigation. Whatever the challenge, forensic science is equipped to investigate and identify the authenticity or otherwise of the documents under examination. The bottom line is that the pen may well be mightier than the sword, but technology trumps it every time.

32

The Yorkshire Ripper:
Caught by Kindness

One of the first forensic scientists I knew was the renowned Stuart Kind, whom I met when I joined the UK-based Forensic Science Society in the 1980s. Stuart, a forensic biologist, had previously been in the RAF and with great foresight he founded the original Society for Forensic Science in 1959, when it was still a fledgling profession.

Police had been chasing the murderer known as the Yorkshire Ripper for over five years, but had been unable to pin him down. During that time he had murdered at least thirteen women and attacked many more. Stuart Kind was assigned to assist the police with their investigations and give them forensic advice. He joined the team at the Leeds hotel where four senior detectives leading the case were staying.

After less than two weeks on the case, Stuart phoned reception at 3.00 a.m. looking for graph paper. He roused the sleeping policemen and asked them to join him. Over the next few hours he explained what he had in mind. Plotting a graph as he had learned how to do in the RAF – the old-fashioned way of flying between two points, before modern technology and satellite navigation systems were developed – he made a note of each murder, along with the date and time of each attack on a map. The idea was to establish a centre of gravity – a point where all roads led to Rome. He believed that stringing a line from the murder sites to the nearest central point would give him an indication of where the Ripper lived.

His theory was that the Ripper had to get back home quickly after an attack so as not to draw attention to himself closer to the crime scene. The crimes were always committed under cover of darkness. Stuart Kind believed the Ripper was trying to mislead the police as to the area in which he lived. It was beginning to make sense to the detectives. The earlier in the evening the attack happened, the further away from home the Ripper was. It was only a theory, but a good one. It became the basis for forensic profiling in the future.

Stuart brought his graph back to the Home Office Research Establishment at Aldermaston, of which he was the director-in-charge, and ran the calculations through the computer. From the results, he worked out that the Ripper lived in an area between Shipley and Bingley in West Yorkshire. The focus of the investigation moved away from Derbyshire. With the heat still on and the media still directing its attention to Derbyshire, the Ripper felt safe.

Peter Sutcliffe's first known assault was in July 1975. He attacked a thirty-six-year-old woman with a metalwork hammer and slashed her stomach with a knife, but, disturbed by a neighbour, he ran away. The woman survived after extensive surgery but had long-term psychological problems resulting from the attack. In August, he struck again; this time it was a forty-six-year-old woman. Again he hit her on the head from behind and slashed her open but again was disturbed and ran away. She too survived.

A few days later, he killed a fourteen-year-old girl. Although never convicted of this murder, he confessed to it in 1992. Sutcliffe laid low until October 1975 when he killed a twenty-eight-year-old mother of four. Knocking her unconscious with a hammer, he stabbed her fifteen times in the stomach, neck and chest. A forensic examination found semen on her underwear but that was before the discovery of DNA profiling, so could not help in his identification.

In January 1976, the Ripper struck again, this time attacking a forty-two-year-old housewife with a sharpened screwdriver, stabbing her fifty-one times in the neck, stomach and chest, after hitting her on the head with a hammer. His MO was becoming well recognised by investigating police, but on this occasion, he stomped on the body, leaving an impression of his footwear, which was identified as a Wellington boot. Her family, who had fallen on hard times, were shocked to learn that she had been working as a prostitute. That hit them almost as hard as her murder.

Sutcliffe picked up his next victim in May 1976, offering her a lift home. He hit the twenty-year-old over the head, but for some reason, he didn't kill her. He attacked again in February 1977, picking up a twenty-eight-year-old prostitute, beating her to death with a hammer and mutilating her dead body with a knife afterwards. Tyre tracks found close to the body threw up thousands of possibilities, but no results. In April, he murdered a thirty-two-year-old prostitute in her flat; again, he left boot marks on her bedding. The tread-marks from the soles matched the earlier case, when he had stomped on the body.

Another two months went by without an attack, when the Ripper suddenly struck again. This time it was a sixteen-year-old schoolgirl. No one was safe. A month later he attacked again – a forty-two-year-old woman was attacked and left for dead when the Ripper was interrupted. It looked like the police finally had a breakthrough, as the witness described the getaway car. But it wasn't to be. After thousands of interviews and statements, 300 police making door-to-door enquiries and thousands of similar cars checked out, it seemed the eyewitness had made a mistake.

In October, another girl was murdered, but this time, unusually, she wasn't found soon after the murder. It was ten days before police found her body. Pathologists and forensic scientists reported that the body had been moved from the original crime scene and dumped where it was found.

It eventually emerged that Sutcliffe had picked up a prostitute, Jean Jordan. He had paid her £5 straight from his pay packet, but later he realised his mistake. He had given her a brand new fiver from a marked bank batch. Worried it could be traced back to him, he returned to the waste ground where he'd dumped the body to retrieve the money but he couldn't find where he'd thrown her handbag. He then tried to make the murder look different to his "trademark" killings. Not expecting this turn of events, he was ill-equipped for the job. He improvised; using a hacksaw and piece of shattered glass, he tried to saw off the dead girl's head. The partially severed head and mutilated body was eventually found on an allotment by a local dairy worker Bruce Jones, later to become famous as *Coronation Street* character Les Battersby.

Despite Sutcliffe's lack of success in finding the incriminating cash, police managed to find the dead girl's handbag. Inside was what was to become a crucial piece of evidence – the £5. Being brand new, it was a valuable piece of evidence, and could possibly provide fingerprints as well as leading detectives to the owner.

Extensive investigation narrowed the note down to a batch delivered to the Midland Bank. They had split the delivery between their branches in Shipley and Bingley – tying in with Stuart Kind's theory. After three weeks of intensive investigation, police pinned the note down to a number of companies, but between them they had over 8,000 employers.

Over the following three months, police painstakingly went through every employee. Amazingly, Peter Sutcliffe was one of those interviewed. Maybe he got lucky or maybe he was a proficient liar – either way, he slipped through the net and no one thought to check out his alleged alibi. In fact, he was interviewed on several more occasions but incredibly, he was always discounted from the investigation. Someone wasn't following the policy laid down by Stuart Kind: that *any* links to the Bingley or Shipley areas were priority leads and he was to be contacted, but Professor Kind wasn't kept in the loop.

Having fooled the police, Sutcliffe was confident enough to strike again. This time he attacked a twenty-five-year-old prostitute just before Christmas. She managed to get away and gave the police a good description of her attacker. Tyre tracks at the scene matched the tracks found at the scene of his earlier attack on the twenty-eight-year-old prostitute in February. Sutcliffe was growing ever-more confident, as the police seemed to have no suspects.

In January 1978, he killed yet another twenty-one-year-old prostitute. He hid her body on waste ground under an abandoned couch and she wasn't discovered until several months later. With an ever-growing taste for blood, he struck a second time in January; this time it was an eighteen-year-old prostitute and again, just weeks later, he killed a forty-year-old woman in the car park of a hospital.

Meanwhile, police attention was diverted to another part of the country when a taped message was sent to them, taunting chief investigator Superintendent George Oldfield. A letter was enclosed with the tape and copied to a newspaper, claiming responsibility for the "Ripper" murders. The sender also admitted another killing in

Preston, that of twenty-six-year-old Joan Harrison, an alcoholic drug addict found murdered in a vacant house. There were no similarities between the Preston murder and the Ripper's MO, nor was there anything in the letter to indicate the writer had "inside information" known only to the killer. Voice analysis of the taped message indicated the man was local to the Preston area. The victim had been sexually attacked and bitten after death, but it was a case for another team; the Ripper was more than enough to handle. The perpetrator of the hoax was eventually tracked down in 2005, following developments in DNA analysis, which identified him from the saliva on the envelope he'd sent. In 2006, ex-security guard John Humble was sentenced to eight years in prison.

Meanwhile, the Ripper struck again; this time a twenty-year-old university student was murdered. Incredibly, Sutcliffe was interviewed yet again, and despite matching a lot of the profile criteria, again they let the Ripper slip through the net. Worse still, one of Sutcliffe's associates reported his suspicions to police. He told detectives that he believed Sutcliffe could be the Ripper. He had known Sutcliffe since the 1960s when they were teenagers. He told police that Sutcliffe was a truck driver, that he always picked up prostitutes and his job regularly took him to the areas where the attacks occurred. He fitted the newspaper eyewitness description of the attacker and he was one of 300 people who'd been paid with the new £5 notes in the Shipley/Bingley area. It wouldn't have taken Sherlock Holmes to work that one out. At the very least, it was worth following up, particularly as, unknown to the informant, the same boot prints were identified in three of the attacks. Had police checked out the footwear of the 300 employees at an early stage, they may well have picked up Sutcliffe a lot earlier and prevented several more rapes and murders.

For some inexplicable reason, the report made by Sutcliffe's associate was never filed, lost among the myriad of information coming in from all over the country. In a time when police had little recourse to computers, paperwork was piling high and there was a distinct lack of communication or co-ordination surrounding the case. Given that it was local to the area, and Sutcliffe had been interviewed a total of nine times, this was the unacceptable face of incompetent policing. It was even more alarming given the fact that forensic scientist Stuart Kind had pinned Bingley down as being the most likely area – it was more than just a coincidence. Because of sloppy policing, people were dying a terrifying death.

In 1980, Sutcliffe was arrested for drink-driving. While out on bail awaiting a hearing, he killed twice more, murdering a twenty-year-old college student and a forty-seven-year-old woman; he also attacked a sixteen-year-old girl and a thirty-four-year-old doctor from Singapore. Both survived.

His final arrest was a stroke of good fortune – he was caught in his car with a prostitute. When police ran a check on the number plates they realised they were false. Before being taken away, he said he needed to go to the toilet and the police allowed him to go behind a storage tank to urinate before putting him into a police car. He gave his name as Peter Williams. He was taken to the local police station and routinely questioned about the Ripper murders – the word had filtered down about the links made by Stuart Kind and his "geographic profiling", as it became internationally known.

Survivors of the Ripper had described him as being 5'6", with dark wavy hair and a beard. It finally triggered a reaction with a detective, who ordered that Sutcliffe be strip-searched. Police were aghast when they found he was wearing a V-necked jumper upside down under his trousers. His legs were through the arms of the jumper and he had extra padding in the knee area, making it more comfortable for him when he knelt over his dead victim, which was part of his MO. The open V-neck of the jumper exposed his groin area, making his penchant for necrophilia easier.

Now certain they had their man, police got a search warrant for his house. During the search detectives seized Sutcliffe's boots. The tread marks were later forensically matched to tread marks on one victim and on another's bed. Sutcliffe's car tyre tracks also matched those found at two crime scenes.

Police brought in Sutcliffe's Czech wife Sonja, who was horrified at what she heard. She had supported his alibi when he had been questioned previously, saying she was with him at the time one of the murders was committed. She left Sutcliffe and later filed for divorce.

Sutcliffe was booked, fingerprinted and charged with multiple murders. The following morning police made a daylight search of the area where Sutcliffe had been arrested. They found a knife, a ballpeen hammer (the sort used by metalworkers) and rope, all dumped by Sutcliffe under cover of darkness behind the tanker, when he supposedly went to the toilet. The murder weapons were covered in the Ripper's fingerprints. They finally had their man.

Questioned intensively for two days, Sutcliffe had little to say. He denied everything. Shortly after detectives produced the ballpeen hammer, rope and knife, he appeared to have a change of heart. He told them in detail what he had done, savouring every moment as he recalled his gruesome murders. He showed no remorse or emotion of any kind, other than when he was questioned about the girl in Preston. He was quite annoyed to be associated with this murder, saying it wasn't "his".

Despite his admission, in his trial he pleaded not guilty to murder, but guilty to manslaughter by reason of diminished responsibility. He said he heard voices, claiming that God made him do it. He pleaded guilty to seven counts of attempted murder. The prosecution were happy to accept the plea of diminished responsibility but the Judge, Mr Justice Boreham, wasn't having it, despite the prosecution pushing to accept it. The Attorney General himself, Sir Michael Havers, argued his case for almost three hours in favour of a quick solution. Allowing Sutcliffe to plead guilty by virtue of diminished responsibility would ensure that the gory details would never have to emerge.

Mr Justice Boreham ruled against the AG and the plea of diminished responsibility, deciding that the case should go to a full trial before a jury. The two-week trial was full of graphic and sordid accounts of Sutcliffe's numerous murders and mutilations and it shocked even the most hardened police and lawyers. Much of the evidence was not released or published by the media, being considered beyond the pale of decency. The Herculean efforts of his defence counsel could not save Sutcliffe. The jury found him to be both sane and guilty on all counts.

Mr Justice Boreham in summing up said he considered Sutcliffe "beyond redemption". He sentenced him to life imprisonment with a minimum of not less than thirty years before parole should be considered, while clearly stating that he hoped Sutcliffe would never leave prison. That would see Sutcliffe released in 2011 – a frightening thought.

After the trial, Sutcliffe admitted to several other attacks but was never prosecuted for them. Even other hardened criminals, themselves murderers and rapists, abhorred Sutcliffe's actions and he was attacked many times in prison. In Parkhurst a fellow prisoner stabbed him in the face with broken glass and he was moved to Broadmore Hospital for his own safety in 1984. Twelve years later a prisoner tried to strangle him with the cord from his stereo headphones, but was prevented from doing so by other prisoners. A year later he was attacked with a pen, losing the sight in one eye and damaging the other. Amazingly, he still receives hundred of fan mail letters from female "admirers".

In February 2009 the *Telegraph* newspaper reported that doctors have now said Sutcliffe, a former grave digger, is "fit to be freed". He is expected to be released on a short-term basis initially, to allow him to get used to life in the twenty-first century, before he is permanently released into the community. Regardless of his age, should Sutcliffe be released? Look at Josef Fritzl and other examples of evil old men. Would you want to live next to him?

Epilogue

All in a Day's Work:
The Life and Crimes
of Jimmy X

Forensic science – sounds very technical and complicated. You don't hear many kids say "I want to be a forensic scientist when I grow up", but perhaps they should. It's safer than being a cop on those mean streets and, although the job can be hectic and pressurised, with an ever-increasing variety of crimes and criminals, it still gives a great sense of satisfaction, a buzz, that "eureka" moment, when a criminal is "banged to rights" by forensic science.

Imagine what a police technical team or a forensic scientist could do with the following scenario. Now that you have an insight into forensics, see what "evidence" you can pick up along the way.

A criminal decides to break into the home of a glamorous well-known businesswoman, "Ms Joanna B". He knows she brings home the takings from her exclusive jewellery shop at the weekend. He's been staking the shop out for a while to check out her movements, find out what time she leaves, what car she drives. In fact, that's how he knows where she lives; he's followed her home a few times to make sure she really does live alone.

She lives in a large house in its own grounds, outside of town, so there are no nosy neighbours to spot him. The house was featured on television recently, and while it didn't say where it was, Ms B was only too delighted to show off the house. Viewers were treated to a guided tour of the interior, which "Jimmy X" made sure to record, giving him the layout of the house. The house still had its original timber windows and doors, and all the "old-fashioned" original locks – she'd "never part with them," she'd said. The new stuff might be more secure, but she bought the house for its original features, and anyway, she had a good alarm system.

Jimmy X agrees. It's not a bad system; he should know, he used to work for the company, so he knows the system backwards.

He parks the van out of the way, hidden by a big apple blossom tree in the paddock. He waits until the early hours of the morning, until he's sure she's asleep. It's almost 3.00 a.m. before the lights go out – he'll give her another half hour to be sure. He then texts his wife to tell her he'll be back late. He pulls on his balaclava and climbs over the low timber fence, the one she'd raved about on television – she'd "always wanted a white picket fence," she said – before he bypasses the alarm system, so as not to trigger an "interference" code back at the monitoring company.

That done, he breaks into the house the old-fashioned way, with a screwdriver; she'd like that, he thinks. He always keeps it in his toolkit in the van. It's handy, as he still does a few "nixers", fitting alarms for people.

Once inside, he is amazed at the expensive antiques. He fingers one or two before deciding to take some of the smaller pieces. They're easier to "shift" and, anyway, he has plenty of room in the van. He's not worried about prints. He's got that well covered; he made sure to bring his latex gloves. He always a keeps a box in the van.

He does a quick recce of the house before going into her office. It looks exactly the same as on television: the beautiful wooden floor, the leather chairs; they're all there. The woman's briefcase is on the floor by the desk. He rifles through it, delighted to find her credit cards, €1,000 in cash and a fancy leather diary. It really *is* his night, as a quick check of the diary turns up a number that looks very much like a safe combination. He checks out the painting on the wall – a portrait of Ms B – and to his delight finds a safe built into the wall behind it. He laughs to himself, thinking, "Some people are so predictable". If the numbers get him into the safe without the bother of having to crack it, he'll definitely buy a lottery ticket; his luck couldn't get much better.

He's worked up a sweat getting into the house and, with the adrenaline rush, his throat is dry and his glasses have steamed up. He has time to slip into the kitchen, get a drink and clean his glasses; he'll need them to see the numbers on the safe. Heading into the kitchen, he crosses a vast tiled floor to the huge American fridge and decides to treat himself to a bottle of the cold beer he spots inside. Just the one; after all, he has to keep a clear head.

Hanging around so long, waiting for Ms B to go to bed, has made him hungry. Finding a chunk of cheddar, he takes a big bite. He could never resist cheese and it'll keep him going until he gets home. Rooting around in the kitchen drawer for a bottle opener, he finds one and opens the beer top, which flies off; luckily, he catches it before it hits the ground. He pulls off the balaclava; it's too awkward to eat the cheese and drink the beer with it on. He puts it back on a minute or two later.

Back to business: he returns to the office, tries the combination and, hey presto, he's in. He's definitely stopping off for that lottery ticket after this.

He scoops everything out of the safe, throwing it all into an old rice sack he brought with him. Always handy, it's strong enough to carry most things, even the laptop computer he took from the briefcase. He decides it's getting late and he's got what he came for, so time to get out. He'll check on the loot later.

Just as he is about to leave the office, he hears a noise. Someone is coming downstairs; he can hear the wood creaking beneath the carpet. What to do? Does he stay quiet and hope Ms B goes back to bed? Perhaps she's thirsty; when she gets a drink, she'll go back upstairs. He starts to panic as she heads towards the office. He picks up the heavy glass paperweight, just in case he has to knock her out. She walks in and puts on the light. Seeing the safe open, she turns around, spots him and screams, grabbing the phone. He rushes at her, shouting at her to be quiet and she won't get harmed.

She struggles with him, tearing at the balaclava and scratching his arm. She even manages to poke him in the eye with her long nails, before he hits her with the paperweight.

It's a fatal blow and she falls to the ground, covered in her own blood.

It's time to get out of there, but first, he moves the body. Dragging it across the hall, he locks it into a broom cupboard, hoping that it won't be found for days. Her car is in the garage, so no one will see it. They'll probably think she's gone off on one of her exotic holidays. By then, he'll be well away.

Pity about the bird – it was a good night's work but for that. Still, he'll still pick up that lotto on the way home, just to prove to himself she hasn't jinxed him.

He heads back to the van the same way he came in. On the drive back, a few yards down the road, he dumps the paperweight into a ditch, happy to have made his escape unnoticed. Still a bit shaken, he stops off at an all-night garage for petrol, and gets himself a cup of coffee to steady his nerves. While there, he dumps the latex gloves in the bin.

When Ms B doesn't show up a few days later, staff are worried. She had lined up another important television slot, it was great for business and she'd never miss that. This time they were to film from the shop. Mrs B had invited all her best customers, well-known wealthy individuals who would really showcase her business. She'd even arranged a big lunch for everyone, at the most expensive restaurant in town. Last week, she'd been making notes in her diary, phoning everyone to remind them. Now there is no answer to her phone, either at home or her mobile. Seriously worried that she had been taken ill or had been mugged on her way home, they call the police.

A squad car is sent to Ms B's house. When they get no reply to repeated knocking, they take a look around the back, and immediately spot that there's been a break-in. One of the windows has been "jemmied", opened with some force. The Technical Bureau is dispatched and they enter the house and examine the crime scene. They photograph the entry point and dust for prints. The timber has been damaged by the tool used to force the window open. The distinctive marks of the tool are embedded in the window frame – a screwdriver.

Entering the main house, they notice the remnants of muddy footprints going from a room off the hall towards a cupboard. There are also some brown marks which, experience tells them, is most likely blood. When they open the cupboard door, they find the dead body of Ms B. It isn't a pretty sight. By now the body has already started to decompose. The heat from the immersion boiler has escalated the rate of decomposition, and already the insects have found their way in. It is now a murder scene. The State Pathologist is called in.

Crime scene officers photograph everything. As they go from room to room, they discover the open safe, now empty. It appears to be a burglary gone wrong, but you can never jump to conclusions in this game. It could be a murder, staged to look like a burglary.

A postmortem reveals that Ms B died from blunt force trauma to the head. The pathologist also finds defence injuries to the victim's hands and arms. She takes fingernail scrapings, noting that one or two of the victim's nails are broken. She finds evidence of tissue, probably torn from the perpetrator. A forensic entomologist also examines the body to determine the approximate time of death. From the development stage of the eggs and maggots, and the heat of the cupboard, she estimates that Ms B has been dead for three to four days. Immediately drawn to the moist head injury, the bluebottles laid their eggs, which hatched within eight to fourteen hours, developing into small and then larger maggots over the subsequent days.

With no immediate evidence of the murder weapon, gardaí search the surrounding area and find the glass paperweight Jimmy X had dumped in the ditch. Forensic tests match the blood found on the paperweight to Ms B. Surprisingly, there are also two fingerprints, a thumb and index finger, as well as DNA. It looks like Jimmy X didn't want to be seen driving with latex gloves. When he got rid of the murder weapon, he let his guard down and handled it; but then, he didn't expect it to be found.

Scene of crime officers find tyre marks close to the house, under an apple blossom tree. They measure and photograph them, before taking a cast. It may be needed as evidence later. Tracking back to the house, they notice footprint impressions in the grassy area leading to the house. With the recent heavy rain, the ground is soft, and indentations can be clearly seen. Judging by the size of the footprints, the perpetrator is a big man. Again, they measure the shoe prints, photographing them alongside a measure to show their size. It is deep enough to take a cast, if they are careful; damp ground can sometimes be a problem. Even then, it is immediately evident that the sole of the right shoe has two deep cuts, where the rubber base has been damaged.

Back inside the house, the rest of the technical team are working away. More muddy prints are found on the kitchen tiles; they are fainter here, because of the tile colour, but the forensic boys show them up, treating them with a chemical and using specialist lighting.

Even initially, it looks like the same guy, probably acting alone, as no secondary footprints are found – although as yet, nothing is certain.

They also spot bits of grass and soil and some pinkish particles, which had fallen from between the ridges of the shoes' soles. A later examination shows they came from the apple blossom tree by the paddock. The burglar had inadvertently picked them up on his shoes as he left his vehicle.

A discarded beer bottle in the kitchen bin is forensically examined. It is found to have DNA from saliva traces, which match that found on the glass paperweight, recovered from the ditch. A tiny spot of blood close by, where the beer cap had nicked the burglar, is also tested. It too, matches the DNA already found. The blood is identified as O-negative, a relatively rare group, whereas the victim was O-positive.

As the wealth of forensic evidence grows, yet another clue emerges, as the remains of a piece of hard cheese is found discarded in the bin. It bears a bite mark, the size making it unlikely to be female. Given the large and heavy stature indicated by the footprints, it is most likely a man. The bite mark is photographed and measured and the cheese is tested for possible DNA from saliva. Again, it is a match.

An extensive forensic examination of the kitchen area picks up fibres which are later identified as a wool-and-nylon mix used in gloves and balaclavas. Similar fibres are found on the victim's fluffy dressing gown. A swab of the area picks up specks of dandruff close to where the fibres are found, obviously discarded when Jimmy X pulled off his balaclava. The DNA matches the other samples. Specks of rice and minute pieces from a nylon rice bag are found in the office area close to the safe. Ms B had no similar products in her kitchen.

Men's glasses are found on the office floor; they'd fallen off during the struggle, but Jimmy X had forgotten about them, as he was too busy hiding the body.

Detectives check CCTV along the route to and from Ms B's home, and from petrol stations along the way. They spot a very interesting piece of footage from a petrol station, half a mile from the victim's house. It shows a man driving a van, stopping for petrol at around 4.40 a.m. As he walked towards the shop, he threw something into one of the bins. He paid for his petrol and a cup of coffee, and chatted with the assistant while paying with a credit card. He checked a piece of paper, spoke to the assistant again and then put in a pin number. Enhanced imagery clearly identifies the van registration and man's features. Further investigation shows that the credit card used was in the name of Joanna B. The van registration is enough to find the suspect's address.

Detectives recover a pair of latex gloves from the bin at the garage. Forensic scientists find two sets of DNA on the gloves, one matching the victim, while there is another set of DNA on both the inside and outside of the gloves. The DNAs are matched respectively to Ms B and the burglar.

Very soon, Jimmy X has unexpected visitors. Armed with a warrant to search his house, detectives find the victim's credit cards and diary, which have details of her PIN numbers. The Technical Bureau check out his van and find a balaclava, which is later matched to the fibres found at the house and on the victim's dressing gown. A broken nail is also found caught in the fibres of the balaclava; when examined, the nail is found to have the victim's DNA. They also find a box of latex gloves of the same size and brand as the pair found dumped at the petrol station and already identified as belonging to Jimmy X. A used coffee cup sits forlornly on the dash, another silent witness to his crime, along with the rice sack which is found in his van.

A search of the house turns up over €900 in new notes, the balance of the €1,000 he'd taken from the victim. The notes are traced to a batch given to Ms B by her bank on the day she went missing. Boots found under his bed match the size and tread found in the house and around the grounds. The tyre tracks on his van also match those found at the crime scene, and both his boots and the tyres have apple tree blossom embedded in their treads.

His boots have two deep cuts on the right sole, matching the muddy footprints found in the house and the cast taken from the grass. Clothes belonging to the suspect are taken away for examination and are found to have fibres from the victim's dressing gown and white paint flecks. The paint is matched to the white picket fence at the victim's house. A check on Jimmy X's mobile reveals that he sent a text message in the early hours of the morning to another mobile registered to Mrs Jimmy X. The text was relayed from a mast close to the victim's house and was sent at 3.23 a.m., the same day Jimmy X was caught on CCTV at the nearby garage.

And then there were the glasses; had they not already had a wealth of forensic evidence, these could have been traced through his optician. Just one more nail in Jimmy X's coffin.

Detectives notice he is a big man, over six feet tall, and he weighs about seventeen stone. He has scratches and scrapes, not to mention a very bloodshot eye, which is starting to bruise up.

A check with the alarm company identifies Jimmy X as a former employee, although he had been sacked long before they installed Ms B's alarm – he wouldn't have had to stake her out otherwise. The laptop found at Jimmy X's house is checked by forensic computer experts. They discover that Jimmy X had transferred ten thousand euro from Ms B's bank account to his own account, the day after the murder. For several years beforehand, Jimmy's account had never had more than €200 or €300 in it. Ms B's leather diary held all the information he needed for the transaction.

It seems Jimmy X's luck has just run out. Oh, and another thing – his lottery numbers came up, €10 million, with just one winner. Then he remembered – he'd forgotten to buy the ticket. It's all in a day's work.

So how did you do? Can you find any more forensic clues? Ready to join the *CSI* team yet?

NO JOB FOR A WOMAN

Sandra Mara

IRELAND'S FIRST FEMALE PRIVATE INVESTIGATOR LIFTS THE LID ON THE SECRET LIFE OF THE NATION.

Sandra Mara got a taste for the intrigue of the PI world from her father, Ireland's first PI. Despite his warning that it was *No Job for a Woman*, she became the top Private Investigator in the country and highly acclaimed internationally, being voted International Investigator of the Year by the World Association of Detectives.

In *No Job for a Woman*, Sandra opens her case files for the first time to reveal some enthralling cases, providing a fascinating insight into the real world of the private investigator — a world of bugging, surveillance, long cold nights and very real danger. She describes dramatic encounters with criminal gangs or shadowy figures like Martin "The General" Cahill, Tony Felloni and Gerry "The Monk" Hutch, as well as the IRA and UDA.

No stranger to dangerous situations, she has faced knife attacks, death threats, police protection and even looked down the barrel of a gun on more than one occasion. It goes with the turf.

It's not all danger. The job has its share of bizarre, humorous and scandalous cases, such as the missing Jumbo Jet, "Patricia the Stripper" and the Manchester United player, or the client who claimed the CIA were on her tail. Then, of course, there are the inevitable cheating partners. Some cases will shock even the most cynical.

ISBN 978-1-84223-337-5